ROUTLEDGE LIBRAF
AUTOBIOGR

Volume 7

DESIGN AND TRUTH IN
AUTOBIOGRAPHY

DESIGN AND TRUTH IN AUTOBIOGRAPHY

ROY PASCAL

Routledge
Taylor & Francis Group

LONDON AND NEW YORK

First published in 1960

This edition first published in 2016
by Routledge
2 Park Square, Milton Park, Abingdon, Oxon OX14 4RN

and by Routledge
711 Third Avenue, New York, NY 10017

Routledge is an imprint of the Taylor & Francis Group, an informa business

British Library Cataloguing in Publication Data
A catalogue record for this book is available from the British Library

ISBN: 978-1-138-93641-6 (Set)
ISBN: 978-1-315-67463-6 (Set) (ebk)
ISBN: 978-1-138-93948-6 (Volume 7) (hbk)
ISBN: 978-1-315-67460-5 (Volume 7) (ebk)

Publisher's Note
The publisher has gone to great lengths to ensure the quality of this reprint but
points out that some imperfections in the original copies may be apparent.

Disclaimer
The publisher has made every effort to trace copyright holders and would welcome
correspondence from those they have been unable to trace.

DESIGN AND TRUTH
IN
AUTOBIOGRAPHY

ROY PASCAL

LONDON

ROUTLEDGE & KEGAN PAUL

First published 1960
by Routledge & Kegan Paul Ltd
Broadway House, 68-74 Carter Lane
London, E.C.4

Printed in Great Britain
by Page Bros (Norwich) Ltd

Contents

Preface

IT may not be out of place to introduce this book with an autobiographical comment on how I came to undertake it.

I had spent some years in the intensive study of imaginative and philosophical literature, and was continually brought up against the problem of the contrast between the meaning of a man's work and life for us, the "likeness" we make, and his own image or idea of himself. We generally underestimate the importance in a man's life of his "life-illusion", and I wanted to compensate this bias by studying autobiography, the record of this illusion.

Personal experiences reinforced, and perhaps in reality prompted, this purpose. I was frequently startled to find that for other people I was a person with definite characteristics, who in given circumstances could be expected to have certain views and to act in certain ways; while I remained in my own eyes rather indefinite and capable of unforeseeable reactions. I came to realise that I was deluding myself in some degree, but felt that the others were deluding themselves about me also. I am not so fixed as I appear to them, and I am not so indeterminate as I assume. Thinking over recent changes in my thoughts and habits, I found it immensely difficult to decide whether they were foreseeable, as the assertion of a deeper trend over less fundamental attitudes, or whether they were something really new. In either case, it seemed curious that I should be so anxious to persuade myself that I was consistent, that this "I" was an identity; for even if something new had emerged, I tried to prove to myself that it grew organically out of the old. As if freedom could mean something to me only if it was destiny, as if a choice was satisfactory only if it imposed itself as my nature.

This intellectual problem presented itself however as an insistent moral pressure. I do not mean concern for the morality of my behaviour and thoughts, though old faults and follies of course cause sleepless nights. I mean a need for meaning. I do not believe that an individual life has a religious or transcendental meaning, and I cannot even comfort myself with the metaphysical despair, the Angst, of the existentialists. Nor is it enough to prove to myself that I am fulfilling a social purpose in a useful job. The meaning had to be personal, subjective. I did not pitch my hopes extravagantly high, and felt one could be content if one could feel one's self to be consistent, to have developed naturally and organically, to have remained "true to itself", and if within this framework one could order certain intense experiences whose significance defied analysis but which were peculiarly one's own. The terms are vague, and I cannot say where this pressure comes from, but I think I am delineating a state of mind from which autobiography springs.

When I tried to jot down some early experiences that seemed to insist on being expressed, I found however hindrances and problems with the apparently simplest and clearest memories. My own difficulties led me to realise how peculiar is the task of the autobiographer, and to investigate the various ways in which men and women have been able to write the truth about themselves. I was surprised to find that, though there is a huge and growing bulk of autobiographical statements, very little has been written about how the autobiographer accomplishes his task.

It was not easy to find a satisfactory form for this study. To classify autobiographies by motive is psychologically interesting, but does not lead to any decisive insight into the reasons for the specific shape or style of a work—at the same time, motives are usually mixed. A historical account is of great value for the centuries when autobiography was finding itself, but is only confusing in the modern period, when autobiographies of all sorts jostle for attention. The plan I ultimately adopted was devised in order to work towards the secret of autobiography as the account of the truth of a life, and it perhaps needs a little explaining.

After defining what I understand an autobiography to be, I recount in historical chapters its emergence as a recognised and "self-conscious" literary form. From this point I turn to what I take to be the main issue, what is the particular sort of truth to be found in autobiography, and I first face the difficulties by enumerating the numerous ways in which autobiographies are not truthful. Even the best fall short in this respect, if they do not do worse, and yet they impress us with their truth; and I suggest that this riddle is solved if we approach them from the point of view of the author's intention, which itself is determined by his personality and achievement. They are, therefore, then examined by types, for this classification allows us to understand the principle upon which the author builds his story and the style in which he writes. Childhood falls into a category of its own and had to be treated separately. In all cases, the search for a formal principle leads to a discussion of the specific content of the book, just as the discussion of the content leads repeatedly to a problem of form.

The question imposed itself, why have many authors found it more appropriate to probe into themselves through the medium of invented circumstances, in the form of the novel? Hence a chapter on the autobiographical novel.

In my final chapter I have tried to define what is specific and unique in the autobiography—what sort of self-knowledge the autobiographer seeks, and in what way self-knowledge differs from knowledge of other people.

Many autobiographies have been referred to, and many more have been ignored. I have chosen to refer repeatedly to certain significant or typical works, rather than to make passing references to a greater variety, so that I could do greater justice to my themes and the works themselves. I have included what I think are the most important in a list given at the end of the book; in the case of foreign works I quote, as far as possible, from translations.

I

What is an Autobiography?

AUTOBIOGRAPHIES claim our attention for a host of reasons. At the least, they satisfy a legitimate curiosity about the ways of men. It is fascinating to enter into the private life of some-one else, so different from us even if he is a neighbour, to hear of the small circumstances of private and social life, of emotional involvements, prejudices and passions, beliefs and convictions, that are normally each man's secret; in the case of men of notable achievement, to learn the personal story of well-known events, of motives and intentions that are hidden behind them. Beyond the interest of such particulars, autobiographies offer an unparalleled insight into the mode of consciousness of other men. Even if what they tell us is not factually true, or only partly true, it always is true evidence of their personality. Knowledge of this type, direct historical and psychological knowledge, is not simply interesting and instructive; it is necessary to us if we are to get on terms with ourselves. And in autobiographies this knowledge is given in a particularly attractive way, as a story in which, as in a novel, we are won over to the "hero". Not that the author must try to win us by proving that he, the hero, is worthy, morally or by his achievements, of our admiration; if he does so, we tend to feel alienated. But we are won over simply by being admitted to his intimacy. Look at Sargent's portrait of Henry James: James holds you off, reserved, a little ironical, perhaps suspicious of irruption into his privacy, as he would have been if you had called on him at Rye. But in his autobiography James not only confides in you, it seems almost as if he were appealing for your understanding and glad of this intimate communion.

I

Few autobiographies lack some sort of interest, but some have a peculiar quality—"Autobiographies are the most entrancing of books, and sometimes they are works of art" (Bonamy Dobrée). How do we recognise them as works of art? This is the question I want to examine. It is not a matter of examining the "form" as opposed to the "content"; what needs to be discussed is, on what principles is the content of a life organised in this literary form, the autobiography?

Autobiography is only one form among many in which a writer speaks of himself and the incidents of his personal experience. Misch, in his great investigation of the origins of the autobiography, has to include in his account a great variety of utterance, from lyrical poetry and philosophical reflection to accounts of achievement, *res gestae*. No national literature is without these forms. But with autobiography a peculiar step is taken, which does not necessarily follow upon these other forms, many of them of great antiquity; and indeed this new departure scarcely took place at all in the literatures of the Far or Near East. It belongs to Europe, in its essentials to the post-classical world of Europe. In it, the spiritual identity of the personality is sought as it is expressed in what Misch calls "its concrete experienced reality"; the multiple experiences of a life are linked reflectively in the consciousness; there is a realisation that the individual is "ineffabile", as Spinoza put it, and yet may be grasped in his successive collisions with circumstance.

An investigation into the historical and psychological origins of this literary genre must lead one deep into the cultural history of the West; but I am concerned with the genre as it has come to be established and recognised. Misch rightly points out that its form arises in a very special way out of the actual manner in which the author experiences reality; but his over-riding historical purpose leads him to overlook the difference between the shape of life and the shape of an autobiography.[1] There is an autobiographical form, and indeed a convention, which one recognises and distinguishes from other literary modes; writers know roughly what they expect to do if they write autobiographies, and critics are in no great difficulty to define their subject-matter when they write about autobiographies. At the same time, there is sufficient

[1] Misch, *Geschichte der Autobiographie*, i. 4–6.

confusion and uncertainty to make it worth while to see if a more precise and coherent definition may not be discovered.

It is necessary first to discriminate between autobiography proper and other literary forms that have an autobiographical content. Cocteau, when asked to contribute to a volume of studies on autobiography, rightly wrote that every line we write, every blot, "compose our self-portrait and denounce us".[1] But while we are not likely to confuse autobiography and lyric poetry, common linguistic usage indicates that autobiography is frequently confused with literary forms nearer to it. Authors often refer to their life-stories indiscriminately as autobiography, memoir, or reminiscence. Mrs. Burr and H. N. Wethered in their books on the autobiography do not distinguish between auto-biographies and diaries or even letters. I would limit myself to what I hold to be true autobiography, not in order to make things easier for myself, nor I hope out of pedantry, but because auto-biography involves a distinctive attitude on the part of the author, a distinctive mode of presentation—and, if one is concerned with its historical significance, gives evidence of a distinctive psycho-logical characteristic of European civilisation. I do not, of course, wish to imply that this "true" autobiography is the only auto-biographical form to rise to the level of art. There is an art of the letter, and in the hands of a Gide or Ernst Jünger the diary or journal has become a shaped literary form (though when these most private forms are consciously composed as art, which means among other things as something to be communicated, they undergo a somewhat disconcerting metamorphosis).

The formal difference between diary and autobiography is obvious. The latter is a review of a life from a particular moment in time, while the diary, however reflective it may be, moves through a series of moments in time. The diarist notes down what, at that moment, seems of importance to him; its ultimate, long-range significance cannot be assessed. It might almost seem that the best diarists are those least concerned with long-range sig-nificance; Pepys and Boswell are ravishing precisely because they are so diurnal, so devoted to what the day offers. And they are men, one inclines to think, who would have found it impossible to write autobiographies. It is we, the readers, who have to

[1] *Formen der Selbstdarstellung*, ed. Reichenkron and Haase, Berlin 1956.

try to synthesise their characters out of their infinite fragmentation.

The use of diary-material in autobiographies may give them "a remarkable authenticity", as André Maurois says, but it is also full of pitfalls. Autobiographers proceed much more royally with their journals than biographers would dare. I do not mean that they simply ignore a great deal; that is unavoidable. But they alter earlier judgements and detect significances which escaped them at the time. Often a diary-entry will provide the material for a vivid picture which otherwise might have escaped memory—some of the brilliant scenes in Benjamin Haydon's autobiography are taken from his diary; but often a direct impression will be altered in the autobiography. Ruskin notes that the despondent account of his aesthetic obtuseness on an early trip along the Riviera which he gives in *Praeterita* does not conform with his diary—"I see, indeed, in turning the leaves [of my journals], that I have been a little too morose in my record of impressions", and he then corrects any possible misapprehension by inserting a page of the journal.[1] What is characteristic is that Ruskin did not simply amend his autobiographical account, but left the two statements side by side, as if to say, one is appropriate to the autobiography, one to the diary. When Haydon writes: "I write this life [the autobiography] for the student. I wish to show him how to bear affliction and disappointment by exhibiting the fatal consequences in myself, who did not bear them",[2] he is asserting a principle of composition which must radically distinguish the autobiography from the diary, which can never be so systematically retrospective. The difference is summed up in a review of Lord Alanbrooke's diaries, *The Turn of the Tide*, in which vital questions of strategy during the Second World War are discussed. The reviewer states that the journals, however carefully edited leave us dissatisfied: "If this were an autobiography, we should know that it contained the considered judgement of Lord Alanbrooke."[3]

There is no less difference between the whole tone of expression in diary and autobiography, so that, if extracts from diaries are

[1] *Praeterita*, ii. 61.
[2] World's Classics ed., 184.
[3] R. H. S. Crossman, review in *The New Statesman*, Feb. 23, 1957.

quoted in autobiographies, they, involuntarily or not, startlingly bear witness to a change of focus. It is the same with letters. When it was suggested to Goethe that he should embody letters in his autobiography, he refused on the ground that "incoherent *realia* strewn about must necessarily disturb the good effect"; and the remark applies not only to matter in the letters that he considered irrelevant to his account, but also to the incoherence of style, the uneasy juxtaposition of different points of view. Beatrice Webb used, in *My Apprenticeship*, a great number of diary entries, and they are often confusing. From time to time, it is true, she will make some comment to the effect that the entry quoted illustrates some feature of her character in her young days, for instance that she was priggish or snobbish. But often the diary entry is unaccompanied by comment, and is meant to fit into the narrative as an adequate statement of what she was. In such cases we find it very difficult to evaluate the entry, and we want to know whether the mature writer fully accepts it now, or in what sense she would now criticise it. Such entries contrast glaringly with other passages where, in the normal autobiographical manner, she describes her youth from the point of view of maturity. There is of course no difficulty at all when we read her diaries as they have been published; we expect from a diary all the uncertainties, false starts, momentariness that we find in them. From the autobiography however we expect a coherent shaping of the past; and if diary entries or letters are quoted, we need the explanatory, interpretative commentary of the author.

The line between autobiography and memoir or reminiscence is much harder to draw—or rather, no clean line can be drawn.[1] There is no autobiography that is not in some respect a memoir, and no memoir that is without autobiographical information; both are based on personal experience, chronological, and reflective. But there is a general difference in the direction of the author's attention. In the autobiography proper, attention is focused on the self, in the memoir or reminiscence on others. It is natural, therefore, that the autobiographies of statesmen and

---

[1] One could distinguish memoir from reminiscence by saying that memoir concerns itself with public events, reminiscence with private relationships. The difference is primarily one of content, and does not affect the manner of composition or writing.

politicians are almost always in essence memoirs. The usual pattern includes true autobiographical material about childhood and youth. But when the author enters into the complex world of politics, he appears as only a small element, fitting into a pattern, accomplishing a little here or there, aware of a host of personalities and forces around him. If he puts himself in the centre, he falls into rank vanity; it is as an observer that he can make a unity of his experiences, not as an actor. At the same time, the character of public political life imposes itself so relentlessly that there is often no essential relationship between the personal character of the man and his work, so that the childhood and such private life as is described remain detached from the main current, and therefore often run the risk of appearing a sentimental self-indulgence. In political life, too, there is a greater risk than in other spheres of the autobiography's being an apologia, a risk, that is, that it is written to persuade. Of course, even the most biased memoirs of this type illuminate a personality; but the illumination is involuntary. The works of de Retz, Godoy, Metternich, are invaluable as memoirs, thin and unconvincing as autobiography.

However, true autobiographies of statesmen are possible where their political activity stands in an essential relationship to their personality, where it can appear as the efflux of their personality. Even here, the forces of political life are so complex that the statesman may restrict himself to indicating the manner and effect of his intervention here and there, instead of giving a coherent story in autobiographical form. Bismarck wrote his *Thoughts and Recollections* with the intention of justifying himself, and he was in no mood to be modest; yet he confined his account to the "inside" story of particular, separate events, supplementing and correcting what was publicly known. I am not concerned at this moment with the question of the truth of his account; all autobiographies have their problems in this respect. But it is significant that the work is not autobiographical in form, above all since the simple weight and complexity of public issues could not be done justice to in the form of autobiography. More must be said below on the political autobiography; it must suffice now to indicate that its possibility arises, but rarely. The outstanding example is Gandhi's, for his political activity, arising from a deep personal conviction, was creative in the truest sense, so that he could conclude his account of his political struggles in Africa and India with the remarkable words: "To describe Truth, as it has appeared to me, and in the exact manner in which I have arrived at it, has been my ceaseless effort".[1] His work could be autobiographical because his political achievements had meaning for him only in relation to the spiritual source from which they sprang.

Memoirs are common in other spheres than the political. What is characteristic of the best is that, while they have the sharpness due to a particular social position and personal slant, the slant is taken for granted or at least not subjected to prolonged attention. Gossips and hangers-on can write memoirs of interest, if they know they have in themselves little claim to our attention; if not, they devastatingly show up their superficiality, like Ford Madox Ford. But the distinction between the memoirist and the autobiographer can clearly be detected even in those who might have written both. Logan Pearsall Smith leaves us in no doubt as to why he called his *Unforgotten Years* "reminiscences". He does tell us something about his early years, but tersely, with astringent and disillusioned irony, evidently reluctant to take himself seriously: "I detect in myself a tendency to sentimentalise over these early years of my existence. It is not that I wish to recall my youth. It is rather that I feel a kind of impatient pity for that half-baked young fool of an American boy about whom I have been writing." "Existence", "impatient", "half-baked"— they are not terms the autobiographer can use, even if like Henry Adams he intends to show us that his youth was misdirected. Pearsall Smith is at his happiest when he is, in his own words, "saving the places and people one has cared for from being utterly forgotten"—recalling them not because of any influence they had on him, but simply because they were lovable.

Appearances here may easily deceive, for it is not always possible to distinguish the autobiographer from the memoirist by the amount of external life that is described. A reviewer said of

---

[1] *Mahatma Gandhi, His Own Story*, ed. C. F. Andrews, 1930, 333–4. This is a condensed version of several autobiographical writings of Gandhi, which have such significant titles as *The Story of my Experiments with Truth* or *Satyagraha (Soul-Force) in South Africa*.

B

Yeats' *Autobiographies* (a collection of the poet's autobiographical writings) "It is probably better to take these papers not so much as an account of the man who was all the time a poet . . . but as a record of people and things he thought important".[1] This is more true of the later papers than the *Reveries over Childhood and Youth*, yet even this consists largely of recollections of relatives and friends. Henry James planned his autobiography as a memorial to his brother, his father, and friends like Mary Temple. But in both cases, with Yeats and James, the ostensible form and intention come to serve a different and truly autobiographical intention, since all these objective identities, these other people, become forces within the writer and are referred back, implicitly more than explicitly, to the writer, whom their impact shapes and who develops in subtle response to them. The opposite is true of the five volumes of Sir Osbert Sitwell's autobiography. For though he seems to have set out with an autobiographical intention, and many personal experiences and achievements are recorded, Sir Osbert falls more and more into reminiscence. It is the figure of his eccentric and engaging father that holds the books together and provides their climax, not himself, and, as Stephen Spender rightly observes, these reminiscences "tell us little about what it feels like to be in Sir Osbert's skin".[2] There is in this account a sort of bristly shyness, which we readily respect, but which holds us off.

One must distinguish autobiography too from philosophical reflection on the self, static analysis, and the self-portrait—as in Marcus Aurelius, Boethius, or Nietzsche's *Ecce Homo*, and many journals which note down the changing aspects of a character, like the tortured confessions of many pietists. What is common to all these methods is the attempt, by means of introspection, at a static representation of the personality. The autobiography is on the contrary historical in its method, and at the same time the representation of the self in and through its relations with the outer world. Perhaps one might say that it involves the philosophical assumption that the self comes into being only through interplay with the outer world. It is true of all autobiographies, I think, that they have in them, in some measure, the germ of a description of the

[1] L. A. G. Strong, review in *The London Magazine*, June 1955, vol. 2, No. 6.
[2] "Confessions and Autobiography", in *The Making of a Poem*.

manners of their times, as has been noted even of Augustine's *Confessions*. Autobiographies that are so engrossed with the inner life that the outer world becomes blurred, as is the case with many autobiographies of medieval mystics, like those which at the other extreme restrict themselves to *res gestae*, fail to realise the potentialities of the genre.

These distinctions have led us a good way towards a definition of autobiography proper. It involves the reconstruction of the movement of a life, or part of a life, in the actual circumstances in which it was lived. Its centre of interest is the self, not the outside world, though necessarily the outside world must appear so that, in give and take with it, the personality finds its peculiar shape. But "reconstruction of a life" is an impossible task. A single day's experience is limitless in its radiation backward and forward. So that we have to hurry to qualify the above assertions by adding that autobiography is a shaping of the past. It imposes a pattern on a life, constructs out of it a coherent story. It establishes certain stages in an individual life, makes links between them, and defines, implicitly or explicitly, a certain consistency of relationship between the self and the outside world (or a consistency of misrelationship, as with K. P. Moritz or Denton Welch). This coherence implies that the writer takes a particular standpoint, the standpoint of the moment at which he reviews his life, and interprets his life from it. The standpoint may be the actual social position of the writer, his acknowledged achievement in any field, his present philosophy; in every case it is his present position which enables him to see his life as something of a unity, something that may be reduced to order. Autobiography, as A. M. Clark said, is not the annals of a man's life, but its "philosophical history". There is point in the suggestion that Goethe called his autobiography *Poetry and Truth* because he wished to distinguish between the actual facts of his youth and the interpretation of the old man writing.[1] Collingwood's case is typical. It was only in 1938, when he thought he had come to the understanding that his life had a coherent purpose, that he could write his autobiography. He concludes his book: "I know that all my life I have been engaged unawares in a political struggle, fighting . . . in the dark. Henceforth I shall fight in the

[1] Erich Trunz, in his notes to his edition of Goethe, vol. ix, Hamburg, 1955. 608.

9

daylight"; and this realisation of a meaningful standpoint, the emergence from shadows into daylight, is a condition of auto-biography altogether. It is the reason why autobiographies of younger men are rarely satisfactory.

Autobiography means therefore discrimination and selection in face of the endless complexity of life, selection of facts, distribution of emphases, choice of expression. Everything depends on the standpoint chosen; and it is clear that the more arbitrary the standpoint, the greater is the likelihood that the autobiography will be one-sided, blinkered, or downright false. This is the reason, I believe, why the best autobiographies are by men and women of outstanding achievement in life. Their standpoint is not as it were chosen by them, it is not at all a question for them to decide as it is with younger people, when they come to review their life: it is there, the indubitable result of their life's work, often acknowledged publicly, but at any rate for them the concrete reality of the meaning of their life. They can feel, as Petrarch proudly begins his *Letter to Posterity*: "Perchance you will want to know what manner of man I was, and how my writings fared." Even when they write to defy public opinion of them, like Rousseau, they are significantly helped in creating their pattern by what they have publicly effected and what they stand for in the public view.

What distinguishes the story of people with an established public achievement and personality is a consistent relationship, a sort of harmony, between outward experience and inward growth or unfolding, between incidents and the spiritual digesting of them, so that each circumstance, each incident, instead of being an anomalous fact, becomes a part of a process and a revelation of something within the personality. Experiences acquire a symbolic value—as J. C. Powys says of autobiography, "the only interest in events . . . is a symbolic one". That is, there is not only a consistency in the character described—as one finds in Cicero, in Boethius, in Giraldus Cambrensis, in the accounts of mystics like Margery Kempe as in many political autobiographies —but also an echoing consistency in the outward circumstances of life. The best autobiographies seem to suggest a certain power of the personality over circumstance, not in the arrogant sense that circumstance can be bent to the will of the individual, but in the sense that the individual can extract nurture out of disparate incidents and ultimately bind them together in his own way, disregarding all that was unusable. Painful as well as advantageous experiences can thus be transformed into the substance of the personality. The thesis can easily sound arrogant, and that is why Goethe put the thought into the mouth of Mephistopheles—

> How merit and luck are linked in one
> The fools can never understand;
> If they possessed the philosopher's stone
> There'd be no philosopher at hand.

It is on this principle that in the first great autobiography Augustine selected from the "large and boundless chamber" of memory a handful of experiences that chart the graph of his progress through error to truth. We know that they do not represent anything like all the intense experiences of his early life, and that some of them, like the boyish theft of pears, acquired significance only in retrospect. But they are illuminated and linked by the autobiographer, for whom, as Augustine says, recollection is "re-collection". However much more fully later autobiographers may dwell on particulars, and however much more complex and insecure the "truth" may appear to them, the method remains substantially the same.

Autobiography is then an interplay, a collusion, between past and present; its significance is indeed more the revelation of the present situation than the uncovering of the past. If this present position is not brought home to us (or only feebly brought home to us, for it can in fact never be hidden), there is a failure. Arthur Keith is referring to faulty books when he says: "When reading autobiographies, I have often wished their authors had been more explicit about the circumstances in which they wrote", and his own simple account of his life in active retirement gives a clue to the manner of his recollections altogether. But he was scarcely aware of the intricacy of this interplay of present and past, and it can play strange tricks with the autobiography. Chateaubriand was not particularly perspicacious or scrupulous in his method of recalling the past, but he shows an unusual insight into this problem of the "standpoint". His *Mémoires d'outre-tombe* were written and revised over three decades, often under startlingly changed conditions both public and private. He therefore introduces different sections with short prologues which describe the situation in which he writes and the issues pre-occupying him at that moment. He explains his reasons for adopting this method in the "Préface testamentaire", and continues with the memorable words:

> The varied events and changing forms of my life thus enter one into the other. It occurs that, in prosperous moments, I have to speak of the time of my misfortunes and that, in my days of tribulation, I retrace my days of happiness. The various sentiments of my different ages, my youth penetrating my old age, the gravity of my years of experience saddening the light-hearted years; the beams of my sun, from its dawn to its setting, crossing and mingling like the scattered reflections of my life: all this gives a sort of indefinable unity to my work: my cradle has something of my grave, my grave has something of my cradle; my sufferings become my pleasures, my pleasures become pains, and one does not know whether these Mémoires are the work of a brown or hoary head.

The long duration of Chateaubriand's autobiographical work, the revisions of judgement and of style that he felt himself impelled to make, made him exceptionally aware of this intimate collusion of past and present, but it is not merely a condition of all autobiography, it is its very sense.

If I have so stressed the fact that the beginning is in the end, it is necessary to stress also the corollary, that the end is in the beginning. There are many autobiographical writings that limit themselves to one particular experience or group of experiences that bare the core of the personality, like Saint-Exupéry's volumes. To this category belong many books of travel, books of spiritual experience in war, and so on. They are not usually called autobiographies, and I prefer the term "autobiographical writings". For one seems to expect from autobiography a totality rather than a quintessence; and even if such an experience gives the personality a new dimension, a turn, the autobiography must embed it in a long process. We need to see the sources of a life from childhood; only in this way do we grasp it—though the "grasp" is a peculiar sort of knowledge to which I must return later. One need only compare Goethe's autobiographical writings, the *Italian Journey* or the *Campaign in France*, interesting as these are,

with *Poetry and Truth*, to see how deeply we delve in the autobiography proper, how much more intimate with him we become.
The distinction is illustrated by the extremes. Aksakoff's *Years
of Childhood*, which ceases with his tenth year, is true autobiography; Lawrence's *Seven Pillars of Wisdom* is something else.

Stendhal set out on his *Souvenirs d'Egotisme* with an apparently
genuine autobiographical intention. He asks himself a series of
questions like "what man am I?", and intends to try to see if he
can "discover something positive, something that will remain for
a long time true" for himself. His method is to retrace all the
incidents of the ten years he spent in Paris between 1821 and
1830. There is no need to say that the book is full of illuminating
remarks about himself and his acquaintance, and tells us a great
deal about his mode of life. All students of Stendhal must use it.
Yet there is something extremely elusive about the whole man as
he here appears, an elusiveness which is of a type not characteristic of the autobiography. Perhaps he felt this inadequacy himself, for very soon after writing the *Souvenirs* Stendhal started his
story of his childhood, *Vie de Henry Brulard*, which opens with
similar statements of his purpose. It is the same person, brilliantly
swift and elusively inconsistent, lacking in judgement and in any
instinct of self-protection. But here we seem really to grasp his
personality. I do not think this is due essentially to Stendhal's
subtle analysis of the influence on him of persons near to him. He
makes us fully aware of the effect of the loveless home, the forced
piety and the snobbery of his father and aunt, their admiration of
his gifts and their well-meaning obstruction of his natural needs;
we see how isolation intensifies the self-assertion, conceit, and
malice of the intelligent and imaginative child, we can trace the
sources of his "Spanish" pride, his horror of the bourgeois, his
loathing of hypocrisy and rhetoric and so forth. Yet *Henry
Brulard* is true autobiography not simply because of Stendhal's
brilliant insight, but also because we are intimate with him from
the beginnings of his life, we see a historical consistency of
character which would satisfy us even if we could not trace its
psychological consistency. We are at home with him in the way we
are at home with childhood friends.

The subtle penetration of the past by the present affects not only
the shape of autobiography, but also the mode of description, the

style. Rousseau claimed that he would give the past as it was in its utter truth: "the likeness of a man in all the truth of nature". He, like a host of writers since, tried to evoke circumstances and experiences as they actually were for the child and young man. We do not need to consult psychologists as to whether this is a feasible task; it is clearly impossible, and even Rousseau's most innocent, unpolemical passages betray the man writing. The description of the boyish ruse of watering the willow, the idyllic day with Mlles de Graffenried and Galley, the picture of the Abbé tightening Mme de Warens' stay-laces, have the sharp stab and lingering aroma of remembered delights rather than the blurred naïvety of actual experience. Croce suggests that "recollections" in the narrow sense, evocations of the past, are possible, though only to poets, but he is surely making a mistake.[1] It is true that writers with a poetic gift come nearer to a reconstruction of the "feel" of past experiences than do other autobiographers, but this "feel" is always composite, and J. P. Sartre is nearer the truth when he says that autobiographers recollect their past passions in order to inter them in "a calm cemetery".[2]

It is not the author's greater or less capacity to evoke the past that significantly distinguishes types of autobiography, but much rather a differing appreciation of what is desirable to be recalled. A Darwin may find his "passion for collecting" the outstanding feature of his childhood; Franklin, barren as far as sensuous recollection goes, recalls vividly early practical and moral problems. The unassuming description of Philip Snowden's Yorkshire childhood is entirely appropriate to his purpose of showing the "formative influences" in this austere village community. Quite different methods of presentation are involved according to the distinctive quality of the personality involved; and in each case, more or less subtly, the presentation of the past is controlled by the character of the man writing.

Though men's mode of experience differs, it is of course possible, especially in modern times, to look on one's story too much as that of a specialised function, and to describe the past in a way that the reader may feel to be evasive or even deceptive. Nietzsche's warning is salutary:

[1] Croce, *An Autobiography*, 22.
[2] Avant-Propos to Gorz, *Le Traître*.

The need to provide for subsistence forces on all male Europeans today a particular role, their so-called profession; some have the freedom—an apparent freedom—to choose this role themselves, for the greater number it is chosen for them. The outcome is strange enough: almost all Europeans, with advancing years, confuse themselves with their role, they themselves are the victims of their "good performance", they themselves have forgotten how very much chance, mood, caprice once disposed over them when their profession was decided—and how many parts they might have played.[1]

From an autobiography we need some indication of this indeterminacy, even if, in the case of marked and outstanding personalities, it may be that they were in very small degree the sports of caprice or victims of their role. Hume's *Life*, important historically as one of the first extended accounts by a writer of his literary progress, fails to reach greatness because of Hume's unwillingness to tell us of anything but the facts directly relevant to his publications; from it one could scarcely guess for instance at the content of his Essays. Gibbon's autobiography is so much greater precisely because he recognised the significance of a larger number of factors of experience. The fault in Hume's conception can readily be recognised by comparing his *Life* with the autobiography of Croce, who was equally terse, equally anxious to avoid dwelling on irrelevancies, and equally determined to restrict his theme to "the history of my calling or mission". But Croce includes in his account factors from outside literature and philosophy, his family and the society of Naples, the impact of social events and personalities at Rome, a sum of experiences and activities that illumine the meaning of his philosophy to him, in that it arose, as he says, out of the need "to assuage my misery and to give an orientation to my moral and intellectual life".

The autobiographer must rigorously select from his life, and perhaps the chief danger is to make the line linking past and present far too exactly continuous and logical. We not only tend consciously to rationalise our lives, but memory, as Maurois points out,[2] operates unconciously to the same end. Gusdorf in his searching essay on autobiography, calls this tendency the

[1] Nietzsche, *The Joyful Wisdom*, §356.
[2] A. Maurois, *Aspects de la Biographie*, 141.

15

"original sin" of autobiographers.[1] The consciousness of the outcome of an experience imposes itself on the experience and distorts it; the completed fact is substituted for the "fact-in-the-making". No autobiography can avoid this sort of simplification altogether since it is the autobiographer's task to view the past in perspective, but we often recognise the point at which it leads to distortion. The danger is peculiarly acute with those who write to show how a particular philosophical attitude has been acquired. When J. S. Mill writes that he has only recorded impressions that were "a kind of turning point, marking a definite progress in my mode of thought", he is warning us that he may be establishing an over-thin line of development, as in fact we discover. Autobiographical apologetics may easily fall into this error, since the writer may be primarily concerned to show what in earlier life foreshadowed his later convictions, and to play down the force of "aberrations". If one judges Newman's *Apologia pro vita sua* as autobiography, it is clear that he does much less than justice to that part of his experience and thought that found its fulfilment within the Church of England—though the complexity of this problem is illustrated by the fact that it was only his conversion to Rome that made him need to write his autobiography. Newman was of course much too skilful a polemicist to suppress entirely the attraction of erroneous beliefs, and the *Apologia* is in this respect much more generous than his letters of the time and his autobiographical memoir. The best apologetics, like the best autobiographies, must evoke the past meaning of an experience, even if only in the interest of throwing into relief the significance of its subsequent repudiation—one remembers how moving is Augustine's account of his repudiation of his loved wife.

We are faced in this respect with the central and most complicated problem of autobiography. For the autobiographer is not relating facts, but experiences—i.e. the inter-action of a man and facts or events. By experience we mean something with meaning, and there can be many varieties and shades of meaning. We may mean the direct emotive response, or the immediate effect in terms of behaviour or thought; but we can also mean significance in the long run, a significance that may appear on the surface only

[1] G. Gusdorf, *Conditions et limites de l'autobiographie*, in *Formen der Selbstdarstellung*, 117.

after much time. Or we may mean a significance that the experience acquires only in retrospect, a meaning it has for us long afterwards as we think of it and try to probe it, irrespective of an actual genetic process. We can legitimately say, of a past experience, "There I recognise myself, a germ that I could not have recognised till today, when I am conscious that I am something that I knew nothing of". All these sorts of meaning may belong to an experience, and autobiography must always include, as a decisive element, the last type: the meaning an event acquires when viewed in the perspective of a whole life. The converse also is true—the position the autobiographer has reached must, in Sartre's words, "disqualify in our own eyes some episodes of our lives".[1] The problem for the autobiographer is to establish some sort of balance between the various types of meaning, a balance that will vary according to his character and intention. Something of the contemporary and perhaps aberrant meaning of an experience must be given as well as something of its ultimate retrospecttive significance. The autobiography is an artistic failure if we say, as did a reviewer of the story of a disabused communist, "its end is assumed from the beginning".[2]

Every experience is a nucleus from which energies radiate in various directions. In any worth-while life there is a dominant direction that is not accidental, so that ultimately the life is a sort of graph linking the experiences. But the graph is an imaginary line, in actuality the movement oscillates, perhaps violently, and the autobiography misrepresents the nature of experience if it fails to indicate these oscillations. It may fail too if the author, while faithfully relating the oscillations, overlays them with commentary that insists too heavily on the present wisdom of the author. With Augustine such interventions are, one can say, the main purpose of his *Life*, and it is only the astonishing novelty and brilliance of the autobiographical passages that enable one to disregard the interpolations. With lesser and later men one resents their unwillingness to let the story speak for itself. Victor Gollancz for instance irritates not so much because one might disagree with his views, as because the autobiography seems to be too undisguised a means of forcing them on us. It may well happen that

[1] J. P. Sartre speaking on his autobiography, *The Listener*, June 6, 1957.
[2] A. J. P. Taylor, *The Observer*, Oct. 27, 1957.

the importance of a young man's work, like Gorz's *Le Traître*, lies in his ceaseless self-analysis and his search for an objective justification of his subjective motives; but we read it not as an autobiography but as a philosophical treatise for which the life-story merely provides a text.

This is a problem for the biographer as much as for the auto-biographer, but the two forms are distinct in purpose as well as in form. Obviously, the autobiography gives us the "inside view", what Rousseau calls the "chain of feeling" for which the auto-biographer is often the only authority. But the author himself tends to remain, in Henry James' phrase, a "blurred image" in contrast to the bright images of the people and things he knows. The portraits of the author published in many autobiographies come as a great shock—rather like illustrations or film-versions of novels—not because they contradict one's idea of the author's appearance, but because one had created no visual idea of him. He exists for himself as something uncompleted, something full of potentiality, always overflowing the actuality, and it is this indeterminateness and unlimitedness that he communicates to us as an essential quality of being. The biographer on the other hand works back, inwards, from the defined personality, the portrait as it were; realised behaviour is for him decisive, not the consciousness of potentiality. The personality that strikes the outer world as most defined must itself be conscious of multiple uncertainties and unrealised possibilities. This consciousness seems to have driven Dürer to paint himself in different roles, as it were. Above all, the very character of his art seems to have tortured the supreme autobiographical artist, Rembrandt, in his sixty-two self-portraits, for he seems to seek ever and again, through new attitudes and disguises, to penetrate to the Protean thing beneath the skin.

There is a further essential difference between autobiography and biography. We are the only authority for the "chain of feeling" in our lives, and we establish this chain mainly through memory. The biographer depends on recorded data and as far as possible checks all subjective memories against records, often in fact rectifying faulty recollections. Inaccuracy is not a serious problem for the autobiographer, and Stendhal writes for all when he says: "I do not at all claim to write a history, but quite

18

simply to note down my memories in order to guess what sort of man I have been". But memory is not only inaccurate, it is treacherous and may profoundly mislead. W. H. Hudson prefaced his *Far Away and Long Ago* with the comment that "it is an illusion to think the few things . . . distinctly remembered and visualised are precisely those which were most important in our life", and one does not need the help of Freud to agree. Every historian knows how critically he must use autobiographies, not only because of conscious polemical intentions in the autobiographer, but also because of the unconscious polemics of memory. Yet, autobiographies are not necessarily better because they are conscientiously based on objective evidence; some of the greatest rely entirely on memory, and the finest parts of Rousseau's are those for which he had no documentary sources. Memory can be trusted because autobiography is not just reconstruction of the past, but interpretation; the significant thing is what the man can remember of his past. It is a judgement on the past within the framework of the present, a document in the case as well as a sentence.

The value of an autobiography depends ultimately on the quality of spirit of the writer. I do not mean, in a simple sense, the quality of truthfulness, about which much more has to be said, and I do not mean the same quality in all. I mean a capacity which differs according to the nature of the personality and life, and which succeeds in creating in us the consciousness of the driving force of this life, what Montaigne calls a man's "master form".[1] Many autobiographies fail to be significant because of triviality or lack of shape in the personality. They may be insignificant too when the personality is not in itself trivial, but for some reason has decided to avoid serious issues in his autobiography. Trollope gives a moving account of his boyhood, but the remainder of his autobiography is mostly trivial, the career-story of a man of letters. He tells us at the end: "It will not, I trust, be supposed by any reader that I have intended in this so-called autobiography to give a record of my inner life"—and one does not know whether to attribute this self-masking to complacency, to man-of-the-world disillusionment, or to a late-Victorian reserve and shyness. Few of the poorest autobiographies are lacking in social and

[1] Montaigne, *Essais*, ed. Villey, Paris 1923, iii, 35.

psychological interest. But one demands from the best more than an account of personalities, events, and circumstances. These must become the framework, in some sense the embodiment, of the personality of the writer as a man pledged to life, and one must be set free from them as historical facts, and from the concern with their accuracy as historical documents, in order to savour the quality of the central personality.

II

The earlier History of the Autobiography

LIKE other literary forms, autobiography has its history. Misch has charted it in Ancient times and in the early Middle Ages, while others have carried on the story into modern times. A full history would necessarily include autobiographical documents that cannot fully or properly count as autobiographies, and my purpose here is only to indicate the qualities of the outstanding examples of autobiography in order to delineate its possibilities and its full emergence as a consciously understood literary form. The process is not understandable within the confines of one particular national literature; more than most genres the autobiography disregards linguistic and national barriers.

It is a creation of European civilisation, and really begins with Augustine. There are numerous autobiographical statements in classical Greek and Roman literature, accounts of things done or works written, communings with the self. But never is the unique, personal story, in its private as well as public aspect, considered worthy of the single-minded devotion of the author. In Oriental and Byzantine literature, as in ancient and modern Europe, there are extended accounts written by men to justify themselves against charges or lament their misfortunes, to plead for clemency or charity—Acciauoli's (1364) can be paralleled by those of the Chinese Ssu-ma Chi'en or Stephanos Sachlikis.[1] These interesting personal documents confine themselves to the relevant issues and are autobiographical merely by force of

---

[1] See the essays on Acciauoli and Sachlikis in *Formen der Selbstdarstellung*, ed. Reichenkron and Haase.

circumstance. It is beyond my scope to suggest why autobiography does not come into being outside Europe, and the existence of such a work as Bābur's memoirs of the sixteenth century, which would occupy a significant place in the history of autobiography had it belonged to Europe, makes one hesitate to generalise. But there remains no doubt that autobiography is essentially European. Where in modern times members of Eastern civilisations have written autobiographies, like Gandhi for instance, they have taken over a European tradition.

No-one can doubt the decisive significance of Augustine's *Confessions* (ca. 400). Its novelty is so astonishing that there is considerable argument about its sources. The customary view that it arose from the Christian concern for the soul and habit of confession leaves much unexplained, and Misch is right in emphasising its debt to Hellenistic and Roman literature and discerning in it the self-assertion of a proud and mighty personality. Yet, despite its display and rhetoric, it surely reveals a feeling of life that is totally different from that of classical antiquity. Here is a feeling of movement in time, of history, a consciousness of an inward stream of forces that becomes evident in, and gives significance to, incidents that in themselves would be trivial. It is the spirit of the Biblical stories, of Abraham going to sacrifice Isaac, of Peter denying his Lord, as Auerbach has so sensitively delineated it.[1] It is in this tradition that Augustine writes, though he gives it a new direction and depth in creating the coherent history of his own soul.

Perhaps the central significance of the *Confessions* in literary history is best illustrated by the awe with which Augustine, in the reflective Chapter 10, speaks of the "large and boundless chamber" of memory. This is the peculiar world of his book: "Lord, I, truly, toil therein, yea and toil myself; I am become a heavy soil requiring over much sweat of the brow". Out of memory he "re-collects" the scattered pieces of his personality. But not in order to demonstrate himself as an Aristotelian entelechy, perfected from the beginning; not like Marcus Aurelius to construct a basic model; but to show his spiritual evolution, the coming-into-being of his full personality—a process of such startling change that he must ascribe it to Divine intervention. It

[1] E. Auerbach, *Mimesis*, Berne 1946, Chapters 1-3.

is not a portrait, but a movement in perspective. Equally remarkable, although it is essentially a spiritual movement, it takes place
through a series of impacts and scenes at specific times and places.
Deeds are not recounted simply because they occurred, but
because they represent stages of spiritual growth, so much so that
his mother grows into a symbol, a guardian angel, and the narrative concludes with their joint adoration of Divine love at the
window in Ostia, and her devout death.

The book is truly autobiographical since it could have been
written only by the man engaged. Many of the events are such
that only he would know them, certainly the feelings involved are
purely private. But over and above all this, it is only he who
could link them and create out of them a coherence and growing
intensity of meaning; only he could shape out of them the coherence of his moral personality. The *Confessions* is the first book,
as Misch says, "to represent plastically the coherence of human
existence in the mother-earth of his story", and thus to establish
the "structural law" of the autobiography.

Augustine's primary purpose was no doubt to write a testimony
to God, and his book has remained a manual of devotion. It
remains too "an epoch in the annals of psychology", as Dilthey
called it. Its peculiar quality as autobiography lies however not
primarily in its religious teaching or its psychological discoveries
—nor in the curious historical information it provides. The
mounting emotive intensity of the scenes, culminating in the voice
singing "tolle, lege" in the garden and in the window-scene at
Ostia, indicates not so much mere remembrance of the past as
poetic re-enactment and creation, that is, a new creative experience
of the author, whereby he grasps himself in a new way, shapes and
re-shapes himself anew. The reader does not merely take in
historical facts, but participates in an integrated succession of
experiences. In this first example autobiography appears as an art.

Though Augustine's work was widely read throughout the
Middle Ages, it had no comparable successor for over a thousand
years. Whether as religious confessions or as chronicles, as "res
gestae", subsequent autobiographical documents lack what
Misch calls the "integration of personal existence" and its
concomitant, "the ethical energy of self-knowledge"[1]; they are

---

[1] Misch, *Geschichte der Autobiographie im Mittelalter*, vol. ii, part ii, 650.

piece-meal accounts, of events or religious experiences, in which the author fails to distance himself from himself. This is true in the main of the vast mass of autobiography which is scattered over the Middle Ages, though there are here and there elements of genuine autobiography.

One of the most remarkable is Abelard's *History of my Calamities*. He wrote this account of his misfortunes and how he had borne them in order to strengthen a friend in distress, and this accounts perhaps for the precision of his narrative. But something else enters in: an involuntary need to relive the past, especially his love for Heloise, and to grasp what had happened. In the famous correspondence with Heloise, which has always been joined with the *Historia Calamitatum,* we notice how anxiously he tries to avoid dwelling on the past which her wonderful letters seductively and passionately evoke. But in the *Historia* (which historically preceded the letters) one detects his need, beyond any immediate pastoral intention, in his banishment and spiritual loneliness, to recall all the circumstances of his raptures and torments, his well-meant plan of living in secret wedlock, and the disaster of his mutilation. Rare too is his awareness of the complexity of his feelings after his brutal castration: "it was a feeling of shame, I confess, rather than a vocation, that drove me towards the shade of the cloister". His account of his subsequent theological controversies tells us less of the issues than of the behaviour of his antagonists and his own feelings of outrage and indignation; and as he speaks again of Heloise, when he appoints her to be superior of the Paraclete convent, there enters again the warmth lingering from their love. The ostensible reason for his account is to demonstrate submission to God's will; the unconscious reasons are truly autobiographical—to recapture the past, to see his life as a whole, to find within its vagaries its one rapture and the one indivisible personality.

Most medieval religious autobiographies lack precision in observation of the outer world and fail to relate meaningfully outer event and inner experience. The religious experience is largely dissociated from the specific personality and in fact rapidly acquires a conventional quality. Suso's (Seuse's) *Life of the Servant* (ca. 1360) is perhaps the finest. It was written, like Abelard's, as a devotional work, for the aid of a "spiritual daughter", but it remains consistently instructional and never becomes confessional in the subjective sense. His life is an example of God's will; and though he describes as historical events the stages of his spiritual growth, they appear more as exemplary devices than as actual occurrences, and have significance chiefly because they may be applied by others: for instance, when he describes how he transformed the popular custom of presenting a bouquet to the beloved to the service of the Virgin Mary. There are occasional vivid scenes, such as his meeting with his erring sister and her shame and repentance, or the trials he suffered when a woman charged him with being the father of her child; but they are events he withstands, not experiences that enrich or change him. The simplicity of Suso's faith and the single-mindedness of his instructional purpose, which made his work so important a book of devotion, limit its value as autobiography.

If autobiography demands the establishment of some sort of consonance between experience and personal values, it would seem that certain historical periods are most unpropitious for this type of literature. In the Middle Ages the chaotic and violent unpredictability of life could scarcely be reduced by an individual to a meaningful coherence, and could be encountered with dignity only by a Stoic or Christian resignation and withdrawal; and in addition the character of Christian belief allowed for no compact with the outer world. History could be no more than chronicle. In the case of *The Book of Margery Kempe* (1436–8) we see the two worlds utterly at variance—an inner life of hysterical urgings and visions, an outer experience of disparate adventures. Here and there, and notably in her encounters with ecclesiastical authorities, there are vivid passages in which we see a moral quality in Margery's determination to fulfil her mission, a self-consciousness which belongs to good autobiography; but usually her actions and her manner of behaviour derive from the obscurest urges. Like so many autobiographies, the work is a precious historical document, particularly as regards the religious feeling of the times, but it is raw, not shaped, material. It has the same sort of self-unawareness as Giraldus Cambrensis' *De rebus a se gestis* (ca. 1200), a title that accurately describes its contents and that ought not to be translated into "Autobiography". The chronical of Salimbene (ca. 1288) is a most fascinating account of things observed and known by this Franciscan monk, and is, at the same time, as Coulton says, a most valuable testimony to the faith of the common people in those times. But its evidence is all involuntary, naïvely gossiped. When Coulton calls it "the most remarkable autobiography of the Middle Ages", he is confusing "autobiography" with "personal evidence".[1]

The concept "Renaissance" has been severely challenged in these last decades. In reviewing the history of the autobiography, however, one is forced to admit what a startling change came over men's thought in this period with regard to themselves. Petrarch's *Letter to Posterity* (1351) opens with words which, reflecting something of Seneca and Cicero, express a new direction of interest and self-confidence. Posterity, he begins, "perchance will want to know what manner of man I was, and how my writings fared". There is no searching of soul here, no confession. He calmly delineates his character, his concern for spiritual matters, his gratefulness for friendship, his need to be free of worldly concerns, his Christian-Stoic philosophy. Petrarch's short account is not true autobiography. He was too intent on displaying himself as a type, in an ideal form, too concerned with generalities—"Childhood deluded me, youth spoiled me, age has improved me". And this general intention made him very reticent with regard to particular events. Later editors found his bare reference to a long-sustained love so inadequate that they supplemented the text with material about Laura taken from his other writings. He founded, or renewed the Stoic tradition of a stylised autobiographical form that was adopted by many later humanists, such as Justus Lipsius, and that often served to hide the actual truth. But he introduced a decisive theme, the untroubled concern for the inward dimensions of the self, springing not from any external necessity, self-defence or whatever it might be, but from a compulsion to meditate upon oneself; and he released the self from the hegemony of faith: "he is less concerned for salvation than for the cult of his soul".[2]

It was not till the sixteenth century that Petrarch's attitude was

---

[1] G. G. Coulton, *From St. Francis to Dante*, 1907, Introduction. In this book Coulton has translated and arranged Salimbene's text.

[2] A. Buck, *Die Selbstdarstellung Petrarcas und Cardanos*, in *Formen der Selbstdarstellung*.

fulfilled in autobiography. Till then, autobiographies other than religious remain rather bare in statement and limited to a particular theme. Ghiberti's, the first autobiography of an artist, speaks first of the history of art in Italy, then very sparsely of his own life in terms of his works, and finally of his theory of art. But suddenly, in the same decade of the sixteenth century, three autobiographies of major quality were written, those of Cellini, Cardano, and Saint Teresa; and even if Teresa could look back on a long tradition of religious autobiography, one cannot but associate her with the others as startling evidence of the fulfilment of a new attitude. All write of their minds, their affections, their soul, but all delineate it also through the concrete detail of their fortunes, without strain, as if it were the most natural thing in the world to do. Montaigne, their slightly younger contemporary, represents the same trend, though he wrote no autobiography. He writes of his opinions with the mock-modest assumption that what he says and does is interesting precisely because it is *his* thought and behaviour; the justification is the portraiture, his own peculiar character. In this "thorny enterprise" the normal attitude and expectation are reversed; Montaigne calls his essays "my fantasies, by which I try to give knowledge not about things, but about myself". Ideas and behaviour claim significance and coherence, however petty and contradictory they are, because they are the expression of the particular man. Of course all these writers claim an objective validity for their achievements, the truth of their ideas or religious vision, the excellence of their art; what is peculiar is that they felt these achievements to be embedded in their specific personality.

Cellini, who wrote his autobiography between 1558 and 1566, was supremely confident of his greatness as an artist, and in part his purpose is to tell us the story of his works. But his famous account of the casting of his Perseus is an astonishing display of a temperament as well as a craft, and a piece of social history besides, and the whole book is the story of a man, not simply an artist. He tells us how he came to write it. Living again in his old home town, his thoughts dwell on the strange identity of the old man and the young—one of the decisive stimuli of modern auto-biography: "Now that I am leaving the age of fifty-eight behind me and find myself in my native place, Florence, my thoughts naturally turn to such a task". Like any old man, that is, he naturally thinks of the incidents of a lively career; but it is not so "natural" that he tells a real story, through the turbulent incidents of which there appears the persistent identity of the teller. His imaginativeness as well as his inveterate vanity often preclude truth, but it is the frankest of accounts, for if he deludes us, he deludes himself as much. He is incapable of "Besinnung", of standing back and coolly reflecting on the truth of situations and motives; but because he is so uninhibitedly candid he does not force us to share his verdict. One can call him a liar and a braggart, yet he is transparent, and Stendhal, who was hard on Rousseau and Marmontel, was right when he said "Benvenuto was truthful ('vrai')". The judgement involves, as often in the case of auto-biography, a statement concerning the man as well as the writer. For "vrai" means that Cellini's life as well as his account comes from the heart, that it has the consistency of a warm and imagina-tive personality—a quality that distinguishes it for instance from the entertaining memoirs of the adventurer Casanova.

The life of this gifted and impulsive man in sixteenth-century Italy and France was fascinatingly eventful, full of accident, and his account had necessarily to be different from Augustine's distillation of a few events heavy with significance. Nor is he general and analytic like Petrarch. Yet he is not broadly discursive like a chronicler. He writes a continuous and dramatic narrative, the incidents of which are held together and linked by the feelings, imaginings, mental responses of a consistent and marked personality. It comes near to the novel, one might say the Spanish picaresque novel, except that the "hero" has a fuller character and a more decisive role, and is always warm in his affections and lovable. How vividly do we see him and his friends in the anecdote which tells of his return to Florence after the plague:[1]

> I arrived at Florence, expecting to find my good old father. When I knocked at the door, a scraggy hunchbacked old woman looked out of the window and began screaming insults at me, telling me to go away and saying that the sight of me made her sick.
> "Good God," I shouted back, "you twisted old cripple, is there no one else in the house besides you?"
> "No, damn you, there isn't."

[1] *The Autobiography of Benvenuto Cellini*, trans. Bull. Penguin Books 1956, 81–2.

"All right then," I said, "I only hope we won't have to put up with you much longer."

Hearing all the uproar a neighbour came out, and she told me that my father and everyone in the house had died of the plague. As I had partly guessed this already I was less upset than I would have been. Then she added that only my younger sister, Liperata, was left alive, and that she had been taken in by a holy woman called Andrea de' Bellacci.

I left her and set off for the inn, and on the way I ran into a very close friend of mine called Giovanni Rigogli. So I dismounted at his house and we went along to the public square, where I heard that my brother also was still alive. I moved off to find him at the house of a friend of his called Bertino Aldobrandi. As we had each been told that the other was dead, when we met we hugged each other with unbounded affection. Then, roaring with laughter all the time, he took me by the hand and said:

"Come along, Benvenuto, I want to take you somewhere you'd never guess. I've married off our sister Liperata again, and she's positive that you're dead."

On the way we told each other all the wonderful experiences we had been through. Then, when we arrived at the house where she was, Liperata was so flabbergasted by such an unexpected visit that she fell fainting into my arms. If my brother had not been there, her fainting like that, without saying a word, would have made her husband suspect that I was anything but her brother; and in fact to begin with he did so. But Cecchino explained everything, attended to Liperata and soon brought her round. Shedding a few tears for her father, and her sister, and her husband, and her little son, she began to prepare some supper. We spent the rest of the evening very pleasantly; we never mentioned the dead again, but talked about weddings and in that way enjoyed a very happy little party.

Girolamo Cardano's *Book of my Life* is in some ways more remarkable, more modern, than Cellini's autobiography. The truth he seeks is not simply the historical truth of actions and events, but the truth of his personality, his feelings, impulses and ideas; his method is analytical and the deeper he penetrates, the more involved becomes his problem. As he compares his enterprise with that of Marcus Aurelius, he becomes aware of the difficulty of his task, for while Aurelius, as he says, wishes to say what he should be, Cardano will tell us what he is in truth, and this truth is a web of contradictions. He defines and illustrates his good qualities—his learning and intuitive skill as a doctor, his prowess as an author, his concern for his sons and attachment to friends—but is ready to confess to "every vice and evil save ambition"—to gambling, spitefulness, superstition, recklessness etc. And confession here does not imply contrition, it is a mere statement of fact. He can prove, with Aurelius, that the longing for fame is fatuous, yet he admits it possesses him; he despises public opinion, yet is proud of his Honours and bitterly ashamed of dishonour. Much is observed that fits into no pattern of values simply because it is part of him, for instance his need of physical pain, which he often inflicts on himself, in order to "overcome the mental anguish" to which he was prone. So that the picture emerges of an extraordinary complex and real man who conforms to no accepted type. The set of things which give him happiness likewise fit no pattern of values, and illustrate his assertion that happiness is not a fixed quality or quantity, but varies with time, place, and mood; his list includes "rest, serenity, modesty . . . meditation, education, piety . . . listening to music . . . water, fire . . . history, liberty, continence, little birds, puppies, cats, consolation of death".

It is perhaps not surprising that Cardano, so acutely aware of the elusiveness of his personality, should have looked under the surface of his temperament and behaviour for the real man. He speaks of an identity, an "essence", within himself that escapes definition, the source as he believes of his intuitive knowledge, of prophetic dreams, of his assurance of God; something that is

> part of me, yet the essence of it I am not able to define. And it is *myself*, although I am not aware that such virtue has originated from myself. This power is present when needed, but not in evidence when I so will. What comes to pass as a result of it is something more than my natural powers could effect.

Here is the hidden centre of his being. It is perhaps to be compared with the soul of the mystic, but with Cardano it appears not only as an organ of the supernatural, but as the essence of his natural personality. Here is the first recognition of Wordsworth's "mystery" of being, of Goethe's "daemon".

Cardano's *Book* then shows extraordinary psychological insight, and it is not surprising that men like Robert Burton should have greatly learned from him (Rousseau claims to have read him, but probably knew him only through Bayle's *Dictionnaire*). In Cellini and Cardano we have two extremes of autobiography: Cellini presents himself, Cardano analyses himself. The comparison is useful, for despite Cardano's infinitely greater insight something essential to autobiography is lacking. He does not entirely neglect narrative, for he uses incidents from his life to illustrate his themes. But his chapters have such headings as "Health", "Sports", "Customs, Vices, and Errors", "Friends", "Marriage and Children", "Religion and Piety". In this way not only is the life broken into pieces, but the personality too. We get to know him intellectually, but scarcely directly and imaginatively, while from Cellini's breathless narrative—as can be judged from the passage quoted above—we know the complex reality of the man without any analysis. The comparison tells us something important about the method of true autobiography and the nature of the knowledge it gives, to which we must return later.

Saint Teresa's *Life*, the third of the great autobiographies of the sixteenth century, was written between 1563-5. It was confessional in origin, composed like two earlier "Relations" for her spiritual directors. But while the earlier accounts were much barer statements of a woman seeking guidance, the *Life*, she tells us, was written in the assured conviction that she had received the "gift of Wisdom" from God and with the knowledge that it would be read by a wide public.

It does not tell, like Augustine's *Confessions*, of the grand outlines of faith. Its theme is the peculiar religious experience to which she was subject, the levitations and visions, her probing into herself and testing of them, with the help of spiritual directors: the progressive purification and "perfecting" of the religious experience. Occasionally she pauses to give a systematic or analytic account of the achievement of true rapture (particularly Chapters 11 to 22); but in the main the account is historical and concrete, embedded in the actuality of her life at home and in the convent. As with Augustine, and in distinction to Suso or Margery Kempe, she thus entwines the story of her inward experience with that of the small encounters of outward life, and her story leads naturally to the actual reform of conventual life and the founding of Saint Joseph's.

Many of the spiritual autobiographies before and after Saint Teresa's dwell abstractly and wearisomely on the raptures of mystical experience and the misery of apathy or sin—men brought up on such reading, like K. Ph. Moritz, could only too justifiably complain of the desolateness of spirit that they produce. When Teresa writes of her sins she too is typically vague. But in her account of her positive religious experience she is not only specific and concrete. What makes this work enthralling is the pertinacity and energy with which she examines herself—usually with the help of spiritual directors—testing her state of mind, weighing up possibilities of delusion, arguing with herself and her directors. She is as much concerned for the quality of her soul as for the actual character of the vision; and in this pertinacious, restless, obstinate self-examination she adds a new dimension to autobiography.

She recalls, for instance, how after a vision in which she had seen Christ "not with the eyes of the body but only with the eyes of the soul", the written account of it she had given to her director "greatly distressed me, for one can say nothing without doing great violence to oneself". She then continues with reference to a previous vision in which she had been conscious of the presence of Christ without seeing Him either with the eyes of the soul or with those of the body:

Those who know better than I say that my previous vision was more perfect than this one, while this in turn is much nearer to perfection than those that are seen with the eyes of the body. The latter, they say, is of the lowest kind, and the one most open to delusions from the devil. I was not aware of this at that time, but as this favour was being granted to me, wished that I could have seen it with my physical eyes, so that my confessor should not tell me that I was imagining it. The moment the vision had passed, at the very instant of its fading, I was myself struck by the thought that these things were all imaginary. It worried me that I had spoken of them to my confessor, and I wondered if I had been deceiving him. Here was more distress. So I went to him, and talked to him about it. He asked me whether I had described the vision as it had appeared to me or if I had meant to deceive him. I replied that I had told him the truth, for I did not think that I had been lying. I certainly had not meant to, for I would not have told an untruth for anything in the world. He knew that very well, and so he succeeded in calming me.

But it worried me so much to have to go over these matters that I do not know how the devil could have put it into my head that I was making them up to drive me into tormenting myself.[1]

The scope of the analysis is confined to religious experiences, and rapidly comes up against impenetrable metaphysical absolutes. But it is, within these limits, intrepid and subtle. At the same time, the method is autobiographical in a very full sense, since it is historical rather than static (like much of Cardano's), and unfolds in a lively dramatic narrative. It is a woman speaking, not a "soul" as in so many religious autobiographies, aware of her need for guidance, often ill and puzzled, but shrewdly distinguishing between poor and good advice, persuasive even when she humbles herself, and always purposeful and energetic. One cannot help thinking that Newman must have learnt a lot from Teresa.

The seventeenth century shows nothing comparable to these three autobiographies. It is a great age of memoirists and diarists— Cardinal de Retz, Saint-Evrémond, Evelyn, Pepys—but not of autobiographers. The "mémoires scandaleuses" of the time are interesting for their scandals, not the personalities of their authors, and none of them compares in quality with Defoe's pseudo-autobiographical *Moll Flanders*. Herbert of Cherbury's *Life* shows probably the more trivial sides of his character, even Hobbes does not get beneath the surface of his life and writings. By far the most interesting are the religious autobiographies, but they cannot be compared in quality with Teresa's. Compared with her, Mme de Guyon is prolix, incoherent, and often hysterically uncertain about herself and her situations. Baxter is diffuse and pedestrian, without psychological insight. The candour and simplicity of Bunyan's *Grace Abounding* (1666) put it above these. It is worthy of an artisan Augustine that he tells us he was arrested in the middle of a Sunday game of tip-cat by a sudden feeling of sin. Most moving is his description of his despair over the almost irresistible temptation to blaspheme that came upon him as he was preaching, or his account of the way in which he was weaned from his (sinful) love of bell-ringing—he was kept away by a neurotic fear first that the bells would fall on him, then that the whole steeple would collapse. But it is Bunyan's mental

[1] *The Life of Saint Teresa*, Chapter 28 (Penguin Classics, 196–7).

inarticulateness, his helplessness, that makes these incidents most moving, not his insight; and like many sectarian, pietistic auto-biographers he fails to recognise the relevance of many experiences to his spiritual progress, so that his account is limited in its range. What would one not give to know more about how he fared as a soldier in the Civil War!—but he makes only a passing reference to it. Even his career as a persecuted preacher and his imprisonment are only cursorily indicated. What we lose thereby is illustrated by the separate little work, *Relation of the Imprisonment of Mr. John Bunyan,* of 1665. Nothing in *Grace Abounding* compares in clarity and vivacity with this account of his arrest and trial, of the bearing of the magistrates, and the intercession of his wife before the Assize court. It gives sharp contours to a personality that in the autobiography remains somewhat blurred.

These religious autobiographies, themselves part of a long tradition, brought in their train countless others in the eighteenth century, particularly of Protestant pietists. Germany has a whole series of them, from A. H. Francke to Hamann, and some remain case-histories of remarkable interest. Particularly worthy of mention is the *Lebensbeschreibung* (1738) of the defrocked Lutheran pastor, Adam Berndt, which, interesting as a social document, is outstanding as an account of imaginary fears and obsessions, the appalled self-observation of a melancholic. But all these authors, brooding on sin and salvation, fail to see clearly either the outer world or themselves as persons.

These pietistic autobiographers, in their attention to the slightest shades of religious feeling, illustrate a trend to give a new importance to the details of personal life, and there is evidence of the same trend in the secular autobiography. Men like Colley Cibber uninhibitedly tell of the details of their private and professional existence. Writers, in particular, feel an obligation to render some account of themselves. Hume's *Life* (1776) is the most extended account of a writer till that time, and can stand as the last of an old tradition which reaches back to the Romans. It does not claim to be more than "the history of my writings" but is more than this, since it shows how consistently Hume followed his bent for "literature". It is however strictly limited to his literary purposes and work, and ignores all his activity outside these limits—for instance, he passes over his two years of service with "great lords" with the remark, "I passed them agreeably, and in good company"; and he does not mention his dramatic experiment with Rousseau. Hume's dry, sceptical terseness is a delight, but it hides as much as it reveals, and is free of all rumination and confession. His younger contemporaries were to discover quite new dimensions for the autobiography.

III

The Classical Age of Autobiography

I USED the term "history" instead of some such term as "evolution" in the title of the last chapter because the concept of an "evolution" of the autobiography up to the eighteenth century is scarcely, if at all, to be justified. There is certainly no simple line of development, and the great achievements seem to stand out like erratics. The religious tradition is the most coherent, but here too there is nothing like a development, steady or unsteady. One may establish the emergence, with the Renaissance, of a bolder and more untrammelled curiosity in man's mind and behaviour, yet this takes curious forms, and does not necessarily lead to autobiography—Pascal's *"le moi seul est haïssable"* belongs to the seventeenth century. So that a historical consideration of early autobiography seems to resist the notion of evolution, and remains at best a history of changing values and forms.

But there would be few who would doubt that in the later eighteenth century and the early nineteenth we ought to recognise, not only that a large number of great autobiographies were written, true "classics" in the usual sense of the term, but that this period may properly be called an "age" of great autobiography.

One thinks primarily, no doubt, of Rousseau, Goethe, Wordsworth, amongst the many significant autobiographers of this age. All these were men inwardly turned, deeply concerned with their sensibility and imagination. But there were others of different character, and I would speak first of Franklin and Gibbon.

It is a pity that Franklin's book became a handbook to success, for its use as a moral primer obscures its marked and attractive individuality. He himself is partly responsible, for he repeatedly recommends his mode of behaviour to others, and he evidently believed the moral principles that he drew up for himself would be useful to his son, to whom the book is addressed, and to other readers. He was a man of many abilities, and is concerned to tell us how he made his way—as a printer, a social reformer, a scientist and inventor, a statesman. There is something of vanity in his whole enterprise, he humorously admits, but what holds his narrative together is his need and desire to give an example of how one can make a success of things, so that his didactic intention is the most important structural element of his story. Of his childhood and youth, for instance, he recalls only those incidents which illustrate some useful problem of personal relationships and give a lesson on how to get on with or manage others. Yet his didacticism is not oppressive, and we need not choose between accepting him as an admired model or rejecting him for the base cunning of his commonsense, as D. H. Lawrence did with indignation. His narrative is always tolerant and humorous, and indeed his whole attitude to himself is the same; eminently practical and "sane", he tells of his errors and faults with the same simplicity and ironical equanimity as he does of his achievements and wisdom.

Franklin's *Life* was begun in 1771, and though not completed till 1789 it shows no trace of Rousseau's influence. He mentions emotional problems only in passing, and never dwells on stresses of conscience. But one does not feel that such experiences were not observed or deliberately hidden by him, but rather that they played little part in his life. This autobiography is the first narrative of a man as a practical social being.

We can hear an echo of Rousseau in Gibbon's *Memoirs* when he writes: "Truth, naked and unblushing truth . . . must be the sole recommendation of this personal narrative"; but it is only a flourish, for there is nothing in the *Memoirs* which could possibly bring a blush to Gibbon's or our cheeks. He began them long before Rousseau's *Confessions* were started, and one may legitimately discuss his work before Rousseau's. It is more tightly organised than Franklin's, since he undertook to show the making of the author of the *Decline and Fall*. It belongs thus to the long established genre of author-autobiographies. Its distinction might best be established by a comparison with Hume's.

Gibbon, like Hume, although more fully, tells us of his literary and historical studies. But the peculiar significance of his account lies in his inclusion of numerous types of experience that contributed, he recognises, to his development as a historian. Thus his irregular schooling, his ill-health, his misfortunes at Oxford, his temporary conversion to Roman Catholicism, are all linked as steps that detached him from the ordinary run of English eighteenth-century thought and prejudice. His service in the militia, trivial in itself, gives him an insight into military matters and a feel for a nation's destiny. His membership of the House of Commons and his life in Society bring him into touch with great affairs and leading statesmen. Even his reticence about his feelings, his meek acceptance of his father's veto on his love for the later Mme Necker, help us to understand how his passion and imagination were fired that day in Rome, as he brooded over the ruins and conceived his great task. For the first time we have an autobiography which reviews a whole life as the shaping and fruition of a specific skill devoted to one absorbing enterprise.

Both Franklin and Gibbon call their works "memoirs". Yet they are true autobiographies, since they not only centre in a personal history, but also delineate the manner in which the man mentally organises the world round him in relation to his own personality and tasks. They may be contrasted with Goldoni, who as a very old man wrote his *Memoirs* between 1784–7. This is an entrancing book, of signal importance for the history of the Italian drama and theatrical life. Goldoni himself appears as a charming character, not only through events which show his skill, equanimity, patience, amiability, but also in the whole style of writing, so simple and unassuming, yet intelligent and alert. But it falls short as autobiography, largely because Goldoni sees himself too completely in this role of the affable, complaisant craftsman, because one cannot see the driving force of his personality. Perhaps he thought, as have many autobiographers since, that his readers know so much about his work that he can devote himself, in his memoirs, to the incidents and accidents of his life. At the other extreme lies Alfieri, his fellow-countryman and fellow-playwright. Alfieri, looks for what is specific to his personality, but always drives towards generalities about his psychological make-up, his pride, desire for fame, his passionate love for the Countess of Albany, his passion for horses. It is a fascinating picture of a man who is always extreme, yet unsatisfactory as autobiography because he so rarely sees things or people in their concrete reality. One would guess that a few specific incidents from his childhood, that illumine his touchy pride, his love of justice, or his prejudice against the French, are directly due to Rousseau—for Alfieri wrote the major part of his autobiography in 1790 in Paris, only eight years after the appearance of the *Confessions*.

ROUSSEAU

All these writers show an alert interest in the specific course of their lives. Franklin's and Gibbon's are outstanding in that, with a secure confidence that before them had belonged almost exclusively to religious autobiographers, they recognise in themselves a dynamic inborn quality, their innermost personality, and see their story as its unfolding through encounters with the outer world. Both without further probing, almost complacently, accept their achievement as a worthy standard by which their lives may be evaluated and their narrative made coherent. With Rousseau something new is added, a question about the personality which cannot be answered, at any rate not simply, in terms of outward achievement, a question about the innermost nature of the self; and with this questioning and questing, something else, a feeling, one might call it a metaphysical compulsion, that one must be true to this innermost nature. Autobiography becomes not only an account of things done or known, an exposition of a personality, but a search for the true self, and a means to come to terms with it.

Several motives can be detected behind Rousseau's *Confessions*. First and foremost is his own opening proclamation of the complex uniqueness of his personality:[1]

> I desire to set before my fellows the likeness of a man in all the truth of nature, and that man myself. Myself alone! I know the feelings of my heart, and I know men. I am not made like any of those I have

[1] I quote from the anonymous translation in the privately printed edition of *The Confessions*, 1904.

D

seen; I venture to believe that I am not made like any of those who are in existence. If I am not better, at least I am different.

But Rousseau immediately slips over to a statement of a further motive, that of self-justification:

> I have told the good and the bad with equal frankness . . . I have shown myself as I was, mean and contemptible, good, high-minded and sublime, according as I was one or the other. I have unveiled my inmost self even as Thou hast seen it, O Eternal Being. Gather round me the countless host of my fellow-men; let them hear my confessions, and lament for my unworthiness, and blush for my imperfections. Then let each of them in turn reveal, with the same frankness, the secrets of his heart at the foot of the Throne, and say, if he dare, "I was better than that man!"

The book is then an apologia in the most general sense. Several times Rousseau insists that it is not an apology in the narrower sense, a self-defence against the charges of his contemporaries. At the beginning of Book VII, when his trials come thick upon him, and he has to speak of "misfortunes, treachery, perfidy", he writes: "I have no fear that the reader, forgetting that I am writing my Confessions, will ever imagine that I am writing my Apologia". But he is here not consistent, for only a page later he appeals to the reader's "sincere affection for truth and justice", and much of the second volume is in fact a presentation of his side of his "case". The *Confessions* are, among other things, a self-defence and counter-accusation.

There is, and prominently, another motive, an urgent need for confession of guilt. After the famous passage in which he describes how he had despicably charged a servant-girl with the theft he had himself committed, he tells us how haunted he is by this memory:

> This burden has remained to this day upon my conscience without alleviation; and I can affirm that the desire of freeing myself from it in some degree has greatly contributed to the resolution I have taken of writing my Confessions.

The motive is referred to on other similar occasions; the auto-biography takes the place of the confessional. His work is therefore linked with the religious autobiography, with Augustine—but with the significant difference that Rousseau speaks not of sins against God, but primarily of sins against his own true self. Thus his confession of sin is essentially associated with his declarations of his virtue, and becomes poignant to him because of his own conception of his true self—of what one might call his super-ego. The necessary correlative of the base Rousseau is Rousseau the virtuous, the Citizen of Geneva, the Roman, the legendary Jean-Jacques with his selfless "enthusiasm for truth, liberty, and virtue". When he is somewhat uneasily clearing himself of the charge that it was "depravity of heart" that brought him to place his children in the Foundling Hospital, he cries out:

> No! I feel and loudly assert—it is impossible. Never, for a single moment in his life, could Jean-Jacques have been a man without feeling, without compassion, or an unnatural father.

There are other motivations too, including obsessive memories and neurotic pressures. But underlying all is a tenacious concern for the quality of his soul. It led him to write of psychological processes up till then hidden, of moral perversities whose mention still provokes shocked reproof from some critics. Croce puts this criticism in its most general form when he rejects the confessional autobiography altogether. While affirming the value of "confessing oneself hourly", he says he sees no value "in passing a general moral judgement upon one's life as a whole". It only flatters one's vanity, he continues, the vanity of self-approbation or that of self-accusation, "vanity in either case because based on an exaggerated opinion of one's own importance".[1] Croce does not mention Rousseau, but it is unquestionable that he had Rousseau in mind; his view is not so very different from Diderot's criticism of Rousseau's character.

The *Confessions* answer with a plain counter-assertion: the soul—not the religious soul but the innermost nature, the human entelechy—is of supreme importance, and the objective is to discover it and display it to others: "I should like to be able to make my soul to a certain extent transparent to the eyes of the reader". Rousseau tells us his life-story, describes his friends, his activities, the genesis of his books, but underneath all this he recaptures what in defiance of the public evaluation of himself

[1] B. Croce, *An Autobiography*, trans. Collingwood, 1927, 19.

41

he considers to be his truest self, that innocent, happy-go-lucky youth, the "child" of Mme de Warens. The period of his fame, the whole second thirty years of his life, seems to him to be an aberration, when "destiny thwarted his inclinations", and its true sense lies in his sporadic efforts to recapture that innocence, in the Hermitage, Montmorency, and Neuchatel. But he does not simplify, and one is perpetually astonished at the insight which enables him to recognise that his assumed, public self almost became his real self, and that his real self was so elusive.

In Book IX he analyses his behaviour after his literary successes had brought him into touch with the leading intellectuals of his time and had inaugurated the period of the legendary Jean-Jacques:

> My continued attention . . . soon convinced me that there was nothing but error and folly in the doctrine of our philosophers, and misery and oppression in our social arrangements. Deluded by my foolish pride, I thought I was born to destroy all these illusions, and, believing that, in order to gain a hearing, it was necessary for my manner of life to harmonise with my principles, I adopted the singular course which I have not been permitted to continue, in which I set an example for which my pretended friends have never forgiven me, which at first made me ridiculous, and would have ended by making me respectable, if it had been possible for me to persevere in it.
>
> Hitherto I had been good; from that moment I became virtuous, or, at least, intoxicated with virtue. This intoxication had commenced in my head, but had passed on into my heart. The noblest pride sprang up therein on the ruins of uprooted vanity. I pretended nothing; I became really what I seemed; and, for the four years at least, during which this state of effervescence lasted in all its force, there was nothing great or beautiful, which a man's heart could contain, of which I was not capable between heaven and myself. This was the origin of my sudden eloquence, of the truly celestial fire which inflamed me. . . .

After describing the brilliant role he then played, Rousseau continues:

> If anyone desires to recall one of those brief moments in my life during which I ceased to be myself, and became another, he will find it again in the time of which I speak; but instead of lasting six

days or six weeks, it lasted nearly six years, and would perhaps have lasted until now, had it not been for the special circumstances which put an end to it, and restored me to Nature, above which I had attempted to elevate myself.

This change began as soon as I had left Paris and the sight of the vices of the great city ceased to keep up the indignation with which it had inspired me. . . . If this revolution had merely restored me to myself, and had gone no further, all would have been well; but unfortunately it went much further, and carried me away rapidly to the other extreme. From that time, my soul, in a state of agitation, no longer kept its centre of gravity, and its oscillations, ever renewed, always destroyed it.

The theme of the *Confessions*, and the standard by which Rousseau judges his actions, is his idea of his true self and his recognition of how elusive it is—elusive in his actual life, elusive too to his retrospective grasp. It could be grasped only in a historical narrative, not analytically, as he says in the discarded early preface to the book: "this bizarre and singular assemblage [his character] needs all the circumstances of my life to be truly revealed".[1] Or, as he puts it at the end of Book IV, "to know me in my advanced years you must have known me well in my youth". It is this general insight into the nature of the personality, and not simply the accompanying brilliant psychological observations, that makes this work the opening of a new era in autobiography.

WORDSWORTH

Narrower in psychological and social range than the *Confessions*, *The Prelude* is obviously like the earlier work in that Wordsworth's life and values return to their starting-point in nature and innocence.[2] Like Rousseau—and undoubtedly following Rousseau— Wordsworth asserts the supremacy of private experience. Even more consciously than Rousseau he feels the decisive significance

[1] *Oeuvres complètes*, Paris 1959, i, 1153 (Bibliothèque de la Pléiade).
[2] The first version of 1804–5 was considerably altered by Wordsworth for the final version of 1839, but my remarks here apply to the first as much as to the last. See E. de Selincourt's excellent introduction and edition, *Wordsworth, The Prelude*, 2nd imp. 1928.

of what is unique to him, something within him that asserts itself willy nilly, beneath his consciousness and will. It was this that dedicated him to poetry:

> I made no vows, but vows
> Were then made for me.

Concern for this deeper self has here freed itself from vanity, or any suspicion of vanity, because Wordsworth feels it is nothing of his doing, it is there unasked and undeserved, and he is only its trustee. It, not he, creates those moments of insight which become poems, and it is essential to *The Prelude* that it is a poem in which we participate in as well as observe these moments of vision—as in the passage at the end of Book XII, when in the boy, parted from his guide and in terror, the scene condenses into such a vision:

> Then, reascending the bare common, saw
> A naked pool that lay beneath the hills,
> The beacon on the summit, and, more near,
> A girl, who bore a pitcher on her head,
> And seemed with difficult steps to force her way
> Against the blowing wind. It was, in truth,
> An ordinary sight; but I should need
> Colours and words that are unknown to man,
> To paint the visionary dreariness
> Which, while I looked all round for my lost guide,
> Invested moorland waste, and naked pool,
> The beacon crowning the lone eminence,
> The female and her garments vexed and tossed
> By the strong wind . . .
> Oh! mystery of man, from what a depth
> Proceed thy honours.

This awed veneration for something within that invests an experience with significance goes beyond Rousseau's tenderness for himself; it is indeed austere rather than indulgent. It is much more, too, than the mere recognition of uniqueness. Wordsworth discovers that something within him selectively and mysteriously creates values out of his experience, and thus builds out of his life a myth, the telling of which is the purpose of his autobiography. It is a conception, or an attitude, that becomes decisive with certain later autobiographies, in Yeats or Henry James; Proust, in his semi-autobiographical novel, systematically traces his life as the development of the myths of Swann and Guermantes. Wordsworth is the first autobiographer to realise—and the poetic form of his autobiography is this realisation—that each man constructs out of his world a unique framework of meaningful events, and that the deepest purpose of autobiography is the account of a life as a projection of the real self (we call it personality but it seems to lie deeper than personality) on the world.

Wordsworth's account of his "education"—in boyhood, at Cambridge, in France and London—is more coherent than Rousseau's. But one cannot be content to put this down to his being a more placid and educable person. There is terror and despair here, inspired by nature and man, and often coming from mysterious depths within him. Above all, there is growth before he reaches

> The calm existence that is mine when I
> Am worthy of myself.

And this growth, which reaches towards a position determined by his inner values, issues not only out of outward experience, but also and essentially from the inner self:

> Oh! mystery of man, from what a depth
> Proceed thy honours. I am lost but see
> In simple childhood something of the base
> On which thy greatness stands: but this I feel
> That from thyself it comes, that thou must give,
> Else never canst receive.

Thus the giving makes experience fruitful, makes his development cumulative. His errors become profitable. His enthusiasm for the French Revolution, he recognises even in the first version, was misguided, but it also enriched him, as an expression and deepening of his love for humanity. Of his first journey through France and the Alps, from which he learned "lessons of genuine brotherhood", he writes characteristically:

> Finally, whate'er
> I saw, or heard, or felt, was but a stream
> That flowed into a kindred stream.

He recognises too that the significance of such experiences may be overlooked or misunderstood at the time, and can be valued truly only later:

> I was lost;
> Halted without an effort to break through;
> But to my conscious soul I now can say—
> "I recognise thy glory".

Thus he tells of the development of a soul. It is not a circular movement, but a spiral; the latest stage is richer in scope, his love of nature and man is an achievement of maturity, not a return to childhood. It is not so much the Wordsworth of the *Intimations of Immortality* that we have in *The Prelude,* as the author of *Tintern Abbey*, who distinguishes stages of growth and who celebrates the man's appropriation of the past in a fuller understanding. *The Prelude* is usually not considered in histories of autobiography, I suppose because it is a poem; it is however a landmark as a history of a soul's growth, and as an exposition of the shaping of life by the soul.

GOETHE

Goethe's *Poetry and Truth* is far broader-based and more factual than the autobiographies of Rousseau and Wordsworth. And here is no question of a return, in circular or spiral form, but of an irregularly moving expansion, the ultimate end of which cannot be defined. It closes with the departure of the twenty-six-year-old for Weimar; but one can say, had it been continued, it would have had to proceed in an ever widening arc, and one inclines to believe that this vast life could never have been enclosed in autobiographical form.

If the possibility of autobiography were to rest on a fairly clear conception of the self, on knowing the self, Goethe's sporadic efforts to continue *Poetry and Truth* must have been frustrated by this never-ending development in himself, and by his own scepticism concerning the possibility of knowing oneself:

> I must confess that I have always been suspicious of that great and so fine-sounding task, "Know Thyself", as something of a

stratagem of a secret conspiracy of priests who wanted to confuse men by making unrealisable demands of them, and to seduce them from activity directed towards the outside world to an inward and false contemplativeness. Man knows himself only in so far as he knows the world, and becomes aware of the world only in himself, and of himself only in it. Every new object, well observed, opens a new organ in ourselves.[1]

Goethe is not of course denying the worth of man's attempts to know himself; it is the purely contemplative, introspective method of which he is sceptical. Being is for him becoming; one is never oneself, one becomes oneself. Through the impact of the outer world, through activity, what was hidden or non-existent comes into being, and then only to enter on further change, in which the writer of the autobiography as well as its hero is involved. Thus his book ends not with a state of rest, but at that moment when Goethe, entering a new life at Weimar, is going (as all his readers knew) to become something startlingly different from the younger man. The book is also, as a consequence, more descriptive and narrative than analytical—in fact many critics have complained of the lack of psychological curiosity in it.

It is characteristic that Goethe undertook his autobiography under an external, not an inner, stimulus. A new edition of his complete works had appeared 1806–8, and as it was not arranged chronologically Goethe responded to a public demand by explaining how and in what order his works originated. He seeks, as he says, "to fill in the gaps of an author's life". In this respect *Poetry and Truth* is a most conscientious and exhaustive literary history. Goethe describes his characteristics as a child and young man, his friendships, his intellectual and practical interests. We see the formative influence of the domestic circle and kindred spirits. The help he received from great minds of the past, such as Shakespeare and Spinoza, is gratefully acknowledged. Local, national and world circumstances and events are given their place. His private life is represented as moving in a complex network, and every significant poetic achievement seems to knot together innumerable strands.

But this acute historical consciousness of Goethe's does not lead only towards a historical narrative, like that of Cellini's, which

[1] Goethe, *Maximen und Reflexionen*, VI.

47

Goethe had translated into German; it leads also to philosophical reflections and establishes a philosophical focus for the work. In the Preface he writes:

> As I endeavoured to describe in right order the inner stirrings, the external influences, the stages through which theory and practice had borne me, I was thrown out of my narrow private life into the wide world. The figures of a hundred important personalities who had exerted a near or remote influence on me emerged into prominence; indeed I had to pay particular attention to the immense movements of the general political world which had had the greatest effect on me as on the whole mass of my contemporaries. For this seems to be the chief task of biography, to depict a man in the circumstances of his times, and to show to what extent the whole stood in his way, to what extent it favoured him, how he shaped out of it an outlook on the world and on mankind, and, if he is an artist, poet, or writer, how he in turn reflects it . . . so that one may well say that each man, were he born a mere ten years earlier or later, would have become a quite different person, as far as his own inner development and his effect on the outer world are concerned.

The uniqueness of a life is therefore the outcome of the interplay between innate character and circumstances. In *Poetry and Truth* there is no quarrel with circumstances, as with Rousseau; nor is there room for remorse or self-accusations. "A man," Goethe writes elsewhere, "is not only what he possesses as his innate characteristics, but also what he acquires".[1] The story of a man is therefore that of the inter-action of self and event in the changing world, of which the changing self is a part.

Goethe's immediate object is to tell how he became a poet, and again his theme is the fusion between the self and the world, for poetic creation appears here as a vital function. His poetry issued out of the pressures of his experience, out of his pain and rapture; he describes how, by projecting himself into his images, he was able to release himself from almost unbearable pressures, "as after a General Confession", and resume his practical life. In this respect *Poetry and Truth* is a major statement of the psychology of artistic creation. But behind this there lies a more general problem of the interplay of the individual and the whole into

---

[1] *Maximen und Reflexionen*, VII.

which he is born. On the one hand Goethe recognises how much our lives are conditioned by circumstances outside us:

> Few biographies are able to show a clear, tranquil, constant progress of the individual. Our life, like the whole in which we are contained, is inextricably woven of freedom and necessity. Our willing is an announcement of what we shall do under any circumstances. But these circumstances seize us in their own peculiar way. The "what" lies in us, the "how" rarely depends on us, we may not ask after the "why", and therefore we are always rightly directed to the "because".

But, on the other hand, Goethe seems to have recognised, as he proceeded with his autobiography, that this willing, this "freedom" itself, is governed also by another sort of necessity, a necessity within one, a profound and coherent will that lies underneath the conscious will and eludes the grasp of mind. It is with this that he is much concerned in the last Book of *Poetry and Truth*, written much later than the earlier. He calls it the "daemonic" element—"it was like chance, since it evinced no sequence of causality; it resembled Providence, for it hinted at coherence". It is illustrated by his play *Egmont*, on which he was working at the period of his life to which this last Book refers, a tragedy in which the hero is destroyed not simply by circumstances, but also by the "daemonism" of his own personality; and he fittingly concludes *Poetry and Truth* with Egmont's own words:

> Whipped as by invisible spirits the sun-horses of time break away with the light carriage of our fate, and there remains nothing for us to do but, composed and courageous, to grasp the reins firmly, and to guide the wheels now to the right, now to the left, from the stone here, the abyss there. Who knows whither he goes? For he hardly remembers whence he came.

IV

The Classical Achievement and Modern Developments

THIS short period, stretching roughly from Rousseau's *Confessions* (1782) to Goethe's *Poetry and Truth* (the last volume of which was completed in 1831), seems decisive in the history of autobiography.[1] Its ground-plan was now laid and subsequent writers have had little more than modifications to contribute—though Misch is too severe when he states that later autobiography is only of sociological importance.[2] Not that some ideal form of autobiography is established; we have different forms appropriate to the nature and achievements of different men. Even so striking an innovation as Goethe's feeling for change and development—a remarkable example of the growth of a new historical consciousness in Europe—does not invalidate Rousseau's obliviousness to change, to historical factors in general. What is common and new is (in spite of occasional flurries of complacency or self-congratulation) a devoted but detached concern for their intimate selves, a partial yet impartial unravelling of their uniqueness, a kind of wonder and awe with regard to themselves; and at the same time an appreciation that this uniqueness is also the uniqueness of the circumstances in which they lived, hence their attention to the concrete reality of their experiences. They stand to themselves, as Goethe wrote to Schiller

---

[1] Apart from Franklin, Gibbon, Rousseau, Wordsworth, and Goethe, one should mention Sterne, James Stephen, Hazlitt, Goldoni, Casanova, Alfieri, Marmontel, Restif de la Bretonne, Jung-Stilling, Moritz. Chateaubriand is only partly, Stendhal only just, outside the limits of these dates.

[2] *Gesch. der Autobiographie*, vol. 2, i—*Mittelalter*, 8.

(16 August 1797), as his theme stands to the poet. They are conscious, too, of their aim, they write reflectively, philosophically, and order their narrative according to their conception of their task; in all the concreteness of their accounts they are searching for man, not simply for themselves, for the essential constituents of human being. With them autobiography becomes a conscious genre, not simply in the sense that what they write could only be written by a man about his own life and never by another person; but also in the sense that it serves a purpose all its own of self-discovery and reconciliation with self. In *Vie de Henry Brulard* Stendhal repeatedly remarks that he remembers things only as he sets about writing his autobiography; the character of certain people, and their influence on him, become clear to him only as he writes. One can extend his observation and assert that autobiography now becomes an instrument for understanding life. It demonstrates that it can be, not just the log of things known, but a voyage of discovery, and a means of reconciliation.

Why autobiography should have suddenly grown to full stature in this period is a fascinating question that can hardly be broached here. It accompanies the break-through that is called Romanticism, though it transcends any of the narrower definitions of this term. It is borne up by a belief in man, in his inherent significance, and while it knows his limitations and faltering, yet sees confusions and wants as fruitful. It asserts the claims of the subjective self, but at the same time those of concrete circumstantial reality. It justifies the particular as against the general, as Blake did, but also seeks for law, for the law of the individual soul and the law of its inter-action with the outer world.

One may understand its break-through in the eighteenth century as a significant element of the process of self-assertion and self-realisation of the European middle class, shaking itself free of the values and forms of an aristocratic culture, and boldly probing into its own spiritual foundations. In this decisive period autobiography is both exploratory and self-confident. The inner self of the earlier religious autobiographies owed the justification of its worth to a common religious belief. The self that is now the object of devoted attention, valued likewise for its peculiar inner quality rather than its outer achievement, asserts its worth for its own sake, without a transcendental prop. Yet there is still something of a religious assurance in these great autobiographies. It is felt that the self that is sought expresses some fundamental and true reality, that in its ultimate nature it belongs to the essence of life, to Providence or God. A feeling of confidence and trust guides the search, confidence in the ultimate wholeness and integrity of the self and in the meaningfulness of its destiny. In later autobiography this trust seems to fail, for the theme tends to become more limited, more modest, more specialised.

The significance of the autobiographies of this period can be recognised from their impact on other forms of literature. Perhaps because it was bound by no literary convention, the autobiography became a medium for new insights into man. There is no need to enumerate the debt we owe to Rousseau's psychological candour, but there are other accessions of understanding, to which all later literature is indebted, which may be mentioned as having been directly due to autobiography.

The most striking discovery is that a man is not a state of being but a process of development, and that he can be known only in the story of his life. Wandering attentively through their childhood, recalling events and persons that are important only because of their complex effects on the child, these authors are the first to see themselves as a complex process of "becoming" in which the past always resounds in the present. The nineteenth-century novels that delve deep into childhood, from Dickens and the Brontës onwards, are unimaginable without the great autobiographies, and their importance lies not just in the discovery of the child's world, but in the recognition that the obscure urges and vivid impressions and affections of childhood are so decisive for the adult.

But equally significant is the discovery, through the autobiography, of the great complexity of the human psyche, and this is intimately related with the discovery of the relationship between self and circumstance. Only through the uninhibited description of the concrete situations through which the "hero" passes can the great variety of his impulses, affections, moods, thoughts, be made evident. Things speak of the soul, often more clearly than thoughts, and sometimes they speak of spiritual regions almost inaccessible to thought. The debt of the realistic novel to the autobiography is unmistakable, especially in its appreciation of the historical moment—and one can add, in the style too. For a style had to be invented, as Rousseau was acutely aware, that would do justice to this concrete world in its detail, its pettiness, and at the same time to its spiritual meanings, exaltations, tortures.

Free of literary conventions, and directed towards the specific truth of the self, these great autobiographies transformed the conception of the psyche, particularly in their realisation of its complexity. I would mention as an example the recognition that allegedly exclusive feelings can exist simultaneously. In Book 6 of the *Confessions* Rousseau describes how he leaves his beloved Mme de Warens in order to take a cure at Montpellier. On the way he is attracted by a charming fellow-traveller, but at first behaves absurdly, involuntarily doing everything to keep distant from the woman he seeks to approach. After a few days of happy intimacy he returns home, without feeling that this love was in any way a betrayal of his affection for Mme de Warens. This self-observation however means a shock for conventional moral psychology and for Romantic idealism. Poets like Catullus and Tibullus have recorded simultaneous love-affairs, and Ronsard was even perplexed by his simultaneous love for two girls.[1] Richardson's Grandison too is "perplexed by what some would call (particular as it sounds) a *double love*". In the autobiography the problem becomes more insistent and has wider repercussions.

Restif de la Bretonne had every reason to dwell on the problem. He finds that, at the age of 19 or 20, he was in love with a dozen or more girls, not counting his supreme passion for his master's wife, and most of these passions are actually documented in his poems and journals of that time. He comments:

My behaviour astonishes me today . . . For when I told all these girls that I loved them, I was telling them what was in my mind; my declarations . . . were true. And, if I had not before my eyes the original documents, dated, this tangled mass of likings, of passions that were even extreme, I should hardly be able to persuade myself that I am not mixing events up.

[1] See R. E. Hallowell, *Ronsard and the Conventional Roman Elegy*, Urbana 1954, 66–7 and 104.

Restif is not referring to sudden transitions of love from one person to another, like Romeo's switch from Rosalind to Juliet, nor to the co-existence of different types of love, e.g. an idealistic and a sensual. Nor is he of course referring to the dalliance of the conventional libertine. He is speaking of "true love", of a tender, devoted passion that feels itself to be exclusive, true, everlasting. He sums up his thoughts on the matter:

> The variety of my feelings and love-affairs, their strength that was not enfeebled by their variety, prove how far the most accredited novels are from verisimilitude, with their well-worked-out logic which never fails. Fatal symmetry, which throws an infinity of young people of both sexes into error, and makes them distressed, since it transforms in their eyes quite natural beings into immoral monsters.[1]

There are instances of similar contradictory feelings in the autobiography of the German pietist, Jung-Stilling, and a most curious account of a double love-affair in the life of James Stephen which goes right against the character and principles of this strictly religious member of the Clapham Sect.[2] Both of them were helped to write with candour because they felt that Providence was watching over their every step. One can claim that the modern novel's insight into the emotions, its recognition of the asymmetry of the human personality, owes much to the self-reporting of the autobiography.

And we can perhaps ascribe to the autobiographies of the classical age a large part in the transformation of the whole concept of "literature". Raymond, the co-editor of the latest edition of Rousseau's *Confessions*, claims that this work is primarily responsible for the new concept of literature, "centred henceforth not on the work, a being or object existing for itself, but on the author, and less on the author than on the man with his personal drama and his irreplaceable person ('figure')".[3] There are other

[1] Restif de la Bretonne, *Monsieur Nicolas*, i. 304–5. This is an abbreviated version of the vast work that was written between 1794 and 1797. Among the delusions and lies of this autobiography there are some things that are startlingly true.

[2] The first three volumes (the best) of Jung-Stilling's *Lebensgeschichte* appeared 1777–8. James Stephen, the ancestor of Leslie Stephen and Virginia Woolf, was born in 1758 and wrote his memoirs of childhood and youth (up to 1783) for his family. They were not published till 1954.

[3] Rousseau, *Oeuvres Complètes*, Paris 1959, i. xv. (Bibliothèque de la Pléiade).

evidences of such a change, independent of the autobiography—in the earlier novel above all, in *La nouvelle Héloïse* and *The Sorrows of Young Werther*, in Goethe's poems, and in his plays which so disconcertingly disregard conventional dramatic principle in order to probe a moral dilemma.[1] But there can be no doubt that the autobiography, a symptom of a general movement which has led for instance to the perpetual experimentation of Brecht, has most pronouncedly expressed and influenced this general trend of literature away from objective forms, and has helped to turn it into a spiritual experiment, a voyage of discovery that knows no conditions but the principle of exploration.

*   *   *

Since this classical age of autobiography, there have been developments in manner and technique, and a significant growth of awareness of the problematic of its truth; but relatively little enrichment in the conception of its central purpose and its scope. Pryce-Jones attributes the great expansion of autobiographical literature in the twentieth century to the fact that "that was the moment in time when mankind [he means, the man of Western civilisation] first became aware of its own fragility . . . The one thing which remained constant in a shifting world was the human personality".[2] Yet this perception goes back at least as far as Cardano and the religious autobiographies of the seventeenth and eighteenth centuries; and in some respects it is the trust in the constancy of the human personality, so marked in the classical age, that begins to fail in modern times.

In later chapters of this book I shall discuss the main modern forms, so that I do not need to do more here than mention modern trends in autobiography (I pass over the great mass of auto-biographies whose interest lies essentially in the peculiarity of the circumstances described or the information provided). The most common type is that which tells the story of a particular profession or calling, the steps by which public achievement was reached; this type is securely rooted in the older convention.

[1] See the very instructive investigation of Ronald Peacock in *Goethe's Major Plays*, Manchester Univ. Press, 1959.

[2] A. Pryce-Jones, "The Personal Story", in *The Craft of Letters in England*, ed. John Lehmann, 1956.

55

Autobiography as the story of a man's theoretical understanding of the world is perhaps new as J. S. Mill or Henry Adams
understand it, though it links on to the purpose of Augustine
and Franklin. The essayistic autobiography is also new, when
personal circumstances are used as the basis for reflections on
contingent matters, as with De Quincey, Renan, Stefan Zweig, or
Somerset Maugham. The autobiography which restricts itself
to childhood, as with Aksakoff, and the autobiographical novel,
are modern forms in the main. In a number of autobiographies
innovations of method indicate a significant scepticism about the
traditional form, particularly in regard to the focus of the author.
Thus we have oblique approaches, like that of George Moore,
who works backwards and forwards from a given moment, or
the deliberate adoption of a third-person narrative, as with Sean
O'Casey. Gertrude Stein adopts an ingenious device. From the
account of her visit to U.S.A. in 1934–5, *Everybody's Autobiography*,
we can see how determined she was not to speak of her inner life,
and for the account of her life-story she chose to write the fictitious autobiography of her intimate companion, Alice Toklas.
In this way she could confine herself to outward appearances,
bar us from intrusive and as she thought meaningless familiarity,
and incidentally, too, present herself as the genius she was for
her devoted Alice. Many writers betray a distrust of continuous
narrative, and are content with impressionistic sketches, as truer
to our mode of experience, like Yeats in the *Reveries*, and some
limit themselves to a particular significant relationship, with his
father like Edmund Gosse or his wife like Havelock Ellis.
Illuminating as these different methods are, they usually indicate
a certain hesitancy or renunciation in regard to the task of grasping the whole range of experience and development. On the whole
I would single out only two developments of outstanding importance, which affect both the scope and the technique of autobiography: the feeling of time lost, and the consciousness that
one's life is representative.

By "time lost" I do not mean lost childhood or youth, which is
so central a theme with Rousseau, and the sentimentalised recreation of which has since become a favourite exercise of leisure
hours. What is new in the nineteenth century is the historical
consciousness that the time described has now altered, gone

beyond recall. Countless autobiographies set out to describe circumstances that are altogether vanished. The fantastically rapid transformation of Western society, above all through industrialisation, has affected everything—the old community of village and small town, ties, tools, manners, religious and moral outlooks and behaviour. Over and over again men write about their childhood and youth, often for their grandchildren, to explain historical circumstances utterly remote from the experience of later generations. In recent times, the fearful dislocations caused by revolutions and civil wars, by ideological wars and dictatorship, have brought a great crop of autobiographies of exiles and refugees, who remember and try to understand their past. Modern Spanish literature was wholly lacking in autobiographical statement until the Civil War of the 1930s; from refugees like Arturo Barea and Ramon Sender remarkable autobiographies have come.

Under this impulse autobiography may easily become memoir. The most popular German autobiography of the nineteenth century, Kügelgen's *Jugenderinnerungen eines alten Mannes*, is in the main a recollection of lost characters and circumstances. Osbert Sitwell seems almost to shy away from himself in order to invoke the past, against the destruction of which he bitterly protests. So pervasive is this consciousness of change that one can say it is never absent from modern autobiography, even when it is by no means a primary motive. One may link with it the consciousness of the significance of an upbringing in remote parts, as with W. H. Hudson or Edwin Muir, where it enters into the specific substance of the personality and has a distinctive and formative function.

Along with this awareness of the impact of historical change has come the realisation that the individual's development is also a part of a general social process, that he is a focal point of historical forces. This in no sense reduces the uniqueness of the individual character and fate; on the contrary, the more marked the personality, the more he seems to sum up a whole social trend, a generation, perhaps a class. It is this that seems to be the central theme for J. P. Sartre, to judge from observations he made concerning his forthcoming autobiography[1]—

[1] Reported in *The Listener*, June 6, 1957.

My experiences are significant inasmuch as they may be similar to those of many people like myself . . . I am not only concerned with the particular meaning of one life. I want to recall the rather curious evolution of a generation.

H. G. Wells's *Experiment in Autobiography* combines the personal and representative meaning of his life in exemplary fashion. Here the lively sense of his own personality evolving from the old-fashioned world of his childhood to the modern world of science and industry, is fused with that of the evolution of a new age. "My story will be at once a very personal one and it will be a history of my sort and my time." Thus, paradoxically, Wells refers to himself as "a sample human brain", "a sample person"— not because he was or considered himself to be an average person, of course, but because his experiences and purposes were memorable in his view only in so far as they corresponded to a general social process.

This attitude must be strong in men who have participated in social or political movements, and it has been well put by Arturo Barea, the Spanish revolutionary socialist, in the Foreword to *The Track*, the second volume of his autobiography:

A very distinguished critic of *The Forge* [the first volume of the autobiography] pointed out that "the experiences chronicled by the author" are not "at all singular", and that "the conversations, the discoveries and the disillusionments of experience are such as could be described by millions". This is perfectly true of the present book too, and it is as I think it should be . . . As I was one of them, I have attempted to be vocal on their behalf, not in the form of propaganda, but simply by giving my own truth.

There are stories, true stories, which I love to tell to my friends, but have not included in this book . . . These would have been suitable tales for an anecdotal autobiography which puts the highlights on the spectacular and amusing; but to me they carried no deeper association, either personal or general, and so I left them out. Yet the filth of the hospital, the gory nightmare of the massacres, the technique of petty graft, the boredom of endless marches, the boredom of night life, the noise of taverns, the unquestioning comradeship of the army, the smell of the sea at dawn, and the glare of the African sun—all this made us what we are, and this I have chronicled.

Many autobiographies in modern times, that arise from this historical and social consciousness, have a purely sociological interest; many of them of course are very trivial. But in the best one can detect a new motivation which is properly autobiographical. They are written from an inner necessity; this weight of experience is a burden that cannot be borne until it is composed in the autobiography. It is not a burden of guilt, as with Rousseau, but a burden of memories and experience. Yeats for instance writes in the *Reveries* how he is haunted by memories until he can find "somebody to talk to" about them. Somerset Maugham tells that he wrote his semi-autobiographical *Of Human Bondage* because he was oppressed by youthful memories; and having relieved himself of this burden he had little occasion to refer to them in his book of retrospective reflexions, *The Summing Up* (see p. 195–6). This is not the irrepressible urge of old men to talk about their childhood; it is not primarily, I believe, an urge for communication, for telling others. It seems to arise from the oppression one feels that all this past experience has not been absorbed, digested, into the system of one's life, that it has not been grasped and utilised. Schiller's general statement is relevant (in a letter to Goethe, 7 September 1797): "It is a need of poetic natures, if not of the human spirit altogether . . . to appropriate through their feeling as much world as is at all possible"; and the autobiography is the means to review one's life, to organise it in the imagination, and thus to bring the past experience and the present self into balance. The object is not so much to tell others about oneself as to come to terms with oneself, not necessarily explicitly and morally, but simply by grasping oneself as a whole. This is why Gandhi or Wells, different as they are, can speak of the peace that writing their autobiography brings them.

Autobiography has become a significant and ubiquitous element of modern culture. All manner of people feel impelled to write their life-story, and there is a most grateful market for these works. My concern is not with those which arise from vanity or showmanship, and satisfy the much stimulated craze for "personalities". Nor is historical information or even psychological documentation a test of quality in autobiography. I am concerned with the manner in which autobiography becomes something intrinsically significant, not as information but as a literary work. The first condition is the seriousness of the author, the seriousness of his personality and of his intention in writing. And the overriding problem is that of truth. The autobiography claims to be a true story, and it must qualify in respect to truth if it is to qualify at all. The decisive question is, how can a life be truthfully narrated? And it is desirable, first of all, to face the fact that, in one way or another, truth is very curiously handled in autobiographies.

V

The Elusiveness of Truth

TO give the truth about oneself has always been the aim of true autobiography, but from Augustine himself, who "toiled" at re-collecting the past, it has been realised that this means selection, discrimination. And selection, in its turn, implies some principle. With religious autobiographers the truth may mean the truth of belief, other writers may choose as their purpose the truth of some outlook or some professional achievement, and the type and scope of the incidents they describe will be defined accordingly. With Cardano, and more emphatically Rousseau, the truth envisaged becomes not only that of the inner personality, the deepest truth, but also that of the behaviour of the person, the facts and events of his life, "the likeness of a man in all the truth of nature"; but the purpose has only to be proclaimed for it to become questionable. We know only too much about the inner censor, that acts so perfidiously because it acts automatically. And even when it cannot hide unpleasant memories from our consciousness, we are often still incapable of speaking of our secret shame, however well we may know it is nothing abnormal or shocking to others.

Yet this sort of inhibition or reserve injures autobiography less seriously than might be thought, and often not at all. We could not, and do not want to know everything about a man, but only what is distinctive and essential. And when we are worried about the possibility of truthfulness, it is not so much this that makes us apprehensive, as the possibility of a truthful, an objective relationship to oneself. It is this apprehensiveness that I see behind Stephen Spender's words, "if I am able to write with truth about what happened to me", which is typical not so much because it expresses a doubt about his will to truthfulness as because of his uncertainty about the possibility of seeing himself truthfully. Yet the autobiographer must believe in this. When Lord Gorell writes that he will tell "the truth, yes: the whole truth, no", we are disturbed and suspicious. Gorell could well believe that he was only being more honest than most autobiographers, yet we are legitimately alarmed at a deliberate self-limitation of this type, and more at ease with writers who perhaps delude themselves with the belief that they are writing the whole truth. To adapt Gorell's nonsensical distinction, we would rather have the whole truth than the truth.

What order or type of truth we expect from autobiography can be recognised only if we enumerate some of the main types of untruth that are to be found. Leslie Stephen remarked long ago that distortions of the truth belong to the values of autobiography and are as revealing as the truth,[1] and it will become apparent that we are concerned here in the main with untruths which do not damage materially the value of the autobiographies concerned.

ERRORS OF FACT

Obviously, every autobiographer must leave out the humdrum details of everyday life. Yet even this indicates something of the peculiarity of his task, for it is not so with the diarist, who may interest us with an account of a meal or his changing moods throughout a day. The smallest incident, some childish illness, may acquire autobiographical significance in that it reveals or foretells some marked feature of the character—so Yeats tells us of the athletic English boy he so admired, who to his disgust could not stand the Irish boy's disregard of meal-times. Detail in autobiography is demanded when it reveals the features of the personality.

A more serious hampering condition arises from scruples with regard to other persons—and, in some cases, from fear of a charge of libel. It is curious that relatively few authors postpone publication till after their death, when, they may well think, these considerations would weigh less. They are mostly as anxious to

[1] Leslie Stephen, "Autobiography", in *Hours in a Library*, 1892, vol. 3.

publish their autobiography as any other work—I should say, not for money or to interest the public, but because the work, like any other literary production, acquires its full significance only when it is cut off from the author and has become public. Posthumously published autobiographies are on the whole no more indelicate or scandalous than those published during the author's life-time. There is of course little security in using fictitious names, as Gide does in his. Friends, enemies, and industrious research-workers soon uncover the facts.

People who have been intimately and equivocally involved with others must inevitably suffer most from this need for reticence. H. G. Wells, for instance, who tells us a great deal about his relations with his first and second wife, drops a heavy cloud over his later liaisons, informing us only that he was sexually of a promiscuous type. The autobiography loses thereby as a memoir or biography, even as a social and psychological document. Yet one does not feel that Wells's reticence has damaged his essential purpose, the essential truthfulness of his account. What would be harmful would be a reticence in respect to others which is a cloak for discretion on one's own behalf. The most frequent cause of failure in autobiography is an untruthfulness which arises from the desire to appear admirable, especially when the standard set is conventional propriety. Even here, however, as I shall point out later, the purpose of many autobiographers may quite legitimately justify them in ignoring whole aspects of their being. In many autobiographies this scrupulousness and scruple remains decisive, and it needs daring to be truthful. When discussing with André Gide *Si le grain ne meurt*, Proust was of the opinion, "You can tell anything, but on condition that you never say 'I'." Gide disagreed, even though the subject they were discussing was the possibility of frankness in regard to homosexual practices. And Gide had his revenge when, reading Proust's *Sodome et Gomorrhe*, he wrote in his journal, "It is hard for me to see in them [Proust's latest pages] anything but a pretence, a desire to protect himself, a camouflage of the cleverest sort".[1] In the abstract, the argument remains undecided, autobiography may be a means of revealing the truth, it may be a means of hiding it. One or two examples will

[1] A. Gide, *Journals*, trans. O'Brien, 1948, ii. 265 and 276.

illustrate normal motives for reticence and in what way this reticence affects the quality of autobiography.

Harriet Martineau's decision to omit from her (posthumously published) autobiography almost everything pertaining to her brother James was due not only to a feeling of delicacy in regard to him, but also to the painfulness of their estrangement. Even in her private letters there is not a single reference to their rupture, which sufficiently attests her feelings.[1] She dearly loved this younger brother, she tells us, and was accustomed as they grew older to ask his advice on all important matters. But apart from these brief remarks, and a general comment that the brother-sister relationship is in principle a difficult one, she speaks no more about him. In actual fact, the more independent and prominent Harriet became, the more the tension between them grew, partly because James disapproved of some of the things she did and believed, partly it seems because of a certain male and brotherly jealousy. The real rupture came when, after Harriet's famous confession of agnosticism, her brother, a distinguished professor of theology, published a fierce attack on her philosophy and, by implication, on her morals. Harriet did not hesitate to indicate in her autobiography the difficulties she had with other members of her family, notably her mother and sister, but about James's attack and the hurt it caused her she remains silent. James himself did not much appreciate his sister's delicacy, for he continued their quarrel after her death, when reviewing the autobiography. It is revealing of their relationship that, in particular, he takes the trouble to challenge the truthfulness of her statement that in early life she had loved, and been loved by, a young friend of his. What injures Harriet Martineau's autobiography, a work far better than it is usually held to be, is in fact the appearance of hardness and impersonality in the young woman, though with age she mellows greatly. By omitting the story of her attachment to her brother she has left out one of the important clues to her character.

Something similar in Beatrice Webb's *Apprenticeship* must however be judged differently. When Margaret Cole published

---

[1] Vera Wheatley, *The Life and Works of Harriet Martineau*, 1957, 311. Harriet in her will directed that her letters should never be published, so I rely here on Mrs. Wheatley's statement.

Beatrice Webb's Diaries, general interest was aroused by the revelation that she was at one time in love with Joseph Chamberlain, who wished to marry her. From the autobiography one would know that as a young woman she knew and admired Chamberlain, and that, at about the same time, she had a distressing love-affair. The two items of information are however separated by many pages, and one would not have guessed they belonged together. Whether this was due to Beatrice's reluctance to "display herself like an actress", or to Sidney Webb's dislike of "personalities", or to consideration for the Chamberlain family, the facts of this relationship were suppressed. Yet, I believe, nothing of value was lost. Her confessed admiration for Chamberlain has its due importance in her own social and political development; the distress of an unhappy love plays an important part in her search for a purpose in life. It was not necessary for the autobiography that we should know Chamberlain was the man she loved.

Quite different is another omission, to which I think reviewers paid no attention. An entry in the Diary for December 5, 1925, reads:

> Somewhere in my diary—1890?—I wrote "I have staked all on the essential goodness of human nature"—I thought of putting the entry into the book [*My Apprenticeship*]—I did not do so because it was too near the truth!

When Beatrice Webb wrote this she had been painfully cured of her optimistic belief in her fellow-men. She had no doubt, and needed to have no doubt, that her choice of life and work was right, but she now needed other reasons to justify it. In any case, as we read her impressive and moving story, we do get some glimmering of this idealistic belief of hers, that inspired in her such determination in assertion and devotion. Yet in sidling away from this statement and its implications Beatrice Webb deprived her book and her character of a central and dramatic theme.

These examples from Harriet Martineau and Beatrice Webb have not been chosen to prove that their autobiographies are faulty in comparison with others, nor to suggest that women are incapable of great autobiography. Their accounts prove the contrary, that women can write autobiographies of high quality.

Faults like these are characteristic of autobiography altogether, and few authors escape them.

Take for example the autobiographies of W. B. Yeats and Henry James, both in the first rank. In a letter to his father, Yeats wrote, concerning his *Reveries over Childhood and Youth*, that he felt he could be objective in regard to these early years— "While I was immature I was a different person, and I can stand apart and judge". Yet even in respect to these old events, and to people long since dead, he has to assure his father that his treatment has been "amiable" and "discreet".[1] To make matters more complicated, Yeats writes in the *Reveries* themselves, "I have changed nothing of my memories to my knowledge; and yet it must be that I have changed many things without my knowledge". The latter part is unexceptionable, and is the right of every autobiographer; but how reconcile the first part with his statement that he has been amiable and discreet?

Henry James's three volumes are governed much more systematically by the determination to be kind. He wrote to his nephew, in reference to *A Small Boy and Others*:[2]

> The general purpose was to be a reflection of all the amenity and felicity of our young life of that time at the highest pitch that was consistent with perfect truth—to show us all at our best for characteristic expression and colour and variety and everything that would be charming.

It is a frank recognition of a distinction between his intention and the "perfect truth", and a somewhat puzzling claim that the two can be reconciled. Occasionally in fact the reader detects crosscurrents in the smooth stream of his narrative. Towards the end of the second volume, *Notes of a Son and Brother*,[3] James inserts a letter from his cousin Mary Temple to a friend in which she happens to say, about Henry James himself, "I hope Harry will enjoy himself in Europe—which he hasn't done for several years". The phrase gives us a shock. It is the only time in the autobiography that we are allowed to know that James was unhappy as a young man. It may be that James deliberately left in this casual

[1] W. B. Yeats, *Letters* ed. A. Wade, 1954 (26 Dec. 1914, *passim*).
[2] H. James, *Letters* ed. P. Lubbock, 1920, ii. 358.
[3] *Notes of a Son and Brother*, 1914, 435. The three volumes have been published in one volume as *Autobiography* ed. F. W. Dupee, 1956.

allusion in order to alert us to the presence everywhere of a hidden theme. But there is no doubt that he has almost completely obliterated what was in actuality an important psychological characteristic.

Of course, an author's conscious and expressed intention is not always realised. Ruskin alarms us when he writes in the Preface to *Praeterita* that he will write "at length on things that give me joy, passing in total silence things which I have no pleasure in reviewing, and which the reader would find no help in the account of". Fortunately, though he is reticent, he tells us a good deal of the painfulness of his repudiation of the evangelical orthodoxy of his parents, and in a bleak, reluctant phrase, "I had nothing to love", illumines the distress of his childhood quite suggestively enough. In itself, the author's lack of pleasure in recollecting certain aspects of his experience is by no means an indication of their lack of significance.

Authors may be reticent about the opposite, about their joys, perhaps because of a feeling that they are too intimate to be shared. Stendhal prefaced his autobiography, *Vie de Henry Brulard*, with a statement that is probably more generally valid than is recognised:

> I feared to deflower the happy moments that I have encountered by describing and anatomising them. Well, that is what I shall not do, I shall jump happiness.

Stendhal too was not so consistent in practice as he intended. But the point I want to make is that there is no rule-of-thumb procedure to judge of these omissions or distortions. All of them damage the historical or psychological truth of autobiography; but they may not damage the true value of the autobiography. Whether they are faults can be judged only in relation to the personality and autobiography involved. On the one side are the truths of fact, on the other the truth of the writer's feeling, and where the two coincide cannot be decided by any outside authority in advance, as Goethe ruefully put it when reviewing a collection of autobiographies some years before he sat down to his own:[1]

[1] Quoted by E. Trunz in his edition of *Poetry and Truth*, *Goethes Werke*, Hamburg 1955, ix, 602.

Truth belongs to all written accounts of one's life, either in relation to matters of fact or in relation to the feeling of the autobiographer, and God willing in relation to both.

We find indeed open admissions in autobiographies of the conflict between the two truths. Ruskin, after a passage describing his early lack of response to Italian art, tells us that, on consulting an old diary, he finds his account is "too morose", and quotes the diary to show that his response had indeed been more sensitive and discriminating than he had stated. Renan makes a similar correction in respect to an odd character he describes, and embodies the correction in a note. Gide appends to his book a letter from his cousin which corrects some statements of his. What is interesting in these cases is not that the authors made mistakes and corrected them, but that they left the original error intact in the text, alongside the contrary statement. Clearly what they felt is that their false impression was as important as the truth, and that the autobiographer has to tell us as much what the writer is as what the facts were.[1]

There is an amusing and typical example of this unresolved conflict between fact and feeling in Henry James's autobiography. This is in part a memorial to William, his philosopher brother, and from time to time he quotes from William's letters, which had been placed at his disposal by his nephew. The latter wrote to him, protesting that in one place Henry had actually altered a phrase in a letter. Henry wrote back in self-justification, arguing that he had been concerned to "do his best" for William, "that is, do with him everything I seemed to feel him like". The deleted phrase he felt could not have come from the real William, was not like his truest self. He admits: "I daresay I did instinctively regard it at last as all *my* truth, to do what I would with", and he goes on, "never again shall I stray from my proper work", i.e. from novel-writing.[2] His alteration, his defence of it, and his bad conscience

---

[1] Ruskin, *Praeterita*, 1899, ii. 61; E. Renan, *Souvenirs d'enfance et de jeunesse*, ed. Nelson, 10; Gide, *Si le grain ne meurt*, Paris 1928, Appendice. That Renan's work is a highly romanced account of his early life does not make the correction less remarkable. Gide no doubt appreciated the opportunity of indicating how subjective any point of view necessarily is, and his correcting Note belongs to the theme of *Les Faux-Monnayeurs*.

[2] H. James, *Letters* ed. P. Lubbock, ii, 359.

about the alteration, are characteristic of the dilemma of the auto-biographer.

PROBLEMS OF STRUCTURE AND STYLE

But errors of fact seem to be mere friendly difficulties compared with those that belong to the very nature of autobiography. All autobiography, whatever help may be provided by documents, is recollection, and Augustine himself recognised how much re-membering depends on the conscious mind and will, and how much the memory is dissociated from the feelings that the original experience engendered (Book X). Autobiographies are suspect to historians not so much because of particular incorrect facts as because of the perspective of the writer, who must see the past from his present standpoint, in the light of all his experiences and knowledge since the facts recorded took place. These later ex-periences will sift the past and determine what was important and worth talking about from what merely seemed important then, will therefore give the author his coherent theme.

This type of distortion is glaringly true of many autobiographies that depict the "education" of the author. In *The Education of Henry Adams*, for instance, the lessons of his early upbringing, particularly the democratic conceptions of his family and friends, are drastically dismissed as misleading error; the insight he won into the true nature of American society when visiting the Chicago Industrial Exposition imposes a peculiar shape and colour on his account of his whole earlier life. Lionel Trilling rightly remarks, when reviewing an edition of Adams's letters: "The reader of the letters gets what the reader of the *Education* does not get, the awareness of how late in coming was Adams' disillusionment with democracy".[1] But the same sort of distortion is true of all autobiographies, even of those which seek primarily to restore the past as it was. Even Aksakoff's account of his childhood is coloured by his adult attitude to life, and not only because he fills in the gaps of the child's knowledge with author's explana-tions. Yeats's *Reveries* could have been written only by the adult poet.

[1] L. Trilling, *A Gathering of Fugitives*, 1957, 121.

Earlier writers like Rousseau or Gibbon had a naïve notion of the truth about themselves, and believed that, even if the truth of some facts might escape them, they were the indisputable authorities on what Rousseau called "the chain of feeling" in their lives, "feeling" here including motivations. Modern autobiographers are more sceptical. This inward knowledge is not necessarily truer than public knowledge, it may even not be the truth; one knows more about oneself than anyone else does, but also one knows less about oneself than other people may know. And one's self-knowledge may be illusory; the more one probes, the further the truth seems to recede—it is as elusive as Kafka's Castle. Gide, who announces that his only purpose is to be truthful, shows himself frequently quite perplexed about his motivations as a child and young man. Armed not only with an unusual alertness and intrepidity, but also with the resources of psycho-analysis, he admits from time to time to being at a loss. For instance, he is tempted to ascribe his childish nervous attacks to a deliberate will to escape the school where he was unhappy; but other evidence forces him to think they may have occurred despite himself. So that some modern autobiographers, like Edwin Muir or Stephen Spender, give up the hope of knowing themselves. It is true that the latter, in an essay on autobiography, seems to suggest that some autobiographers do reach self-knowledge, while others do not. The works of Schweitzer, Freud, and Croce he calls examples of "objective, depersonalised autobiography" in contrast to those "that remind us how little objective human beings, who set themselves up as measuring instruments, really are".[1] But while there are great differences between types of autobiography, especially between those which conceive a life as a specialised mission and those which have no such single-minded a theme, this distinction between objective and subjective will not stand a thorough-going test. Schweitzer's story, impressive though it is, is full of unlit recesses which leave one from time to time at a loss—not because we need to know all, but because we need to understand.

Memory itself performs this sifting process, and is the most powerful unconscious agent in shaping the past according to the will of the writer: "memory is a great artist", in Maurois' phrase.

[1] S. Spender, "Confessions and Autobiography" in *The Making of a Poem*, 1955.

It is likely that autobiography is at its happiest when reconstructing childhood, that is, when it is based almost solely on memory. Yet it cannot be maintained that these memories are reliable, either in their factual truth or in regard to their relative importance. It is true, as Stendhal discovered, that by concentration one can remember an extraordinary amount of the childhood that one believes utterly lost; but what accent and tone does the rememberer give it? and what does he persist in forgetting? W. H. Hudson observes that "it is an illusion to think the few things distinctly remembered and visualised are precisely those which were most important in our life", and no-one could refute him. Often it is precisely the most important events that memory rejects. Yet, though the biographer cannot be excused for errors in this respect, it is otherwise with the autobiographer. From him we want the past as it appears in his mind, in his present mind. This may reject certain facts, it may alter others; it is their reflection and refraction in him that is important, and that is shaped in his narrative.

The autobiographer has in fact a double character. He exists to some degree as an object, a man recognisable from outside, and he needs to give to some extent the genetical story of this person. But he is also the subject, a temperament whose inner and outer world owes its appearance to the manner in which he sees it. Thus Hudson was not restrained from writing his autobiography by his doubts about whether he did actually remember the things of most importance in his life, and his statement is completed by the outright claim of J. C. Powys that the truth remembered is the only truth that matters—"A person's life-illusion ought to be as sacred as his skin". The events recorded in autobiography have a double relevance, a relevance to the author's historical life, and a relevance to his present self; they are symbolic of both. So Goethe, on a visit to his native city of Frankfurt, long before he settled down to write his autobiography, recalled his grandfather's patriarchal house in Frankfurt and its subsequent vicissitudes, and sees it as "a symbol of many thousand other cases".[1] When passed on to us in autobiography, such a memory becomes symbolic both of a past situation and of the quality of mind that recalls it.

[1] In a letter to Schiller, 17 August 1797.

F

The distortion of truth imposed by the act of contemplation is so over-riding a qualification of autobiography that it is indeed a necessary condition of it, and it will demand our attention when we consider more fully what autobiographers actually do. Here I am concerned only to point out how elusive historical truth is. Consider only the effect of the age at which the autobiography is written. Many autobiographers write in old age, when there is little chance of any change in their outlook or position, so that it may seem that they have come to a point where they may give a definitive assessment of their lives. But it is clear that this very remoteness from times of stress and uncertainty may lead to distortion; at the same time, the fact that they have reached a stable goal may bring them to depict the past as leading too inevitably to its outcome, they may see their lives too much as a sort of theodicy. G. H. Lewes, in his excellent biography of Goethe, rightly pointed out the "inaccuracy of tone" of *Poetry and Truth*—"The turbulence of a youth of genius is not indeed quite forgotten but it is hinted at with stately reserve. Jupiter serenely enthroned upon Olympus forgets that he was once a rebel with the Titans." In his autobiography, which was written in his high old age, Henry James is much milder to America than he was in earlier life, for instance in the *Daisy Miller* period, as his editor points out.[1] Of course, in some instances, the writer is so old that he lacks the mental energy to grasp the driving force of his life—like certain death-masks which, when the man is very old, seem to express little more than the general stamp of age. The latter part of Goldini's *Memoirs* is rambling and trite, no doubt because he was so old when he wrote. J. J. Thomson's also suffer from age, except in the sections devoted to his purely scientific work.

But many autobiographies are written in middle life, by men still vigorously engaged in life and work. Yet how subjective too is their view! Croce wrote his in 1915, when he was established as a philosopher and a personality. If he had written it in 1945, with the experience of two world wars and the Fascist régime behind him, and in a new and appalling world-situation, perhaps his account of his philosophical development would not have been altered, but at any rate the relation of thought to practice, the

[1] Henry James, *Autobiography*, 1956, ed. Dupee, X.

72

function of thought, would have appeared to him in a new light; the moral obligations of the thinker and the importance of his own liberal roots would have loomed up larger. H. G. Wells's *Experiment in Autobiography* (1934), in which his life is seen as the working out of "a practically applicable social science", was written in the full conviction that the physical and social world was being progressively understood and mastered by mind. But what would Wells have made of his life had he written his autobiography in his last years, when in despair he wrote in his *Mind at the end of its Tether* (1945) that mind was doomed to extinction? Or what could Henry Adams have said about his "Education", if he had written in 1914, when he saw so many of his confident beliefs refuted, instead of 1907? One is tempted to say that he could not have written it at all if the propitious moment had not been seized.

Few people have written more than one autobiography, but there is material which allows us to leave speculative questions and consider what actually happened. Different purposes may impose variations in autobiography. Saint Teresa wrote two accounts, "Relations", before embarking on her *Life*. The earlier bleak accounts are dominated by her need for guidance from her confessor; the later, much fuller, betrays her confidence in her visions and chosen way, and was written less to ask for guidance than to show the way. Keller, the Swiss writer, wrote two short autobiographical essays, one in 1876, the other in 1889, and the differences in his valuation of his early life arise not only from a difference of age but also from a difference of readership, for one was written for an avant-garde German public, the other for the readers of a Swiss parish magazine. The various drafts of Gibbon's *Memoir* differ primarily because of his uncertainty of purpose and, to some extent, his uncertainty of what public he was writing for —whether "discreet and indulgent friends" or the "public" at large. We can trace, in the successive redactions of Chateaubriand's autobiography, very marked changes of judgement of events and persons, as well as of style. Wordsworth's *The Prelude* is an outstanding case of an autobiography of which there are two complete versions, and it repays examination as illustrating a typical process.

Wordsworth's method illustrates a number of points already

mentioned, for example, the wilful suppression of personal facts such as his love for Annette and the birth of their child. But I am here concerned only with changes due to time. We have, for the *Prelude*, three sources: first, the actual events and all contemporary testimony; second, the account Wordsworth gives in the version written in the main between 1804 and 1805, when he was still near to the situation described in the later Books; and third, passing over a number of intermediate alterations, the version prepared by Wordsworth for publication in 1839, when he was an old man. I mention only a few salient points; the differences have been fully enumerated in Ernest de Selincourt's scholarly edition.

In theme the poem remained the same. But there are many not insignificant alterations, due partly to the fact that the earlier version was addressed to Coleridge, while in the latest Wordsworth, though retaining in places the direct address to Coleridge, had the public more in mind; but due mainly to their embodying "criticisms directed by a man of seventy winters against his own past" (de Selincourt), i.e. against the double past of the boy and man who had lived through these experiences, and the man who had written them down in the first version.

The changes are most notable in the account of Wordsworth's religious and political beliefs as a young man. Now, in 1839, he deliberately alters his earlier statements in order to tone down his Hartleyism and nature-mysticism, and to introduce definitely Christian beliefs as a balance. Some of these changes, writes de Selincourt, were "entirely alien to his thought and feeling" in earlier life and in the earlier version. If, in that earlier version, he was reticent about his political opinions during the years in France, in the final version he is much more conservative than ever before, much more patriotic—for example, he modified his earlier attack on the English government of 1792 and added a tribute to Burke.

Some of these alterations are simple comments of the older man, which do not, or ostensibly do not, disturb the statement of what actually occurred. But even such comments affect the general impression. In the first version, he attributed his return from France (Book X) to lack of funds:

Compell'd by nothing less than absolute want
Of funds for my support.

This not particularly poetic expression is replaced in the final version by a more dignified one, and supplemented by a comment expressly made by the older man:

Dragged by a chain of harsh necessity,
So seemed it—now I thankfully acknowledge,
Forced by the gracious providence of Heaven . . .

Even here, where the "so seemed it" and the "now" clearly differentiate between the young man's view and the old man's reflexion, the more general form of statement, "necessity" instead of "want of funds", and the acknowledgement of Providence, induce in us not only a different feeling, but also a different picture of the young man. Often enough, Wordsworth was much more ruthless with his earlier version, deliberately substituting his idea of what he should have been for what he was or for what in 1804–5 he had thought himself to be.

One might become indignant with Wordsworth the old man— and certain emendations are hard to excuse. The bearing and sweep of the whole however are not altered. And even where the old man inserts his interpretation (and the young author had after all done the same), the discriminating reader can see the three layers of the palimpsest in lively engagement with one another and enjoys the text all the more for it. For this is one of the joys of reading autobiographies, since we take them not as factual truth but as a wrestling with truth. I suppose few autobiographers have so deliberately altered the facts of their feelings and opinions as did Wordsworth, but few have had such a skeleton in their cupboard as an early version of their autobiography. Other literary sources, like diaries and letters, are much easier to tamper with, since one has in any case to select from them and fill in gaps, so that one makes one's pattern with a good conscience. But *The Prelude* remains, in its final version, in spite of everything, one of the great autobiographical documents, and one must conclude that Wordsworth was doing, only much more deliberately, what in the main all autobiographers must do, and that this tampering with the past, with the truth, simply belongs to autobiography.

A comparable alteration in a modern autobiography is worthy of mention since the earlier account was published and the later amendment discussed by the author. During the Spanish Civil War, Arthur Koestler was captured by the Nationalist insurgents, and released only after some weeks spent in daily expectation of execution. He published an account of his experience, *Dialogue with Death*, in 1937, while he was still a Communist. Later he realised that his experience in prison decisively contributed to his repudiation of Communism. This is what he writes in the second volume of his autobiography, *The Invisible Writing*, of 1954:

> I intended to incorporate *Dialogue with Death*, with a few cuts, into the present volume. But this did not prove feasible. The book is written in a different style, and from an entirely different perspective, by a man fifteen years younger, still under the impact of a shattering experience, and while the Spanish War was still on. The last-mentioned circumstance was responsible for a deliberate under-playing of the spiritual side of the experience, as it would have been frivolous to indulge in introspective reflections while my comrades fought and died in Spain—or so at least it appeared to me at the time. Also, the transformation that I underwent during that experience was at first an unconscious one, and it took some time before it seeped through and altered my conscious outlook; thus, for instance, I only broke officially with the Communist Party nine months later.

He adds later:

> *Dialogue with Death* is an autobiographical sketch written at the age of thirty-two; the present chapter is an 'explanation' of the same events, written at the age of forty-seven. I wonder what shape and colour they would take if I were to re-write them after yet another fifteen years have elapsed. Yet in intent each of these versions represents the truth . . .

No-one can doubt that it was necessary, and in the interests of truth, that Koestler should alter his earlier account. In an opposite case, it is with disappointment that one finds that Robert Graves, re-issuing *Goodbye to All That* after nearly thirty years, makes such slight and inconsiderable alterations. It was not necessary for him to bring the story up to date and tell us what had happened to him since; what we really want is a re-shaping of the older material.

If this conclusion seems paradoxical enough, one finds oneself driven to the complementary paradox that too scrupulous an adherence to the factual truth may injure an autobiography. When Edwin Muir hesitated between describing his life in terms of his dreams and intuitions or in terms of actual events, he was at grips with a basic problem of autobiography. Of course he cannot avoid, and does not try to avoid, interpreting his life. When he attributes his taste for watching football on the waste lots of Glasgow to "the grimy fascination in watching the damned kicking a football in a tenth-rate Hell", he is imposing a later judgement. When he dismisses his early Nietzscheanism as a simple "compensation", he gives no idea of its profound and positive influence as one may discover it in his early poetry. But he did not feel entitled to follow his method through, and after mentioning his wish that he could "show how our first intuition of the world expands into vaster and vaster images", he decides reluctantly that he must "stick to the facts", to the sort of truth we call simple. As a result, his autobiography lacks the power and sweep that the early chapters promise, and perhaps the deepest impression it leaves is his consciousness that the story of his outward life is what he calls "a dry legend, which I made up in collusion with mankind".

Muir was perplexed by the problem of evoking the whole sense of his life. But even the evocation of a particular, well-remembered and well-attested event is a problem. Events have a rightful place in autobiography by virtue of their significance for the author, and where the event is a purely intellectual one, or has a primarily intellectual significance, it is not so difficult to describe. Thus it was that Gibbon's account of the impact of Rome—"After a sleepless night, I trod, with a lofty step, the ruins of the Forum . . ."— is so satisfying. But many events have a most complex structure and multiple associations, and often defy evocation. Gide, a writer of evocative skill, often refers to his despair at reproducing the truth of significant experiences. He admits his incapacity to reproduce the quality of the effect that the reading of Heine made upon him at the age of sixteen:

> It is the fatal defect of my account, as of all memoirs; one presents what is most apparent; the most important things, without contours, elude one's grasp.

The linear, narrative form of the autobiography imposes a distortion on the truth of which Gide was again particularly conscious. He found himself forced to write in separate sections of his religious, intellectual, and emotive development, though he was conscious that they all occurred together as one process, and he quotes with approval in his *Journals* the comment of a friend[1]:

> As soon as one knows you well, one understands that all of the states which, out of regard for art, you depict as successive can be simultaneous in you; and this is just what your Memoirs do not make us feel.

The "art" spoken of is here not something dispensable, but the art of literature, the art of autobiography. Even the most natural of its conventions, the division of a life into "periods" or "chapters", can be misleading, an infringement of the truth, "façade-architecture" as it has been called.[2]

These difficulties are different in quality and severity according to the nature of the autobiographer. Where the author has a distinct theme, such as the development of his philosophy or his scientific work, "periods" are more readily recognised and signalled, and the experiential factors involved are altogether more simple. The autobiographies of scientists like Francis Galton, above all Freud's masterly account, satisfy even though they are stripped down to a bare theme. Everything depends on a consonance of method and style with the personality and theme. It is dangerous for autobiographers of this type to introduce more personal matters, since these can easily seem complacent trivialities. A three-volume collection of autobiographies of psychologists, published in 1930 in USA, illustrates the dangers— on the one hand, dull academicity, on the other, trivial *personalia*; one is surprised when one comes across the contribution of William McDougall, an essay of outstanding worth.[3] The most fatal error, in all types of autobiography, is not untruthfulness, but triviality of character, such as appears so devastatingly in Havelock Ellis's *My Life*—in his pervasive vanity, his continuing

[1] A. Gide, *Journals*, trans. O'Brien, ii, 257.
[2] H. von Doderer, *Die Strudlhofstiege*, München 1951, 323.
[3] *A History of Psychology in Autobiography*, 3 vols., 1930. McDougall's contribution is in the first volume.

apologetics, his complacent obtuseness. A critic called this, "an almost unique lesson in the difference between candour and insight";[1] but I think this is too kind, the autobiography lacks candour as well as insight.

The quality of a personality is perhaps most rapidly detected in the style. Style is of course as varied in autobiography as in any type of literature, and it must vary according to the personality and his mode of experiencing. The terse, vigorous language, the taut structure of Croce or Freud, strike us immediately as entirely consonant with their theme and entirely truthful. Much greater difficulties loom up when the author's purpose must be to recreate a complex emotional development. He may fail through underwriting. Trollope, after the admirable description of his early years, deliberately hides himself from us in order to speak about his professional career; the failure lies in the fact that we feel that the professional aspect of a writer, as opposed say to that of a scientist, is the least significant part of his life. Earl Attlee likewise seems deliberately to have underwritten his experiences. He attempts to treat of social and political activities as if they were simply all in the day's work, and hides from us the powerful personal and public emotions that were involved, doing justice neither to himself nor to the public issues. We have to call such accounts untruthful, as we do those in which the author imputes to himself excessive self-importance or dwells on emotional experiences which play no functional part in his life and are mere decoration; the untruth of under-writing is of course much more bearable, since it is allied with qualities of modesty or shyness that in their turn win our sympathy.

Over-writing is certainly more common, and more dangerous as regards the total effect of an autobiography. Gide was brought face to face with this danger. His object in writing was in a major sense confessional, even if he varied the normal approach and wrote, not in order to be excused, but "in order to be accused".[2] He rightly felt therefore that he had to evoke, with all the literary art at his disposal, the ardour of his feelings at certain moments. Yet Valéry, in his sympathetic and sensitive comments on Gide's text, expressed his distrust precisely of those passages "where the

[1] Alex Comfort in the *Observer*, February 1, 1959.
[2] Gide, *Journals*, trans. O'Brien, 1948, ii, 194.

art is still noticeable". These "virtuoso passages", he wrote to Gide, are dangerous, because "to spin words to one's confessor is a serious matter; it will make him forget to absolve you".[1]

There are much simpler and more representative examples of the danger of over-writing, the most common resulting from the complex temptations we undergo when attempting to bring the remote past of childhood into focus. It is clear that every man's memory of childhood is different from the actual experience of childhood, and it is not easy to decide when an autobiographical account slips over into illegitimate distortion. I have chosen two passages from books of good quality in order to indicate where the boundaries may be considered to lie. The first is a famous, often reprinted passage from Chateaubriand's *Mémoires d'outre-tombe,* describing springtime in Brittany (it is obviously best to leave it untranslated):

> Le printemps, en Bretagne, est plus doux qu'aux environs de Paris, et fleurit trois semaines plus tôt. Les cinq oiseaux qui l'annoncent, l'hirondelle, le loriot, le coucou, la caille et le rossignol, arrivent avec des brises qui hébergent dans les golfes de la péninsule armoricaine. La terre se couvre de marguerites, de pensées, de jonquilles, de narcisses, d'hyacinthes, de renoncules, d'anémones, comme les espaces abandonnés qui environnent Saint-Jean-de-Latran et Sainte-Croix-de-Jérusalem, à Rome. Des clairières se panachent d'élégantes et hautes fougères; des champs de genêts et d'ajoncs resplendissent de leurs fleurs qu'on prendrait pour des papillons d'or. Les haies, au long desquelles abondent la fraise, la framboise et la violette, sont décorées d'aubépines, de chèvrefeuille, de ronces dont les rejets bruns et courbés portent des feuilles et des fruits magnifiques. Tout fourmille d'abeilles et d'oiseaux; les essaims et les nids arrêtent les enfants à chaque pas. Dans certains abris, le myrte et le laurier-rose croissent en pleine terre, comme en Grèce; la figue mûrit comme en Provence; chaque pommier, avec ses fleurs carminées, ressemble à un gros bouquet de fiancée de village.

This passage deserves its fame; it is admirably concrete and terse, like much in the *Mémoires,* not "romantic", sentimental, or rhetorical. It is completely suited to a volume of "mémoires" of the normal type, and I should not criticise it if I thought of Chateaubriand's work merely as such. But the work is also autobiography, and the passage occurs in the account of his childhood, the most directly autobiographical part of the *Mémoires*. It is only in this connection that it raises doubts.

It in no sense interprets the impact of Spring on the boy. It is a composite picture, the result of reflection on many Springs in the mind of a man far away from childhood and Brittany. The references to Paris, Rome, Greece, even to Provence, bring in relationships meaningful only to the travelled man; even the comparison of the apple-blossom with a country bride's bouquet introduces a sophisticated element alien to the boy as he was. It is misleading about Spring in general, for the whole point of Spring is that it makes its impact successively, changing every day; the birds do not return together, the flowers are not all suddenly there. There is actually little evidence that the boy himself observed these things attentively; he was, as Chateaubriand describes himself, more likely to be absorbed in violent games and dreams and reveries. In this passage past and present are not successfully fused, the present overlays and obscures the past. By contrast, Chateaubriand's account of the return of the fleet to Brest, and the turmoil set up in the boy by the tales of the sailors, is real and true autobiography (Partie i, Livre 2, Ch. 10).

My second example is taken from Richard Church's *Over the Bridge*. This is the story of a boy of unusual sensitivity who becomes a writer, a poet, and it is therefore essential that we should be able to feel his peculiar manner of taking in the outside world. It needed therefore an evocative style. But on several occasions Church is, I think, guilty of over-writing. In the first chapter, the account of a moving incident entails the description of the small family:

A lesser power, but wholly trustworthy, was my brother Jack, whose taciturnity I took for granted, never questioning the oddness that made this lad of eleven so different from both our parents. They were happy people; my father a perpetual boy. He seemed to be a creature released, like a colt from a stable, and he galloped about the paddock of life with a thunder of hoofs and a flashing of nostrils, drinking the very air and intoxicating himself on it.

My mother, the fountain of Father's confidence and hilarity, was demonstrative, passionate, and subject to storms of jealousy. But her mind was cool, and her moral courage infinite. It was she, therefore, who made the home and held the world in place. In spite of this

Atlas-burden of responsibility, she was capable of gaiety, moods that suffused her brown eyes, parted her lips, and revealed her faintly prominent teeth, so that she became sylvan, a woodland creature, with just that small reservation of autumnal reminder that woodland creatures can never wholly discard.

There can be no objection to the attempt at summing up characters which the boy at that age (Church was then seven) would not know except close to, successively, and blurred. Comprehensive descriptions of this kind do not necessarily disturb our consciousness of the way the child sees other people, and may indeed help our understanding. What is disturbing here is the way in which the bird's eye view is expressed, in particular the images—the father like a colt, the mother a woodland creature. These suggest a manner of seeing parents which must be utterly alien to the child, and which we feel to be foisted on him. The retrospective vision here blots out the real relationships. A little later in the same chapter Church shows his awareness of the problem when he writes: "No doubt in recalling those distant scenes I am translating them into the language and concepts of adult life"; and this is not only true but unavoidable. But in some passages it is not translation that takes place, but embellishment, writing up. It is not at all the same as building out the knowledge of the child with information and judgements acquired later, as with Aksakoff, Goethe, James and the rest, where the different layers of childhood and age are clearly discernible. Embellishment of the sort one finds even in a work that is in general so sincere and candid as *Over the Bridge* is perhaps the most insidious threat to the truth of autobiography.

I suppose it is the biographical, historical approach to autobiography that has led to the opinion that the chief test is factual truth. It is however surprising to find how little our aesthetic judgement is affected by such distortions of the truth. Benjamin Haydon, one can see, is as partisan a writer as could be imagined, and no-one would dream of accepting without scrupulous examination his account of his quarrels, nor his descriptions of persons. Cellini is clearly a braggart, a liar. It will usually be the case that where a lie is the result of a calculated intention to appear right or important, damage is done to autobiographical truth. But when, as in the cases of Haydon and Cellini, we see them from the beginning as "exaltés", when the whole sweep of their lives has something extravagant, inventive, Quixotic about it, when their imaginations determine their behaviour as well as their accounts: then we take their inventions, their distortions, as part of their being, as their truth, which is in fact revealed in their autobiographies with greater candour than we find in many more "truthful" works.

Are we then to conclude that truth does not matter overmuch in autobiography? We cannot believe this. Not only does the reader expect truth from autobiography, but autobiographers themselves all make more or less successful efforts to get at the truth, to stick to it, or at least try to persuade us they are doing so. Writers know perfectly well what they are doing when they write autobiographical novels. We have then to define what sort of truth is meant, and this we can discover only in relation to the author's general intention. It will not be an objective truth, but the truth in the confines of a limited purpose, a purpose that grows out of the author's life and imposes itself on him as his specific quality, and thus determines his choice of events and the manner of his treatment and expression. For this reason we now proceed to examine certain types of autobiography which correspond to the specific personality and intention of the author, as a scientist, a statesman, a poet, and so on. Only the autobiography of childhood escapes this classification, and accordingly we turn our attention first to it.

VI

The Autobiography of Childhood
Aksakoff and Moritz

MOST autobiographers succeed better with their childhood than their later life, even their youth. This success must be ascribed partly to the strength of an established literary tradition. However different children and their circumstances may be, their mode of apprehension and growth is much more similar than in later life, so that all "Childhoods" can profit by traditional treatment. Two such different Scotsmen as Carlyle and Lord Tweedsmuir can write childhoods that are recognisably related; and it is understandable that Stephen Spender was unwilling to give an extended account of his childhood because he felt it would throw little light on what was specifically himself—"autobiographies of childhood are chiefly important for the light they throw on childhood in general, and they are not especially illuminating on the autobiography of particular individuals".

But Spender partly refutes himself since, in later parts of *World within World,* he returns to his childhood. Although all childhood has much in common, it is in fact here that the specific source of later drives is discovered, and it is therefore essential to true autobiography. Later illuminations, rational insights, or moral resolves do not compare in weight or substance with the quality of the early temperament; or, as one might better put it, they become momentous only as the realisation and shaping of what was there, indistinct and unformed, in the child.

The common structure of accounts of childhood is given by its common theme—growing up. It is a theme peculiarly appropriate for autobiographical treatment, since the inner development is so embraced in outer events. In this state, when the child scarcely scrutinises himself, he comes to be and know himself through his awareness of others, of the outer world. The process of growth therefore takes a lively, concrete form, through observed things and people; the widening consciousness is this widening world. The choice of events is decided in the main by memory—usually there is no other authority—and what remains in memory is still alive and vivid. It may not be rationally important, that is, not important within the line of personal development; more important experiences may be forgotten; but it is the past as we possess it now, it has significance in being *our* past. And because in childhood we move outwards in all directions, every experience seems worth while and is accompanied in memory by feeling. Later, as the character becomes more precise, specialisation of various sorts occurs, and there is abdication. Later therefore, as the autobiography moves into adult years, much of the childhood may seem superfluous, disconnected from the later man—like those photographs of chubby children in sailor suits that contrast rather painfully with the men of substance and importance they become. Within the framework of childhood, however, recollection has a good chance of creating that concrete homogeneity of subject and object, of past and present, of mental image and external event, that makes good autobiography.

When the childhood is merely the preface to the account of the mature man, experiences tend to be singled out that fore-shadow the later development. There is then a double selective principle, on the one hand what is remembered, on the other, what is considered of relevance to the later achievement. One can admit that the latter principle is never utterly absent, but in autobiographies that are limited to childhood it is much less imperious. Such autobiographies show the formation of a temperament, not a public or even a private character, and for this reason they can be taken as the purest form of autobiography. One thinks of Stendhal's *Vie de Henry Brulard,* Tolstoy's *Childhood* (though this is not strictly autobiographical), Gorki's *Childhood,* Hudson's *Far Away and Long Ago.* I take as my examples S. T. Aksakoff's *Years of Childhood* and K. P. Moritz's *Anton Reiser.*

AKSAKOFF

Aksakoff's masterpiece reaches only to his tenth year. Although it was written shortly before his death in 1859, when he was a well-known writer, it was not primarily meant to show the father in the child. True, he is an unusually sensitive, emotional, and imaginative child, who loves to tell stories; but his particularity is treated not with prophetical intent, but as a means to render with extraordinary vividness the situations through which he passes. Aksakoff does not, however, confine himself to impressions of particular vividness; he seems to try to recall all he can. After giving a few typically dissociated memories of earliest childhood, he then maintains a continuous narrative, using knowledge acquired later to fill in gaps and explain matters which were beyond the child's knowledge or comprehension. He himself had some misgiving that "the detail of narrative will seem to many trivial and worthless".

But precisely from this abundant and sometimes apparently inconsequential detail there appears the image both of this particular child and of childhood in general. As a small boy Aksakoff was often ill, and the habit of illness sharpened the natural observancy of the child, of childhood—the attentive observation of the world, the longing to participate, together with the habit of imaginative compensations. We see how this enforced passive watchfulness grows, as he grows stronger, first into a timid and restricted activity, then bit by bit into a fuller active life, just as the early meagre games he invents grow into the richer delight of reading and story-telling. Embracing all is the slow discovery of the world as he grows older, and this is signalled by a series of journeys, momentous enterprises in the remote Russian province, which are exciting revelations.

It would have been easy for Aksakoff to have exploited these journeys for their intrinsic interest, the risky crossings of the great stormy rivers, the manner of life during the country journeys in the Ufa district, the character of the barbaric and nomadic settlements in which they sometimes had to rest. The work has all these things, and Aksakoff might have seized on them as a grateful substitute theme. It is the description of the life and people on the Blasket Islands that makes O'Sullivan's *Twenty Years A-Growing* so charming and memorable a book of reminiscence, not an autobiography in the full sense. But with exemplary discretion Aksakoff directs us firmly to what the child knows or feels, so that all events become the substance of his awakening consciousness. For him, in the excitement of travel, all details are absorbing, the ordinary as well as the extraordinary—the evening fishing that he so passionately loved, the crossing of rivers, peasants harvesting, his first water-mill, the pictures in his room. All is vivid; and the indiscriminateness of attention tells us of the outer world, but also, and always, of the child.

The line of the child's development is not simplified by an artificial arrangement of experiences. The places to which they travel do not correspond to a steady graph of inward development; it is the child that imposes his pattern. They visit Chourassovo, a great manor-house where the child is first introduced to a grander, aristocratic world. But they then return to their own estate at Bagrovo, in all respects a less interesting place, and for Aksakoff's mother a place of boredom. But here the child makes of the quietness itself an immense enrichment; and here, in some of the finest pages of the book, he first consciously experiences the Russian Spring, from the break-up of the ice to the onrush of the harvest.[1]

The adults are observed much more closely than children. Because of his illness Aksakoff had difficulty in making friends, but there is also no characterisation of the little sister who was his constant and loved playmate. The adults have that finishedness and plasticity that they can have only for the child, for whom they are the given, established world, accepted as such, whether with affection and admiration or with fear and hostility. His relations with his father and mother are described with wonderful delicacy. For the mother he was all in all. Her devotion saved him in his illness, and her almost obsessive protectiveness becomes,

---

[1] In *A Russian Schoolboy*, the account of his school-days that Aksakoff wrote and published before *Years of Childhood*, Aksakoff attributes to the end of his school-years his first real experience of Spring—"this was the first time I had really seen and really felt that season". It is a nice problem; was he, in *Years of Childhood*, anticipating? My own suggestion is that this, the later account, is true, and that either he had temporarily forgotten it when writing *A Russian Schoolboy*, or meant that a different and fuller consciousness belonged to the adolescent.

G

as he grows, a source of tension with his father and himself. Gently, with the most considerate respectfulness, the father tries to make the boy more robust and independent, to interest him in country affairs and sports to which the city-bred mother is indifferent and contemptuous. The tension in the boy, his passionate love for his mother and his longing for the sports and knowledge she despises, is most delicately delineated in small details, for instance the struggles that always occur when he begs leave to go fishing. Towards the end we see how he begins to grow conscious of the tension, how the bonds with his mother begin to loosen as he realises that at times he cannot unreflectingly tell her all that is in his mind but must be discreetly silent. He begins to see his mother as a person in herself, and this is the same as realising his own separate identity. All the relationships in this book, specific and in part exotic as they are, seem archetypal, childhood-in-itself.

It is curious to compare this book with Aksakoff's account of the following period of his young life, *A Russian Schoolboy*, which was written earlier. As a document of the time it is as interesting and genuine, and it too is freshly and gracefully told. It is however much less profound as an autobiography, since the mother and boy enter ready-made, and the sources of their almost neurotic affection are hidden. Even if we read it after the later volume, as a sequel, it is weaker. The unity of world and child is broken, and breaks up into the world here and the boy there. Things happen, but they do not become experiences. This is an inevitable process in all lives, as one grows more complex and develops interests that do not fit on to the world that is given. What at this stage of life can make a unity of an autobiography is the knowledge of the future man, the line of development into the future; and this is lacking in this volume. The Childhood is sufficient to itself; the Boyhood needs something more.

Years of Childhood is unsurpassed as a revelation of childhood. Such a judgement, however, raises a central problem to which we shall have to return. Can one speak here of conscious psychological insight? Not, certainly, as one can in respect to Rousseau's *Confessions*. There is no attempt to reveal psychological processes conventionally ignored, little objective comment or analysis, no theorising. It is a question whether Aksakoff was aware of the wider bearing of his relationship with his mother, which he describes solely as something peculiar to them. But this lack of scientific insight in no sense harms the book. It shows the kind of insight that is however essential. What we are given is imaginative reproduction of the child's inner and outer world, inner and outer vision, a knowledge and truth that comes home to us in tingling awareness and self-awareness; truth that is plastically formed, not analysed.

K. P. MORITZ

In Aksakoff's *Childhood*, experience is assembled organically into the personality. Clearly, not every childhood is so lucky, and autobiography is not limited to such lucky childhoods. Experience and personality may be at variance, the child's development may be torn, harsh, frustrated. K. P. Moritz's *Anton Reiser* (1785–90) is an outstanding example of the story of a child whose nature is poisoned by outer circumstances.

Moritz was a scholar, aesthetician, and educationist. His own unhappy upbringing made him acutely aware of the distress and errors caused by ignorance of child psychology, and he wrote his autobiography in order to provide material and guidance for educationists. It was in part published in his own *Magazine for experimental psychology,* in which during the 1780s he published a series of autobiographical documents to serve his pedagogical purpose. Clearly therefore, although it is his own particular story, his ultimate objective is not what was specific to him, the character of Moritz the man, but what is representative of childhood. Perhaps for this reason he wrote it in the third person, and called it an "autobiographical novel"—though he also stressed that it is "a true and faithful representation of a man's life, to its finest nuances". It closes with the end of his school-days, before he had discovered his true bent, and it is important to bear in mind that Moritz began it before he was thirty (he died before he reached forty), that is, before he felt he had found his own way, so that the indeterminacy of the autobiography's close corresponds to the uncertainties of the author.

In the Introductions to the four Parts of the book Moritz makes his intentions clear. It is "primarily the inward history of man" and is intended "to make his individual existence more important to him"—i.e. to make each individual more confident in the intrinsic worth of his being, irrespective of public judgements. It asserts the significance of the apparently trivial and disconnected details of a life, since when the life is surveyed as a whole these details become connected, consistent, important. Particularly in the Introduction to Part 4 Moritz shows his general purpose, for through an analysis of his character he throws light on children in general. The hardships of his life drove him he says, to find compensation in "fantasies", but at the same time "he had a certain feeling of the real things in the world around him and was unwilling to renounce them completely"; so that he was, as a result of his constant struggle with existence, "in constant struggle with himself"—"a struggle of truth with illusion, of dream with reality".

Born into extreme poverty, the boy suffers throughout his life from uncomprehending oppressive powers, parents, tradesmen, clergymen, teachers, who misguide him and bully him, whose charity is humiliating, and who drive him to find compensations in his imagination. He traces his failure to stand up to these pressures to the earliest influence in the home.

His father and mother, cooped up in the straitest circumstances, quarrelled continually; worse still, the boy felt that the father he did not love was more often in the right than the mother he loved. These first impressions, writes Moritz, have never been effaced from his soul and have laid the basis of his hypochondria. He recognises that his raptures over the first meadows in which he lies had something diseased about them, as a flight from reality, and are the basis of all "the illusory images that his fancy paints". In addition, his parents, like many in their position in their time, found comfort in pietism, in highly emotional meetings of the elect, and in literature like the auto-biography of Mme Guyon. And so the boy is brought up, like Edmund Gosse precociously educated in religious exaltation and the feeling of sin, to find joy in tears and melancholy. Games, all simple natural pleasures, are forbidden. Moritz describes how the boy, finding a little handcart and enjoying the pleasure of pushing it round a garden, has to justify himself by imagining that "little Jesus" is in it. He is taught to revel in the thought of his own death, and comes to court injustice in order to have the pleasure of feeling hurt.

This training makes him pathologically sensitive to public opinion, and partly out of an inner need, partly in order to impress, he develops a precocious power of prayer (one is again reminded of Gosse). The idea of becoming a preacher begins to fill his mind, so that he may enjoy the prestige and satisfaction of standing up there in the pulpit righteously wrathful with the congregation. Later, at the school to which charitable but tyrannous patrons send him, he finds in the idea of the theatre a role that will satisfy his vanity. He neglects his school-work, despite spasmodic and sometimes hypocritical movements of remorse and reform, and buries himself in reading, identifying himself with the sentimental and frustrated heroes of contemporary literature such as Werther. Just as earlier Moritz notes that his religious exaltation gave both an outlet to his spiritual needs and a fateful twist to his character, so now his analysis of his literary compensations is remarkably subtle. For while *The Sorrows of Werther* gives him an opportunity to wallow in self-pity, it also gives him moral strength and encourages him to live; it strengthens "his pride in being a man", and rescues him from feeling himself to be "an insignificant and rejected creature". The desire to become a poet seizes him, and he wins credit at school from his poetic efforts; but Moritz points out how characteristic it was that he always rhapsodised on far-fetched, grandiose themes, instead of being able to speak "of what lies close to man". This too is not a genuine calling, but a compensation. The book closes with his journey to join a theatrical company; and it is a symbolical conclusion that when he arrives he finds the company disbanded, and is left face to face with uncertainty.

As a psychological document this autobiography is of outstanding importance. On the one hand, it is one of the most searching analyses of the social and personal sources of pietism; on the other, it reveals for the first time the mechanism of certain psychological processes. Moritz understands the process of compensation, uses the term suppression ("Verdrängung"), and gives a case-history of an inferiority complex. His story is in addition a profoundly interesting piece of social history. Is it more than this, is it a great autobiography?

It lacks on the surface some of the qualities of a work of art. It is written awkwardly, without ease of style, and the narrative is often interrupted by analytical reflection and pedagogic comment. There is little evocative description, and where it is attempted, it easily becomes sentimental, crude. Feelings are in general drily and abstractedly delineated, not presented, and the characterisations of other persons tend to the caricature. At times it seems to be more a case-history than a life-story. For these reasons, and not simply because the life itself is so painful, it cannot be loved like Aksakoff's *Childhood*.

Yet are these faults? It is precisely the theme of this book that, from earliest childhood, the boy fails to come to terms with reality, that he can never see the outer world objectively nor be himself. This painful dissonance enters into the style itself. Charm of description, fluency of phrase and simplicity of structure are necessarily lacking in this book, since they would express not only what the boy, but also the author, lacked. In his games, which often take a masochistic form, in the pretensions which satisfy him momentarily but remove him further from finding himself, this dislocation in his nature is consistently exhibited. His analytical method belongs intimately to this man, who could never free himself from painful introspection and self-doubting, so that he cannot even get absorbed in his own story. We, as we read, almost painfully experience that "laming of the soul" that is his theme. In the Introduction to Part 2 Moritz writes that when one looks closer at a life, the details appear connected and "harmonious". In his case it is not the harmony of classical but of modern music that one finds, full of dissonance, a unity in which the awkwardness of the style is built into the incidents to make the massive impact characteristic of great autobiography.

One may contrast it with Edmund Gosse's *Father and Son* in this respect. It was inevitable that the tone of Gosse's searching and candid autobiography should be different from Moritz's, since Gosse felt that he had outlived the torment of his childhood; he had reached a serenity that Moritz never gained, and looked back on his childhood with detachment and compassion— compassion above all for the father who so oppressed him. As a consequence, however, the pressures, the distortions, never appear to be so appalling, so cruel, as they must have been. Not only is the whole smoothly and skilfully written, but there is at times (only very rarely) a little "fine writing" which acts as a distraction and consolation. When, for instance, Gosse writes that the dreams of the boy "were interminable, and hung stationary from that nightly sky", there is an imported, alien consolation in the final image. The description of the solemn baptism of the boy into the community of the Brethren loses something of its painfulness through the humour with which it is written. Gosse's work is a fine study, in many ways "scrupulously true" as he claimed it to be. But it fails to recreate the experience of dislocation and distortion that is disclosed through Moritz's bleak and ungainly truthfulness.

The autobiographies of Aksakoff and Moritz, like all other autobiographies, acquire their shape through the authors' consciousness of what the child ultimately became. But both are peculiarly distinguished since they attend to the multiple experiences of the child and are aware of potentialities in their own right, and not simply because they lead somewhere, to a career or a position. At the same time, the peculiar drive within the child takes shape, he is not simply a malleable object. One can contrast with them the autobiography of Denton Welch, a story of painful disharmony with the outer world. The weakness of this work is that the dislocations are only evoked, there is no attempt to seek their sources, and the boy seems to have no power to resist, no innate drive. It seems as if the author deliberately reduces himself to almost automatic responses. A philosophy of life, expressed through the manner of writing, seems here to overlay the actual truth, while in Aksakoff and Moritz it is the truth of childhood that determines the philosophy.

There are many excellent "childhoods". These two seem to me to be representative because they are only and fully autobiographical. They are not directed towards the later man, nor centred upon a partial theme, a partial relationship, or some extraneous theme. I was tempted to join with them Gorki's *Childhood,* a powerful and sombre work. But though here we can gather something of what the boy was—independent, sturdy, wilful—he is not the centre of the picture. What is central is the people among whom he lived, terribly reckless and cruel, unreflectingly mean and generous; so violent a world that the child can do little more than withstand. Gorki makes his intentions plain:

> As I remember the oppressive horrors of our wild Russian life, I ask myself often whether it is worth while to speak of them. And then, with restored confidence, I answer myself—"It is worth while because it is actual, vile fact, which has not died out, even in these days—a fact which must be traced to its origin, and pulled up by the root from the memories, the souls of the people, and from our narrow sordid lives . . ."
>
> And there is another and more important reason impelling me to describe these horrors. Although they are so disgusting, although they oppress us and crush many beautiful souls to death, yet the Russian is still so healthy and young in heart that he can and does rise above them. For in this amazing life of ours not only does the animal side of our nature flourish and grow fat, but with this animalism there has grown up, triumphant in spite of it, something bright, healthful, and creative—a type of humanity which inspires us to look forward to our regeneration.

Gorki's autobiography was meant to serve a wider purpose than the discovery of the self; it reminds us that there are circumstances and times which make demands that cannot be reconciled with a pure autobiographical purpose.

VII

The Acquisition of an Outlook

AUTOBIOGRAPHIES that are confined to childhood can uncover experiences and capacities that are inconsequent. Those that continue into adolescence and the adult years almost inevitably narrow their scope to the story of a main achievement, a particular outlook or professional career, that by which the person is publicly known and that often is the actual cause of writing. If in respect to childhood the autobiographer can be largely (not at all fully) empirical in approach, as regards the later years he is guided by a teleological principle. This concern with his later achievement must of course affect also his outline of his childhood, and he cannot escape a painful dilemma. If he treats the childhood without reference to what he has become, it tends to be in many parts irrelevant to his story and to reflect perhaps a sentimental indulgence in his private memories; if he speaks only of what in his childhood presages his later development, the truth may easily be distorted by his polemical bias. This problem of selection is most severe for those men whose career is closely bound to impersonal tasks, for instance scientists.

Interesting and perhaps moving as it may be to see the man behind the work, the private individual behind the public façade, this is not the primary purpose of good autobiography. What we want is to see the man within the work. And the danger in cases of highly specialised achievement is that the talent, the work, may seem to have a self-moving dynamic of its own. An auto-biography such as Freud's advances logically from the statement of a scientific problem to successive solutions and new problems. But even in such a case, the autobiography is of outstanding value precisely because it demonstrates that this is not the truth of the matter, and that a life is the story of a man working, not of work. It is a salutary corrective to those histories of special types of human activity—of political institutions or economic forms, even of literature and art—that almost inevitably suggest too strongly a self-moving law in things and situations. It is easier to define a problem or a theory than imaginatively to recreate a man; but even the narrowest autobiographies can make us aware of the creative impulse in the individual, that individual energy, on which history of any sort depends and that most easily eludes one's grasp. The autobiography of the narrowest scope can make us aware of its reality, and allow us to see a memorable life as what it is, the operation of spirit upon circumstances, as well as that of circumstances upon spirit.

In the first place I propose to discuss that class of autobiography where the author's range of interest and relevance is defined not only by the actual form of his life but also consciously, deliberately, by his formulation of a philosophy. Most religious autobiographies belong to this type, and in modern times many of the autobiographies of philosophers. Few autobiographers do not include the statement of an attitude; but in these cases it constitutes the main substance of their activity, and determines what in their experience they value and record.

Augustine's *Confessions* are exemplary in their structure. We may disregard, for our present purpose, the raptures and exhortations that exerted so confusing an influence on later religious autobiography. Here, with remarkable clarity of purpose, they are for the most part kept separate from the narrative of the events that call them forth, so that they do not obscure the lineaments of the story. Relatively few experiences are chosen, few personal relationships are dwelt on, and these are closely linked as stages in Augustine's spiritual progress. What Augustine manages to do is to enshrine a particular experience in a particular local circumstance and a particular personal relationship, so that the inward religious experience issues from and affects the whole personality —the actual physical man and his actions, the mind, and the personal affections. The scene of ultimate conversion in the garden comes as the outcome of philosophical and religious debate and hesitancy, but also is framed in the atmosphere of friendship and personal intimacy, and has as its background the profound love of and for the mother; all the powers of Augustine are in play, and the physical environment serves as a catalytic agent, to precipitate the decisive event. One does not need to be a Christian to recognise the profound truth of this mode of experience; such events—and there are several such in Augustine's book—illustrate the very method of spiritual progress: knowledge comes from multiple sources in the person, it proceeds by leaps and is accompanied by a mysterious rapture, it is a becoming and yet, at the same time, a recognition of what was always there, and it occurs through the medium of circumstances that in themselves are insignificant and fortuitous, and yet become an all-important and absolutely memorable constellation. There was much in Augustine's life on which the *Confessions* are silent, and much in himself and his circumstances of which he was ignorant. But none of these omissions injures the truth of his work, which reveals most penetratingly and vividly the manner and structure of understanding, which arises from the energetic will and profound feeling, and creates a mental framework for the release of directed energy. Augustine is supremely successful in making us feel that the story of his belief is not the story of one aspect of his being, but that of his whole personality; the narrative convinces far more powerfully than the attendant reflections.

The same co-ordinated energy of personality is evident in Saint Teresa's *Life*. There were numbers of religious autobiographies in the later Middle Ages in which mystics recounted their ecstasies and visions and undertook tasks imposed on them by revelation; but what is characteristic of them in general, and of those of the seventeenth and eighteenth century, is that the intensity of religious experience is accompanied by a loss of individuality. As autobiographies they are not to be criticised because the religious experiences may be deemed to be hallucinations, for these are subjectively as potent as other experiences; nor do such experiences remain without a practical effect, for they may drive Suso, Margery Kempe, Mme Guyon to action, to ascetic practices, to the cloister, to service of the diseased, to pilgrimages and so forth. But the relationship of faith and action tends to be abstract, the action belongs more to the faith than to the person. If such persons are called hysterical or neurotic, as they often must be, the term refers not to the religious experience itself, but to the lack of coherence between the experience and the personality as a continuous entity. What makes Saint Teresa's *Life* a great autobiography is that we see how her mind, submissive yet obstinate, trusting yet critical, wrestles with her visions, and how these themselves become surer, more understood in the sense that they find expression in practical behaviour with others, ultimately in the reform of conventual life and the founding of St. Joseph's.

Religious belief, especially the sort of illumination that characterises Augustine and Teresa, is by definition irrational, incomprehensible. Their object and achievement in the autobiographies could not therefore be rational understanding of themselves and the source of their faith. But this is no handicap; and the closer we look at autobiography in general the truer this seems of all. The distinction of great autobiography is not so much the truth of knowing as the truth of being, an integration and reunion of different aspects of the person, a coherence of the acting and the spiritual personality in the particularity of circumstances.

The danger besetting religious autobiographies lies in the fact that the intensity of a metaphysical revelation tends to obliterate and devalue other sorts of experience. Tolstoy's *A Confession* illustrates this danger in a profoundly moving way. In early life he had written the three volumes *Childhood, Boyhood,* and *Youth* which, though expressly not strictly autobiographical, put us most directly in contact with himself. *A Confession* is a late work of 1874, and was written after his conversion in a mood utterly different from the avidity for life that fills the early volumes. In a later comment about it, Tolstoy wrote:[1]

> When I thought of writing the whole sincere truth, not hiding anything that was bad in my life, I was horrified at the impression such a biography must produce.

And he quotes Pushkin's poem, *Remembrance—*

> As with disgust the record of my life I face,
> I curse, chastise myself, and shudder.

It is therefore not surprising that *A Confession* tends to evade the

[1] *Recollections*. Tolstoy, Centenary Edition (trans. Aylmer Maude), xxi, i.

particular and to move in abstract, general terms. Only here and there is a particular decisive experience recalled, and then only summarily, such as the public execution Tolstoy witnessed in Paris, which confirmed his doubts of the current belief in progress. The most memorable "events" in the book are not incidents, but a fable and a dream. The fable is one of the Buddha Birth stories, handed down through the Golden Legend and through translations of The Fables of Bidpai—a hunted man hangs from a twig in a well, with a ravening beast above and a monster below, watching a black and white mouse gnawing the twig away. In the dream Tolstoy lies in space, with only an imaginary support, between the wide consoling heavens and the terrifying abyss. Fable and dream are harrowing symbols of man's precariousness, but they are general symbols, not particular, and transcend the actuality and meaning of a particular life.

Newman's *Apologia* cannot be criticised on this score; as apologetics it had to be, and is, highly personal—"I mean to be simply personal and historical". Yet, though it is substantially true to the facts, and is written with superlative skill, it too as autobiography has a fatal fault. It is confined in the main to those few decisive years when the Anglican was converted to Roman Catholicism. Newman does not think it necessary to tell much of his childhood or to mention a number of significant experiences in early manhood that do not fit in with, or seem relevant to, his purpose. These omissions served his immediate polemical purpose, and they do not imply any conscious or unconscious intention of untruthfulness. Newman was well aware that a man is not simply an intellect, and that his own conversion came from a deep personal source; his object was, he stated, to set forth "that living intelligence by which I write, and argue, and act". For this reason he chose an autobiographical form for his *Apologia*: "It is the concrete being that reasons". Newman's success can be gauged by the conclusion of an acute critic, that while the *Apologia* is "not psychological biography of a high order", and while there are "no full and satisfactory motivations", in it we have "a remarkable revelation of personality".[1]

What is the fault, then? It cannot be the lack of psychological analysis, for that is absent from some of the greatest

[1] W. E. Houghton, *The Art of Newman's Apologia*, 1945, 107–9.

autobiographies. The fault lies partly in the very skill of the exposition. Its rounded finality, the controlled suggestivity of the writing in all its details, evokes a certain distrust, and this distrust is reinforced by the absence of a full account of the child and young man. One fails to perceive and feel the driving forces in the man, the genetic sources of the personality, the numerous potentialities in him which ultimately led to this great decision of Newman's life. His life appears not as a controlled torrent, but a contrived plan. The "fault" lies in this: Newman represents the great decision as taking place in these few years; but we feel that a true decision of this type must be rooted deep in the man, and from an autobiography we need to find it already pre-fashioned in the earlier life, and affecting the total man, his personality and mode of life. The change of belief which is the centre of Newman's story does not fully engage and decisively illuminate the whole man.

My criticism becomes clearer if we compare the *Apologia* with Schweitzer's *My Life and Thought*. This work is not at all neatly or skilfully composed, and Schweitzer's self-delineation is awkward, even blundering. Probably because he had already written something about his childhood and had published two books on his work at the mission at Lambarene, here the main accent is laid on his philosophical and theological writings, and the autobiography culminates in a statement of his philosophy. The theme is an important one, the underpinning of a religion grounded in feeling, which for that reason has shown itself he believes to be ineffectual, by rational thought rooted in reality. This is the story of his own thought, which passed from the orthodoxy of his Protestant upbringing through his predominantly ethical interpretation of Christianity to his final philosophy of "Reverence for Life", which embraces the Christian ethic in a philosophy of activity. This story of his thought is surprisingly without drama and tension and cannot be compared with Augustine's or Newman's. There is hardly a hint of spiritual crises, for instance of distress when he leaves the traditional position of his father and friends or when he later propounds views in startling conflict with the Church of which he was an ordained member. His determined devotion to what he believed to be the truth gains our admiration, but his account lacks the urge and stress that would make it a great autobiographical statement. If he was so imperturbable, his mind seems to lack the resonance his theme demands; if the calmness belongs only to the way in which he presents his life, we suspect he is trying to make his development seem more logical than it was.

What gives this movement of his thought greater power than Newman's, however, is the account of its embodiment in his life. Interwoven is the life-history of a brilliant theologian, a distinguished organist and interpreter of Bach, who gave up a strikingly successful career at the age of 30 in order to devote himself to Africans as a medical missionary. It is this decision, and the years of work in Central Africa, that give substance to what in his philosophy he calls "elemental thinking", that "spiritual relation to the world" that he considers disastrously wanting in modern civilisation. Both elements—the practical life and the thinking—are necessary, for his ethical decision to serve the distressed could have a general significance, he believed, only if it could be shown to be fully grounded in rational thought.

It comes about, then, that Schweitzer is remarkably reticent about the subjective sources and character of his great decision. His life, as he tells it, pursues a very even tenor until at the age of 21 he decides to "give something in return" for the ease and happiness of his youth. Whatever these sources were—and it is indubitable that they are intimately connected with the Christian feeling of sinfulness and search for grace, with traditional Christian charity—it is Schweitzer's deliberate intention not to dwell on them. At the time the decision was made he was aware that its quality was different from the "call" experienced by men of a simpler, more naïve faith, and it was sustained by him, as time passed, on philosophical grounds as a representative ethical act whereby he was able "to raise his natural relation to the world to a spiritual one", and thus give meaning to individual life.

It is clear that Schweitzer's life was essentially governed by a religious impulse. His service to the Africans, however helpful to them, was primarily important, like charitable activities in general, in respect to his own soul and, as a representative action, to the spiritual welfare of Western civilisation. Because of this, his work in Africa has been sharply criticised. He has been accused of lack of concern for the social and economic advancement of the Africans and of lack of sympathy with their political aspirations; he shows himself paternalistic, if not authoritarian towards them. If this criticism is justified—and I incline to think it is—the goodness of his work is as sharply to be questioned as was the work of the London Charity Organisation Committee by Beatrice Webb and the early socialists.

But does such criticism affect our judgement of the autobiography itself? It does, I believe, in so far as Schweitzer is concerned to justify his missionary activities within the framework of a general philosophy of civilisation. This philosophy is consonant with his life in that its central theme is man's spiritual relationship to himself, his personal feeling of value, his spiritual freedom; it does not take into account social and political freedom except in a one-sided, abstract form akin to nineteenth-century liberalism. We are not meant to read the philosophical passages of the autobiography as a mere personal confession of faith, but as a conclusion of truth; and if we boggle at the philosophy, we tend to view the actual personality with some distrust.

In actual fact, our response to this autobiography must be ambiguous, as so often with autobiographies that bear a direct message, particularly those near to us in time. We tend to take Schweitzer's philosophy, as it is expressed in the autobiography, not as we would take it when we read his philosophical publications. The autobiographical form leads us to appreciate it as an expression of his personality, not as an objective statement about man in general, and thus, even, to invert some of his own valuations. What one sees is the unity of a life impelled by a mighty and scarcely understood force, for which the man, as he reflects, seeks plausible rational grounds. The later philosophy, which he finds satisfying and urges on us, seems to some extent a rationalisation of the original Christian urge, and is far less adequate to the mode of his life than is that original obscure drive. Schweitzer does not understand himself well, and he lacks the psychological subtlety of a Newman; but his autobiography gives what the *Apologia* lacks, the assembly of a man's whole powers in shaping his life.

In this respect, for all its faults, Schweitzer's *My Life and Thought* can be counted a worthy representative of its type. For religious autobiography as the story of the acquisition of a particular outlook has a very special place, since religion is not just an outlook. It involves a complex of emotions and relationships and an energetic principle of living. That is, the best religious autobiographies synthesise multiple powers of a man.

Autobiographies that delineate the acquisition of a philosophy may tend to replace living experience by opinion, and thus lose in plasticity and human substance. It might be contended that such a criticism is irrelevant, if autobiography is the representation of the truth of a life, and if the man was capable of responding to experience only through mental activity. J. S. Mill or Herbert Spencer, one might say, were abstract minds of this type; why should one ask from their autobiographies for anything more than an account of their ideas?

Mill himself gives the answer as far as he is concerned. As a young man he was, as he puts it, a Benthamite "thinking machine", and his account of his grotesquely intellectual education shows how he became so. He had "a well-equipped ship, but no sail", and the crisis of his thought came when he suddenly realised that if all his intellectual and political ideas were to be realised, it would give him "no great joy and happiness". He tells how, deeply influenced by Coleridge, he then came to graft a philosophy of feeling on to his system, the outward signs of his changed attitude being his love of nature and of Wordsworth's poetry, and his devotion with Mrs. Taylor, whom he later married.

Mill's story has the elements of a significant and even dramatic autobiography; his prominence might have made it a representative, as well as an interesting, document. Why is it that it falls short? The immediate answer is that it is dry, and provokes the comment that Harriet Martineau made, "poor Mill". What we miss is the adequate projection of the thematic idea into the form of experience. There are hints that his first, early visit to France awoke his love of the countryside, but he never finds the words to evoke his love. He is so reticent (out of loyalty?) about his involved relations with his father, who trained him to his rationalism, that we get no glimpse of the opposed elements in his make-up. Even the impact of the intuitive philosophers is given in dry, abstract words; only occasionally do his words move as he himself was moved—for instance when he is brought to tears in reading Marmontel's account of his boyish hardships and resolution (it is worth noting that Stendhal saw that there was rhetoric and play-acting in Marmontel's account). When Mill pays his tribute to Mrs. Taylor, his words lack precision. In sum, Mill fails to create an image of his emotive self, though his autobiographical purpose could not be achieved without doing so. It is not sufficient to say his writing lacks evocative, poetical power; it lacks truth, in the sense that the emotive driving force never takes individual shape.

No such criticism can be levelled at Herbert Spencer's *Autobiography*, for there was no emotional crisis in his life. His story shows how, through the systematic study of nature and man, he moved progressively from the recognition of objective problems to truer generalisations. The moral basis is given with his inheritance of religious non-conformity and political radicalism which, emerging with him in the era of modern science and technology, turns into an unrelenting search for an all-embracing, "synthetic" law of life.

It is a weakness of Spencer's autobiography that he recapitulates at some length the actual theme and content of his successive works, instead of taking us behind stage to the hidden processes in himself that called them forth. One suspects curious complications behind this harsh and rather forbidding exterior. Yet Spencer would have said that whatever psychological complications there were had no influence on his main achievement, his scientific study of man, and could properly remain in oblivion. But the real failure of the autobiography results from the fact that he does dwell at considerable length on the detail of his personal life, his friendship, travels, his fishing, even giving his fishing diary; and yet all this side of his life is represented as being truly irrelevant to his work. When Darwin called him an egotist he was suggesting that Spencer failed to admit the help he gained from his intellectual acquaintance, and one must admit he often seems arrogant and dogmatic. But even if one were to accept Spencer's independence, one has to ask, why speak so much of these purely personal interests and affairs? His life, seriously hampered by the nervous illness that prevented him from working except in the mornings, seems to divide into the isolation of the morning and the dissociated sociability of the rest of the day. This dichotomy is amusingly illustrated by his distaste for biography altogether. He always expressed the harshest disrespect for and lack of interest in the actuality of history as contrasted with the general laws that can be considered to govern social development, and yet he found himself, in the autobiography, writing about such particulars. He excuses himself rather lamely, by saying that since someone is bound to gratify public taste by writing his biography, he will in anticipation correct the errors that will occur. If one takes him at his word, one would have to say that the autobiography of the "synthetic" philosopher is an outstanding example of the nemesis of specialisation. But it would be truer to say that it is an example of a failure to understand what autobiography is; if Spencer really believed that only his scientific work was worth recording, he should have written the autobiography as the story of his thought.

This is how Henry Adams conceived his purpose, and few autobiographies have so single-minded an intention as *The Education of Henry Adams*. Whole sections of his life are passed over in silence, for instance his years of fruitful work at Harvard, or the happiness of his married life and its tragic ending, for Adams describes and comments on his experiences only in so far as they related to his understanding of the modern politico-social world.

Education means for Henry Adams "teaching oneself to react with vigor and economy" to the social forces that surround one—to react "not at haphazard, but by choice, on the lines of force that attract one's world". It should enable one "to chart the international channel for fifty years to come", so that personal and social energies can be purposefully directed. The central problem of his education arose from the fact that this New Englander, a scion of a leading American family, was brought up in doctrinaire democratic beliefs that he found corresponded not at all with the real America of the latter part of the nineteenth century, and that gave him, as he says, nothing as far as "education" was concerned. Thus it is that much in his career, his early travels in Europe, his service in the American Ministry in London during the American Civil War, his academic work at Harvard, is summed up by him as useless, or even worse as serving to unfit him for the modern world, "a destructive political education". His account of these experiences is so reluctant, so hostile, so negative, that it has earned him the name of a great "denier".

It was the economic crisis of 1893 that enabled him to begin to "get hold" of his world, and his positive education began when he visited the Chicago Industrial Exposition, and saw what he calls "the first expression of American thought as a unity"— "the whole mechanical consolidation of force" of modern capitalism. His task was to discover the political ideas that corresponded to this social reality, and to embody them in policy. His education was accomplished when, as the intimate of John Hay, the Secretary of State at the turn of the century, he saw the United States intervening powerfully and purposefully in world affairs (the China war); that is, when he saw his government forging a policy appropriate to the character and power of American and world society. As he completed his book (it was first printed in 1907), he believed that all the Great Powers were reaching a similar realistic understanding of the world, the only guarantee of peaceful progress; he was doomed to bitter disillusionment in his old age.

That Adams was wrong in his assessment of the contemporary world limits the value of his work as a political tract; it does not invalidate it as an autobiography, as the story of a man contending with experience. Nor does his silence over many aspects of his life injure its truth and quality. Rather, the single-minded energy with which he pursues what was for him significant makes the account revelatory and forceful. The style itself, which is reflective and general rather than descriptive and evocative, is a true record, for Adams was concerned with his consciousness, his ideas, rather than events, his "adventures", and in this presents the essential truth of his personality. Yet there is a fault in this autobiography, and it occurs at the point where both the man writing and the man whose story is told are involved. From Adams's letters, and other sources, one knows that he remained attached to traditional democratic ideas much later than his *Education* would have us believe; the author of the *Education* harshly denigrates experiences that were held to be of value by the man of whom he writes. This is a typical problem of autobiography as the account of the acquisition of an outlook: the final philosophy too emphatically colours all the past. And perhaps this trend is responsible also for the inadequacy of his political philosophy, for his relative unconcern for domestic policies and his sanguine belief that by 1950 it should be possible to plot "the future orbit of the human race". That is, if he had been more attentive towards aspects of his experience that he rather contemptuously dismisses as useless, his autobiography and his philosophy would have been truer.

How little an autobiography is injured by clear definition of purpose and limitation of scope is illustrated by Croce's short account, a masterpiece in its structure and style. He wrote it at the age of 50, in the midst of creative labour, as a means to collect his thoughts: "I look back on the road I have traversed, and try to fix my eyes on that which I have still to traverse in the years of work that lie before me". "The history of my 'calling' or 'mission'," he writes, is "a criticism, and therefore a history of myself." That is, the review of the past is a means to proceed more confidently with future work. Croce rejects from the outset any attempt at writing confessions, recording memories for their own sake, or evoking descriptively the past.

This history of his mind is therefore highly selective, but it must include the contacts with persons and places which contributed to its shaping. His childhood environment in Naples is described because there, remote from the tides of political life, his mind began to reject conventional and religious beliefs and turned to imaginative occupations, to literature and literary criticism. The shock of his parents' death in an earthquake threw him into a torpor which lasted for some time while he was living in the lively political atmosphere of his uncle's house in Rome, until it was dispelled by Labriola's moral philosophy and his first enthusiasm for Marxism and socialism. A distrust of materialism confirms him in his early taste for literary and scholarly pursuits, but it is now modified by his need to feel that he is "doing good". The success his literary work wins brings him however a feeling of discontent and dissatisfaction, and he is urged on to discover the philosophical bases of historiography and art, and in this work finds "a revelation to me of my true self"—"I was driven to philosophy by the longing to assuage my misery and to give an orientation to my moral and intellectual life".

Still perplexed by the conflict between his desire to do good and his intellectual passion, he was liberated from abstract moralism by Labriola's essay on the materialistic conception of history. The idea that mankind is redeemed "through labour and in labour" came upon him "like falling in love". But his Marxist passion soon burnt out, and it is characteristic of the autobiography that Croce does not enter upon a lengthy refutal of Marxism, but asserts primarily the personal source of his criticism—"mine was at bottom the nature of a student and thinker". He outlines at the end his Philosophy of Spirit, having sketched his aesthetics and his theory of language as steps towards it.

Croce's work is a model of the autobiography of a philosopher. It is only as a thinker, he believes, that he deserves attention, and he keeps strictly to the path of his thought, refusing to dwell on unrelated matters. But he recognises that his make-up as a thinker is complex, and has to include factors of personal and social life. They are however not evocatively described, but reduced to intellectual terms, in which form they enter into the substance of his intellectual activity. A fuller biography of Croce would tell us much more of interest, and perhaps inform us about emotive or intellectual influences that he overlooked. But nothing could so adequately express the specific quality and energy of his mind and personality as does his autobiography.

Croce's autobiography was most ably translated by R. G. Collingwood, the English philosopher whose thought owed a good deal to the Italian's; and it would seem that Collingwood's autobiography also was influenced by Croce's. It could not have the magisterial terseness and clarity of Croce's, since Collingwood was a very different sort of man, but it is also remarkably sure in its structure.

Collingwood was in no doubt about his purpose—"The autobiography of a man whose business is thinking should be the story of his thought". This gives him a principle of omission which he strictly observes. He tells us very little about his childhood, apart from so remarkable a fact that his imagination was captivated at the age of 8 by reading Kant's Theory of Ethics. He hardly mentions the stresses of puberty, and is silent about his private life in later years. But he recognises that thinking does not proceed in a vacuum, and certain facts of experience are signalled out as of decisive importance. For instance, he lays emphasis on the importance of his parents' being artists, so that art was for him from the beginning something that was being made, an ever renewed attempt to solve a problem in painting,

not just the finished museum piece—an experience that influenced greatly his own philosophy of art.

His account of the development of his mind at Oxford and
after is at the same time the account of certain capital experiences.
In London, his daily journeys past the Albert Memorial lead him
to puzzle over the artistic intentions of the creator of this mon-
strosity. His early training and practice in archaeology make him
realise that valuable work in philosophy, as in archaeology and
history, arises only if one sets oneself the proper question; so
that, in the interpretation of the thought of the past, the philosopher needs history if he is to understand what sort of question,
often implicit, was posed by the old thinkers in different times
and places. But he found the answer to his quest could not be
provided by that modern specialist type of historiography that
separates man according to particular activities—political,
economic, social for instance—but only from that which sees
man as a totality in his whole environment; so Collingwood was
forced to become a philosopher of history.

But practical experiences as well as diverse studies contributed
to his thought. The disaster of the First World War, and the errors
of the Treaty of Versailles, confirm him in the view that better
international relations and stable internal systems depend, not on
a change of heart, but on "more understanding of human affairs".
Again he is driven to history, for there is no sharp distinction
between past and present; he sees that the past is not dead, but
"incapsulated" in the present, and that to know yourself you must
know history. And he justifies the study of history on the grounds
of his own understanding of it as the imaginative "re-enactment"
of the thought of the past in his mind. The study of the past will
not give rules for conduct in totally new situations; but it trains
one to recognise the totality and "specificity" of a situation.

A further main stimulus to his work as a philosopher was his
practical profession as a teacher at Oxford. His moral responsibilities towards his pupils were brought home to him with particular force in the late 1920s and the 1930s, the period of economic collapse and the rise of Fascism. His hatred of the deceit
in Fascism, of its corruption of the mind as well as morals, led
him not only to sympathise with the moral passion of Marx
but also to lay stress on the reality of thinking and the relation

between thinking and practice. Now, as he is writing his book in 1938 and 1939, when he embraces his full obligations as a teacher and philosopher, all his earlier work falls into perspective. His continuing efforts to free thought from abstraction, to see it as a constituent of human activity—to see art as something that is being made, history as a living part of the present, research as a response to a question, thinking as a social responsibility—now come to have a coherent meaning. Now his autobiography can be written.

Collingwood's work—which should be recognised I believe as a most illuminating document of the spiritual situation of the late 1930s—illustrates many of the characteristics of good autobiography in general, and in particular of that which tells of the acquisition of an outlook. It is the opposite of contemplative recapitulation or indulgent recollection, for it is an essay in interpretation, a means of discovering a sense in his life of which the author was not fully aware before he began to write. Through it he organises his past experiences according to a scale of value he has only lately established, and extracts from them a meaning of which he was not conscious at the time of their incidence: as he says, he had hitherto been "fighting in the dark". As a result he not only severely discriminates between what is memorable and what is not, but also is less interested in evoking the mood of the past than in indicating what seeds of the future it held. Collingwood's autobiography gives little idea of the aloof and difficult man he was for many of his acquaintance and colleagues. But it does not claim to be the picture of a person, but the core and inner reality of a moral personality that could find its self-realisation through transforming the outer, contingent world into a body of coherent and energetic thought, which in its turn provided a basis for meaningful activity. Above all, it does not misuse autobiography and make it merely an instrument for expounding doctrine. Like Croce's, it shows how the author experiences and reflects on experience, how his thought is enclosed in his life. The sincerity and truth of the personality is primary, and the quality of the doctrine depends on the quality of the personality.

Autobiographies of the type discussed in this chapter are written with a more or less emphatic intention of expounding doctrine, and in the author's mind the justification of the enterprise lies in the rightness of the outlook he has reached. Students of a man's philosophy will read his autobiography as an aid to understanding the evolution of his thought. But if the autobiography is of such quality that it can stand by itself, and be appreciated for itself by readers otherwise unacquainted with the author, our attention turns in a different direction. It would have angered Augustine—and perhaps will have made some religious readers indignant—to think it possible to say of the *Confessions*, as I have put it, that "we may disregard the raptures and exhortations". If that were possible, he would say, then he had written to no purpose. But this is what generally happens. The autobiographical form directs our attention to the personal subjective history, to the ideas and actions as effluents of a personality and a situation; it consistently reduces their claim to objective validity. Not that the philosophy is irrelevant, but it is convincing only within the context of the experiences narrated. If one wants really to come to terms with Augustine's or Croce's philosophy, one studies their theological or philosophical works. The autobiographies themselves direct attention to the uniqueness of their personalities rather than the general validity of their ideas. The autobiography altogether is not an appropriate means to urge the objective truth of a doctrine—though it may reveal more profound and general truths of life which the doctrine only partially formulates.

VIII

The Story of a Calling

THERE is no sharp distinction between the story of an outlook and that of a calling. An outlook is often embodied in a calling or profession, and a calling may be significant only in so far as it embodies an outlook. But there is often a difference, usually very marked in the autobiographical account, in so far as an outlook may be of a most general, comprehensive character, a religious or philosophical attitude, which may not be associated with any particular practical activity; while the calling may be much more specialised and involve a much more precisely defined mode of activity. It is to this latter type that this and the following chapter are devoted.

All good autobiographies are in some sense the story of a calling, that is, they tell of the realisation of an urgent personal potentiality. But in some cases the inner calling merges into a social function, a profession, and a public personality grows out of the private. The autobiography may then be written not primarily for private reasons, but for public, perhaps to satisfy public curiosity about a well-known figure, but, more seriously to illuminate the nature of the public achievement and perhaps to reinforce it. One can of course discover many incidental motives, as in all autobiography. But if one is searching for the secret of the structure of autobiography, the category of the calling or profession is usually decisive. It is this that determines what range and variety of experience are considered to be relevant, and in what form, what words, it is to be expressed. I believe that one can establish a sort of scale of relevance, from those like scientists whose creative being most fully subjects itself to an impersonal, objective task, to those like poets for whom openness to experience is vital.

I must emphasise that I am speaking about autobiographies, not about persons. Though many autobiographies are entitled, "My Life", autobiography does not reproduce a life. If I say that certain experiences are not relevant to the autobiography of a scientist, I do not mean that the scientist did not have them, or was incapable of them. All that is implied is that these experiences may play little or no part in the development of the man's specific achievement. This may be held to be too severe a criterion. The common run of autobiographies in the last hundred years seems to follow the opposite principle, and to delight to take us behind the scenes of the public personality and tell us about his private affairs and thoughts, his home and his hobbies, and so forth; and this can appear to the reader to be a particular charm, and in any case to give us information of an interesting and amusing kind. But I am concerned with good autobiography as such, not merely entertaining and instructive confidential communications. And those autobiographers who have taken their task seriously have recognised that for their purpose they have to be reticent about whole aspects of their life in the interest of their main task. We do not assume that what they tell us is all that could be told, but that it is all that is significant and relevant. Often we can detect them halting and swerving aside—as when Sir Arthur Keith suddenly checks himself as he is beginning to speak of some mistake he made in personal life— "This is not to be a record of my regrets, but a plain account of my thoughts and actions during a critical period of my life". We have seen how severe in their conception of their task are Croce and Collingwood.

It is clear that no schematic prescription can be made of the scope of autobiography, since personalities and achievements and their relationships are of such infinite variety—particularly in societies where there is considerable opportunity for a man to develop a personal gift. An analysis of outstanding modern autobiographies will indicate however some limiting conditions.

THE SCIENTIST

Darwin's autobiography, though the first impulse came from a German editor, was written for his family, and it contains a certain amount of the anecdotal material an old man tells to his grandchildren—like the story of Carlyle's lengthy harangue at a dinner-party on the virtues of silence. Probably, had Darwin been writing for the public, he would have confined himself more rigorously to his achievements as a scientist. But in the main it is a true autobiography; the personal affairs he speaks of belong coherently to his theme, and make it, for all his reticence, a most moving document. One might say indeed that we owe the sketch of his father to the fact that he was writing for his family; it was omitted from the edition in the Thinker's Library. Yet these odd anecdotes about his father give us a valuable clue to the formation of Darwin's moral character, even though he himself thought that he did not gain much from his father intellectually. One can only be glad that Darwin was not misled by his scientific interests to rummage about among his ancestry for traits he might have inherited, as did Galton or Havelock Ellis. Grandparents and parents have a place in autobiographies as persons, not as transmitters of genes.

Darwin speaks only briefly about his childhood, mentioning some of the interests he later lost, like his love for poetry and Shakespeare, and concentrating on those characteristics and habits that seemed to him of significance for the future—his indiscriminate love of collecting, his passion for shooting and the punctiliousness with which he registered his bag, and his laziness, which he attributes to the comfortable circumstances of his home. At Cambridge, in the company of distinguished scientists, he learns that science is more than collecting, and something mysterious happens to him: he is stirred by the ambition to become a great scientist. His training is completed on the voyage of the Beagle, when he moves from collection to classification. From "the collection of facts on a wholesale scale" he moves to generalisations, at first in the fields of biology and geology; and then, under the impact of Malthus, he turns his attention to the general question which was to result in *The*

Origin of Species, always following the "Baconian principle" of observation, and making special memoranda of facts that seemed not to fit in with his pre-conceived ideas.[1]

In the same spirit of scrupulous observation Darwin relates how he lost his religious beliefs, slowly and without distress. It is characteristic that while he is most unrelenting in respect to certain proofs of God that his own scientific work seemed to destroy—e.g. the arguments relating to design in the universe—and rejects on moral grounds the idea of a God who could be the author of the suffering that is characteristic of life, he is content to remain an agnostic in respect to the mystery of the origin of the world. His empiricism and honesty kept him from all dogmatism. His general theory of evolution gave him confidence that the "innermost guide", the conscience, was a vital social instinct and hence universal and infallible. His observations on his religious beliefs, which were omitted from the earlier editions of the Autobiography at the request of his wife, show the same man as the scientist: patient, modest, immensely humble towards facts, yet not dispassionate in respect to goodness and above all truth as far as it was ascertainable.

Darwin writes little about his wife and home-life, partly because the family for whom he was writing would know all about it, mainly I think because as he says "my chief enjoyment and sole employment throughout life has been my scientific work". But he tells us clearly how grateful he was for all the loving care that his wife gave him, and his account of his precarious health and nervous illness shows how he needed the protection the home gave him. The shelter he enjoyed in childhood was thus prolonged throughout his life, and friends like Huxley united with his family in helping him to evade disturbances and controversies which would have hindered the progress of his scientific work. It seems as if his physical nature and the affection and respect that always surrounded him were bent on preserving him for his great task

[1] G. Himmelfarb (*Darwin and the Darwinien Revolution,* 1959) is certainly right in challenging the notion that Darwin's theory arose from mere observation of facts, and in asserting that his earliest observations were guided by theory, often erroneous theory. Darwin at times seems to claim that he proceeded purely empirically, but at other times he clearly shows that he understands his method, which is true scientific method, as the progressive alteration of hypothesis under the impact of observed facts.

as a scientist. He could therefore, without effort, place these personal relationships in their proper position as subsidiary to the task.

If it would have been a mistake for him to have dwelt on them in his autobiography, it was equally important that he should have recognised their existence, and recognised too what effect this concentration on one sort of achievement had on his emotive, imaginative, and even moral powers. With his characteristic scrupulousness he sums up in the most moving passages of the *Autobiography* what influence on his character his exclusive devotion to science had had. He tells regretfully how in his old age he had lost all his taste for poetry, and enjoyed only trivial literature. He writes of "an atrophy of that part of the brain . . . on which the higher tastes depend", and then goes on to a cautious but revealing generalisation: "The loss of these tastes is a loss of happiness, and may be injurious to the intellect, and more probably to the moral character, by enfeebling the emotional part of our nature."

Darwin thought of his story as specific to him, yet it has a general and representative character, not only in the presentation of a scientist's progress through exact observation to wider and wider generalisations. He in general leaves on one side psychological, moral, and social problems, for the interest and value of his life lies primarily, in his own mind, in his relation to science; where he speaks of them, as for instance of conscience, he may reveal an unworldly naïvety. The touching letter from his wife about his moral and religious attitude, published as Note 4 in Nora Barlow's edition, is remarkably to the point. She writes: "May not the habit in scientific pursuits of believing nothing till it is proved, influence your mind too much in other things which cannot be proved in the same way? . . . I do not quite agree with you in what you once said that luckily there were no doubts as to how one ought to act." What is significant about such an observation in the context of this study is that it is typical of this sort of autobiography that this sort of problem hardly enters in, and does not need to enter in, however real a criticism it might be with respect to Darwin's character. Darwin's autobiography can stand as a sort of archetype of the scientist's autobiography, for what it includes as well as for what is excluded. In its artless, unpretentious phrases it seems to restrict itself to what is ascertainably and irrefutably true, and it widens out imperceptibly and involuntarily into a monument to the ethos of truthfulness.

Freud's *An Autobiographical Study* is even more severely restricted to his scientific work. It was written in the first place for a medical periodical that aimed, through autobiographical statements by leading scientists, to establish the actual state of medical science, and for this reason Freud had naturally to be concerned primarily with his scientific work. But its later issue, with some additions, as a separate publication indicates that Freud was content with it as an autobiographical statement.

In it he asserts that his earlier work, *On the History of the Psycho-Analytical Movement*, "contains the essence of all that I can say on the present occasion". Few factors in his life outside science are mentioned, though he tells us enough of the humiliations and difficulties of his Jewish childhood to indicate how the foundations of his "independence of judgement" were laid, and we see too it was a feeling of social responsibility that directed his enthusiasm for scientific discovery towards medicine. The main part of the autobiography however recounts with brilliant lucidity and terseness the steps by which he recognised and overcame problems in the investigation of neuroses. The vigour and fluency of his German style, the clear intellectual structure which absorbs with such ease images and colloquial idiom, assures us as much as anything else of his intellectual mastery.

He goes on to tell how his analysis of neuroses led to novel interpretations of literary figures, Oedipus and Hamlet, and hence to a theory of artistic creations as "the imaginary gratifications of unconscious wishes, just as dreams are". He proceeds to the consequent insight he gained into primitive society and religion. The whole course of his life is represented as a consistent and developing response to objective problems. Only at the end does he suggest the operation of subjective factors. He recognises that his late interest in art and religion is linked with his character and pre-occupations in childhood, so that "after making a lifelong detour through the natural sciences, medicine, and psycho-therapy, [my interest] returned to the cultural problems which had fascinated me long before, when I was a youth scarcely old enough for thinking." But he does not investigate these connections further, jokingly labelling his latest interests as "a phase of regressive development".

It is disconcerting that Freud, of all people, scarcely refers to unconscious impulses and inhibitions, to "Freudian" factors in his life. We have only to read Ernest Jones's great biography to become aware of psychological complexities in Freud on which Freud himself remained silent. Of the man in his personal relationships with his father's and his own family, with his friends and colleagues, we have scarcely a glimmering. No doubt he was in some respects blind, even gullible, for all his self-analysis and rationalism—to judge from his son Martin Freud's *Reflected Glory*, he must have been incapable of seeing what he was as a paterfamilias, and followed a conventional upper-middle-class pattern without thinking it anything but natural. But this blindness, these omissions, do not lessen the value of his autobiography. He roundly asserted his conception of it:

> This autobiographical Study shows how psycho-analysis came to be the whole content of my life and rightly assumes that no personal experiences of mine are of any interest in comparison to my relations with that science.

There is a fault in this definition. No fault can be found in his decision to write his story as the story of his scientific achievement, and to omit all irrelevant personal matter, whether of a psychological or social nature. But Freud does not sufficiently take into account the fact that "personal experiences" may not simply be opposed to scientific achievement, but may also be a factor in regard to both the choice of the field of study and the actual results obtained. It is the dream of scientists to eliminate these factors, but is it ever possible? Certainly in Freud's case his rigour is at certain points misleading, and perhaps a little propagandist, and his jocularity concerning his "regressive development" gives a hint one should not overlook. The failing of this autobiography, so exemplary in its disciplined structure, is that it insufficiently accounts for Freud's ardent interest in art and religion, and for the specific interpretation of both that he made. Other factors enter in here, from the social, religious, philosophical spheres, that demand a fuller account of his personal life than he has given us in the autobiography.

Darwin and Freud were scientists whose work had an exceptionally wide range and impact, so that the severity with which they omitted from their autobiographies whole aspects of their experience is particularly revealing. It does not mean that they did not have fuller lives than they recount, but that they felt that even profound personal experiences were irrelevant to their autobiographical task, and if mentioned at all should only be there as it were in parenthesis. Few scientists have been so reserved in their autobiographies, and few reach their standard of excellence. J. J. Thomson's tells us quite a lot about his life at Cambridge, but the only significant part is his story of the Cavendish laboratory and his work in physics. Though he had important social duties as Master of Trinity and a member of important Government committees, his remarks on other matters often border on the trivial—though one must remember that the autobiography has signs of being the work of a very old man. Arthur Keith wrote his autobiography when, though old, he was still full of vigour, and his account is much fuller than the others I have mentioned. It is indeed a well written and in many ways interesting story of a distinctive and distinguished character. But it sadly fails to link up the different aspects of his experience. This lack of connection suggests frequently a lack of self-understanding in Keith, and there is something endearing in this naïvety itself, though it is involuntary. And perhaps it is not untypical of a man with a rigorous but narrow training in natural science that, when Keith speaks of wider issues like the First World War or the concept of race, his ideas do not merely seem dissociated from other trends in his character, but also frighteningly dogmatic and conventional. If I am primarily concerned here to emphasise how difficult it is for the scientist to incorporate into his autobiography more than a narrow range of experience, unless he wishes it to be simply an interesting social document, it is perhaps permissible to add that his peculiar and intensive specialist pre-occupation also tends to departmentalise his experience itself and to hinder the cross-fertilisation of experience that makes for the full personality. At the same time, the autobiographies of scientists can show in an almost unique manner certain human resources, in particular the purposeful engagement of energies in a developing task, where the task is

I

not given from outside but has to be discerned and defined by the individual concerned.

THE STATESMAN

Few autobiographies of statesmen and politicians can claim distinction on literary grounds, though quite a few are well written. Many of course are written with the plain intention of providing information about public affairs, and the autobiographical element is only incidental. But where the avowed and central objective is the autobiography proper, it seems that the very massiveness of political and social events makes it almost impossible to review them from an individual standpoint. The statesman enters into a complex organism which presents its problems to him piecemeal, irrespective of his will, and usually, at the best, his personal accommodation to realities is rewarded by a very modest modification of them in a desired direction; and even then, who can say the outcome was really his doing? Usually expedience and opportunism must rule the day, and the direction of events, any particular outcome, may have little relation with the personality of the man engaged, with his private character; so that while his personality as a politician may be consistent, it may not have much to do with his private being. Autobiographies of statesmen often serve the salutary purpose of reminding us of the difference between the public and private personality. The temptation to sentimentalise private life is great, but even if sentimentality is avoided, the result lacks the force and unity of good autobiography.

Lord Tweedsmuir's (John Buchan's) autobiography is fairly typical. The rather austere childhood in Scotland in no way prepares us for the public role he played. There is consistency in the private life of the man, in the environment he created and the sort of friends he had, but what he did publicly was the product of chance: the job was given, he did what public policy and circumstances made possible. In Tweedsmuir's case, his success as a writer of light literature corresponds to the dissociation of his private life from his public; literature becomes an intelligent pastime, just as private life becomes a charming refuge.

It is therefore natural and proper that the autobiographies of statesmen are important essentially as memoirs, as historical material—the historian knows how often their truth is comprised by an inordinate sense of self-importance, or by the desire for self-justification.

They can become significant as autobiographies when the personality of the man is such as to have imposed itself distinctively on events, when the outer world has been moulded by his quality, his passion. This is evidently most likely when the man is at odds with his times, something of a rebel. But it often happens that such a man is blinded by the very violence of his passion, or moved by an overpowering propagandist intention, when he writes his autobiography. The extreme case is Hitler's *Mein Kampf*. Partly Hitler deliberately distorts real events, for the purpose of propaganda; but partly too the truth is obscured in the very turmoil of passionate theorising. Sometimes such rebels can give a fairly clear account of their childhood circumstances, which may establish in their minds certain attitudes and values, but the strength of such views frequently changes into rigidity, and they show themselves incapable of further personal response to reality, their views become dogmatic, their personalities rigid, and their story heavily biassed.

The autobiographies of revolutionary socialists all suffer from these characteristics, especially as they are usually written avowedly as propaganda—I am thinking among others of those of Bebel, the German socialist, of Gallacher or Pollitt. Trotsky's *My Life* is a brilliant example of the type. It was written in the first period of his exile from the Soviet Union, when, in enforced leisure, he could use his personal story both as propaganda for Marxism and as a polemic against Stalin; personal reminiscence would have been despised by him unless it could be enlisted in political purpose. His account of his childhood and youth is exceptionally concrete and clear, as are indeed some scenes from his political career. One sees how the child is led through the thickets of confusing experience to a philosophy, Marxism, which releases powers within him and enables him to follow a meaningful line of action. But, rescued from "blind empiricism" through a social theory, Trotsky becomes more and more contemptuous of empiricism, and in certain respects incapable of empirical observation. In some matters he shows brilliant analytical insight—

E. H. Carr, in his great history of the Soviet revolution, has taken over very largely the essence of Trotsky's analysis of Stalin and Stalinism as the embodiment of "reaction", of ossified bureaucratic mediocrity. But the reality of Stalin himself, as a man, is never seen, nor the actuality of circumstances and other persons; all fade into generalisations, all experiences are reduced to elements of a general political struggle, people degenerate into allies and foes. Once Trotsky has his theory, he needs no longer to study reality; his answers are ready-made. Brilliant as is the personality of Trotsky, in his understanding and manipulation of his world, the book is even more fascinating in its unconscious revelation of the way in which a man, released for activity and given power by an idea, can not only subjugate everything to this idea, but can also lose touch with all that will not fit in with it. As a result the autobiography shows a man losing rather than finding himself, especially after the great days of the Revolution.

At the other end of the scale, politicians who recognise that the world they enter forces them to alter their earlier views, or to make continual compromises, also tumble into difficulties. Philip Snowden gives a fresh and moving account of the austere life in the Yorkshire village where he was born, where the basis of his harsh independence of character and his religious socialistic purpose was laid. Genuinely autobiographical too is his story of his part in the early socialist movement. But when he comes to the later period of his ministerial activity, he seems to get lost. Even as memoirs it is unsatisfactory, for he is over-concerned to justify himself, not merely in relation to the expedience of what he advocated and did, but also in relation to his socialist conscience. Here his early independence becomes acrimonious self-righteousness. Lord Attlee could rightly claim much greater consistency of principle, though from the beginning he was much more aware that politics entails compromise. But he is so modest that he shies away from all exposition of principle and subjective drives, and concentrates on particular issues; and even here, he tends to discuss only the immediate, rarely the larger issues. His autobiography does far less than justice to a tough and pertinacious as well as idealistic character, and makes himself, and all issues, seem flat and dull. So practical is he that he makes it seem that the most startling decisions, such as that to explode the first atom bomb, are a normal part of the day's work; and it must surely be a criticism of his character that he never tries to grasp the totality of a situation, for instance, what the outcome of the war meant to Britain as a Great Power. Attlee's failure is all the more surprising since he was borne along by a clear reforming principle.

Churchill, with his rebellious temperament, his imagination and gift for drama, was better equipped for writing his autobiography. His *My Early Life* is a most attractive book, and most revealing about his personal character, such a mixture of conventional prejudice and independence, so ebullient and yet so shrewd. His irrepressible hunger for adventures, his flouting of authority and clever manipulation of the great, are all of a piece with the shrewd accommodation he made between his rational scepticism and his emotive orthodoxy. What is lacking is a principle; it is the story of a temperament, not a statesman. His great theme was given to him, much later in life, by world-events, above all by the Second World War; and of these he had to write as a historian, not as an autobiographer, so much did their importance transcend the personal.

So it is rare that a statesman can write a true and satisfactory autobiography. He depends on luck as well as on himself, though of course the luck also depends on him to some extent. Gandhi's autobiography is one of the few to be really satisfactory. What is distinctive about his life is that he evolved his own moral idea and purpose, had the courage and sagacity to pursue and organise a practical policy towards its realisation, and yet remained devoted to his idea so that he never was submerged in practical politics. Thus, in his autobiography, his personality remains dominant throughout.

Gandhi's *My Own Story* was compiled by his friend and collaborator, C. F. Andrews, from several autobiographical writings with titles such as *The Story of my Experiments with Truth* and *Satyagraha [Soul-Force] in South Africa*. The titles are significant, for they claim that his political story is that of a personal faith. We see how this religious and moral faith takes its first form in youth, and then how it develops along with his growing social and political experience, so that his political activity always appears as the unfolding and embodiment of principle. In childhood he can find inner freedom only in loving obedience to his parents, so that freedom and law come to mean the same to him; later, as his conception of law deepens, all his major decisions take the form of vows, a voluntary submission to a higher purpose. In England he becomes aware of himself as a member of a community, and from Ruskin in particular he learns to think of himself socially, so that freedom and truth acquire a social meaning, and he begins to see that social and political action are necessary to realise them. Faced, as an Indian in South Africa, with the indisputable inhumanity of the colour-bar, his service to humanity becomes the struggle for the human rights of his people; but these rights are never an end in themselves, and justified in his eyes only as a general human necessity, just as the method he adopts, moral (passive) resistance, "Akhimsa", is not a mere technique of political struggle, but the embodiment of, and the means to awaken, moral strength, soul-force, "Satyagraha". As he writes of himself:—"Becoming more and more absorbed in the service of the Indian community, the reason behind it was my desire for self-realisation".

The authority Gandhi won over his followers was unique. On the one hand he showed himself extraordinarily shrewd in his political dealings, and his sagacity alone earned him the respect of enemies and friends. But in the attitude of his disciples, non-Indian, as well as Indian, there was also a religious element, which sprang from the recognition of the spiritual driving force in his character. Throughout the struggles in South Africa and India this spirituality of objective is dominant, and is most impressively identical with his aim of national liberation. The two elements are strikingly fused in his vows of continence and chastity, which he took in order to make his service to others most absolute, and at the same time, most readily comprehensible to them.

Particularly interesting are Gandhi's repeated decisions to fast. The hunger-strike is a tried weapon of political prisoners, but it took a new form with Gandhi. It was the failings of his own disciples to live up to the rules of the first Settlement he founded that led him to fast in the first place, and he imposed it on himself as a penance for faults for which he considered himself, as their "guardian" and "teacher", chiefly responsible. Later he used the fast spectacularly in India. It was a shrewd weapon, effective both in rallying friends and in reducing the opposition, and it justified itself as political tactics. But the autobiographical account fully persuades us that it was not merely a tactical manoeuvre, that it came from that profound religious-moral urge from which all his activity arose, and was a penance for the sins of all, of opponents as well as allies.

As a psychological document Gandhi's autobiography is not revealing. He does not investigate the obscure sources of his beliefs and convictions, and, though the range of events is wide, the type of experience described is limited. Experiences that did not contribute to the evolution and clarification of his moral purpose are ignored. The artlessness of the style betrays a complete lack of concern for introspection, for the private values of friendship or sense-experience. But this is no fault, for in this his autobiography corresponds exactly with his life, and both exhibit that single-mindedness which he states was the purpose of his vows. Thus it is that his political activity bears in every respect the stamp of his personality, and the autobiography has a unity that is rare. It is fully persuasive when he defines his autobiographical purpose thus:

> To describe Truth, as it has appeared to me, and in the exact manner in which I have arrived at it, has been my ceaseless effort. The exercise has given me ineffable mental peace because it has been my fond hope that it might bring faith in Truth and Akhimsa to waverers.

Gandhi's autobiography, exceptional as it is (and as his life was) in its homogeneity and clear purposefulness, illustrates the problems facing the statesman who writes his autobiography. More factors, a more varied range of factors of experience are operative here (not just there in the life, but operative) than in the case of the specialist intellectual worker, though the diversity of his activities means that it is difficult for him to order them in relation to his main drive. The quality of the latter, too, involves more personal, moral elements, and we need to be able to follow the evolution of its moral structure. At the same time, a great stretch of human experience, much of his personal experience and relationships, his private feelings, are irrelevant and have to be left out of the autobiography if it is not to become merely interesting reminiscence or an engaging personal story.

THE SOCIAL WORKER

In some respects the autobiography of the social worker follows a similar pattern, since it must show how a personal moral conviction takes shape as a social attitude and in social work. But here the achievement remains more distinctively personal, and even when the social worker is involved in politics, he is so in a more selective way than the politician. Thus the original, personal impulse may remain more intact, more present to the mind, and more capable of growth. Many such people become rigid, of course, and lose themselves in their task, so that their autobiographies are in the main the story of the work achieved. But the possibility is there that their story is essentially that of their inner life. So it is that James Stephen, the prominent member of the Clapham Sect, whose autobiography goes only as far as early manhood, is engrossed in the problematic of his emotive and moral life.

In this field two of the outstanding autobiographies are by women.

When one reads Harriet Martineau's stories or moral and philosophical writings, one may easily be dismayed by her rigidity, her moral self-confidence or even self-righteousness. Her attitudes often are presented as a "duty" that ought to be recognised by everyone. One may be on her side and admire her campaign against slavery, her energetic championship of the social rights of women, her opposition to the legal victimisation of prostitutes; one must recognise that English political and social life owes an enormous debt to men and women with such fearless energy and conviction. But one quails somewhat before a character that is so ruthlessly confident that her opinions are based on unquestionable principle. If one disagrees with her, say in her religious attitude, or her dogmatic economic liberalism (which she actually modified in later life), or the rather arrogant moralism of her judgements on foreign affairs, one may think she had a real gift for deluding herself. If her autobiography had been primarily an account and justification of her ideas and policies, it would have shared their faults.

In fact, it is something very different. In it she is far less concerned with the actual causes she backed than with the manner in which she came to take them up, and we are far less involved in them than in the quality of her personality itself. The autobiography is not non-partisan; she is still fighting for her causes. But the emphasis is laid on private factors. She wrote it in 1854 and 1855, at the age of 52–3, when her doctors had told her she was likely to die at any moment (she in fact remained alive and intellectually active for another 20 years); and it was to some extent this consciousness of impending death that turned her attention to her inner history. The book is a moving and penetrating story of a spiritual development, written in a style that has the charm of vigour, clarity, and mental ease.

Her childhood is a document of rather unexpected penetration.[1] Brought up in a severely puritanical home, intellectually precocious but clumsy and without girlish charm, she suffered from extreme diffidence and constant irrational terrors. Dreams of divine favour or devoted martyrdom compensate her feeling of inferiority and insignificance, and a longing for punishment assuages her sense of sin—"I always feared sin and remorse extremely, and punishment not at all; but on the contrary desired punishment or anything else that would give me the one good that I pined for in vain—ease of conscience." With remarkable insight she suggests that the deafness which struck her in early girlhood was partly due to this nervous tension and exaltation. To her own sufferings in constant illness, which she could overcome only by severity towards herself, she ascribes the hardness of her attitude in early life towards other people. It comes as no surprise that after her great and single-handed success in social and political affairs, combined with the nervous strain of supporting a carping mother in her London home, she suffered a complete nervous collapse in 1839, and describes it as "a blessed change" from her life in London. Given up by the doctors, after five years on a sick-bed she was cured by mesmerism, and incurred much ridicule and obloquy because she boldly championed the cure.

Harriet's account of her literary, social, and political writings

---

[1] Vera Wheatley (*The Life and Work of Harriet Martineau*, 1957) quotes opinions of recent critics that are remarkable in their obtuseness—the autobiography is called by one "that alien unrevealing work". Harriet's Victorian contemporaries were on the other hand shocked that she revealed so much.

and doings is cradled in this inner history, and without decrying their objective value she endeavours above all to uncover their personal origins and personal meaning for her herself. At the age of seven, reading *Paradise Lost*, she discovers the solace of intellectual occupations, "the first experience of moral relief through intellectual resource". The "necessarian" philosophy she reached in early womanhood, her espousal of the notion of "the invariable action of fixed laws" in all life processes, which she calls "the mainspring of my activity", is traced back to her psychological need to overcome the wild imaginings due to excessive nervous tension. So too she tells us how her notorious confession of agnosticism, that shocked her contemporaries so severely, arose from a necessary effort to overcome the morbid fantasies and fears that had assailed her during illness. Only after her cure, and in the light of this new rationalistic philosophy, does she begin to "relish life", and in the pleasant circumstances of her Ambleside home her character seems to blossom, she becomes gentler, kinder, more generous, without in any way reducing her intellectual labours. So she feels she has shaped herself into a unity. Her philosophy, her social and political work, her relations with others, are "a natural growth of the experience and study . . . the progression of a life". Certainly she could do only what appeared to her to be a duty—even writing her autobiography seemed to her to be a duty. But she reminds us of those ideal figures of Goethe, Iphigenie or Tasso's Princess, in that truth to the inmost self and duty, natural impulse and social obligation, are fused. When she asked herself why she became a writer, she might very well have answered, "Because that was how I could do good", for all her writings have a moral bearing. But in fact she gives the answer that it was not a matter of choice, but "a natural function": "I have not done it for amusement, or for money, or for fame, or for any reason but because I could not help it."

There are two portraits of Harriet Martineau in the National Portrait Gallery. One of 1849, by Richmond, represents a kindly, somewhat grandmotherly person, soft and gentle, and not very different from several other eminent women as Richmond painted them. This was the most popular of her portraits, and the one she herself liked best. The other, by a much less accomplished artist,

Richard Evans, done in 1834, was much disliked by Harriet and her friends. It shows a plain and gawky young woman, determined and even redoubtable in her expression and stance, with challenge and unhappiness in her face. This is the woman whose story was to be told, and the chief drawback of the autobiography is that this woman, capable of strong affections and of grief, was silent about the brother whom she loved most dearly and who hurt her most. But the autobiography is an outstanding work since, in spite of this omission, it is the story of the woman herself. The campaigns she undertook are not the centre, but illuminate the woman engaged; and they illuminate it consistently, since they never arose fortuitously, however accidental the immediate cause might be (the suggestion of a Minister of the Crown, the offer of a voyage to the East etc.). Her own character determines her choice of activity and what she makes of her opportunity, so that the work she did always reveals her personality.

Beatrice Webb began her autobiography, *My Apprenticeship*, with the narrower purpose of showing how she became a social scientist. In the Introduction she even writes: "I have neither the desire nor the intention of writing an autobiography"—and by this one understands that she was not interested in writing memoirs nor in revealing the private concerns of her life (on some of which, as I have pointed out in Chapter 5, she remains silent). But then she goes on to say that she found she had, in the interests of her purpose, to speak about her personal life, for it was her experiences as a child, woman, wife, and citizen that turned her into a sociologist. These experiences, she comments with insight, would not be relevant to the making of a physicist, chemist, or biologist. That is, she felt that her profession grew out of complex personal and social experience, which she recounts not as reminiscences (however interesting they might be as social history) but as formative factors in her development. They are woven with great skill into her story.

Beatrice Webb distinguishes two main elements in this development: the subjective impulse to serve others, and a search through scientific study for law, whereby the subjective impulse would be rightly guided. In Martha, her nurse, she has her first "revelation of the meaning of the religious spirit", and in the family friend, Herbert Spencer, she meets the teacher who showed that social institutions could be "observed, classified, and explained". Her task was to fuse the two elements.

The first fifteen years of her life were spent, she tells us, "not in learning a craft, but in seeking a creed". What she tells about the comfortable circumstances of her home, numerous and distinguished friends, society and travel, is severely limited by her theme of the search. There is even considerable reticence—the causes of which one can guess—in her account of her inner struggles, which are indicated in the main by excerpts from her early diaries. Unable on rational grounds to accept Christianity, but finding the "religion of science" quite insufficient, she comes to adopt, not a creed, but "an intuitive use of prayer". In the stresses of girlhood and young womanhood—she speaks of suicidal tendencies, a love of death—"only the habit of prayer enabled me to survive". She found release from her stresses and the relief of activity in the Comtist religion of humanity and the devoted social service initiated by such people as Arnold Toynbee and Octavia Hill. The spiritual insecurity by which she, like Harriet Martineau, was tortured, and its relationship to their social work and rationalistic philosophy, are valuable evidence of the psychic stresses underlying Victorian solidity.

Characteristic of Beatrice Webb was however the inner need to find an objective justification for her moral and religious impulse. She soon came to realise, as Harriet Martineau had done before her, that much charity is misguided. Charity is not to be justified in relation to the conscience of the charitable (she refers in particular to a newly awakened sense of collective sin in the English propertied class to which she belonged); it must be justified objectively, in relation to its effect on the receivers of charity. Hence she sought to find out facts about the working classes, and it is characteristic that the immediate purpose of the first practical social work she undertook was not to alleviate distress but to investigate social conditions. The charge was raised against her that she was hard, and she had to insist that a general "impulse of pity for the needless misery of man" is as real and effective as the impulse towards personal charity; in fact she was to oppose much personal charity as self-indulgence. *My Apprenticeship* then traces the steps by which she went

beyond the position of the scientist and philanthropist to that of
the active worker for Co-operation, Trade-Unionism, and finally
Socialism.

What gives depth to Beatrice Webb's autobiography is the
fact that the story of her thought, and of the activity that her
thought guided, is also the story of a person desperately needing
to cope with profound spiritual needs. Public work was not the
all-satisfying answer to her spiritual troubles. She herself comments on "the black thread of personal unhappiness" that runs
through her early diaries; what she quotes from them makes it
clear enough. Out of this unhappiness, her torments, her spinster-
hood, there arises, she tells us, "a consciousness of a special
mission". This mission, as social scientist, is a sort of compensation for her despair. A Diary entry that she quotes shows that
she realised this at an early age: "I have originality of aim and
method . . . a sort of persistency which comes from despair
of my own unhappiness". As she began to see a positive purpose
to her science, and drew nearer to socialism, and when she became associated with the Fabians and Sidney Webb himself, the
despair began to recede; but the need for prayer as "a source of
strength" remained. It is a pity that she felt unable to cope with
her belief in "the essential goodness of human nature" (see
above, p. 65), for it has an important place in the drama of her
inward search.

The dramatic tension of these years of young womanhood is
only reticently described by the autobiographer, and appears
mainly through the incorporated Diary entries. As she was
writing it, Beatrice Webb noted that her husband did not like
this aspect of it—"all that part which deals with 'my creed' as
distinguished from 'my craft' seems to him the sentimental scrib-
blings of a woman".[1] The historian of sociological techniques
might agree with Sidney Webb. But Beatrice was quite right in
seeing this theme as a central one in her autobiography, and one
could wish that she could have felt herself freer to develop it. For
the autobiography is the story of the engagement of a personality
in a task, not the story of the task alone (and one might add that
historians go astray when they divorce the story of events from
the personalities who carried them out, or when like Sidney

[1] *Beatrice Webb's Diaries* 1924–1932, ed. M. Cole, 1956, 58.

Webb, they substitute the history of institutions for history itself). This autobiography shows, despite resistances in the authoress herself and in her immediate environment, what factors were operative in her case, and what are necessarily operative in the case of the social worker, whose work however objectively established and scientific in character, must include moral and emotional impulses and results. It seems that Beatrice Webb became more convinced of this as she wrote *My Apprenticeship*, for after completing it she wrote in her Diary: "What troubles me is that before I die I should like to work out more completely than I have done in *My Apprenticeship* my conception of the place of religion in the life of man."[1] I am not at all sure that if Beatrice Webb had written this book it would have been particularly enlightening. But what she says about her own religious impulse within the framework of her own life is not only sincere and moving, but provides a necessary focus for her whole account.

In selecting these few types and examples of the autobiography as a calling, I am not concerned with drawing up a comprehensive list or establishing dogmatic categories. One could enumerate other headings, and many autobiographies lie in between. All that I wish to assert is that autobiography must vary in approach and scope according to the specific achievement of the man, if it is to reproduce the essential drive of a character, and that limitation is a condition of excellence. These categories are meant to be representative, not exhaustive. One further category however demands special attention—the autobiography of the artist or poet—and its literary claims are such that a chapter must be devoted to it.

[1] ibid. 76.

IX

The Autobiography of the Poet

THE autobiographies of poets—by "poets" I mean all imaginative writers—obviously seem likely to have a certain literary distinction, since they are written by men practised in verbal self-expression. On closer scrutiny, the advantage is not so great as might be thought. Practice in writing is certainly an advantage to the autobiographer, but there are few professions which do not give it, and nothing could surpass the style of Gibbon, Newman, Croce, Freud, in their autobiographies; and in many other cases, what had to be said could not have been said in a more appropriate way. Imagination, love of words, and literary dexterity on the other hand may be a pitfall for the autobiographer, and lead to over-writing or irrelevance. What one can expect from the imaginative writer is an unusual skill in the evocation of scenes and characters, and more delicate self-observation, especially in respect to obscure inner urges, imaginings, to modes of perception and apprehension; one can expect too an artistic arrangement of the whole. Only a writer intimately concerned with imaginative literature could have written so skillful and penetrating an autobiography as Gosse's *Father and Son*.

In themselves these qualities do not make good autobiography. What makes them important in the poet's autobiography is that what they reveal is decisive for the nature of the poet. Events and achievements of a public kind are not so decisive for him as the more intimate impressions and responses, and events become important for him not in themselves, but for what he puts into them. His life-story is the story of how his imagination is kindled by occurrences or personalities that may intrinsically be quite insignificant. Edwin Muir dwells so lovingly on his childhood because he is conscious that the "images of childhood" are permanent, and that later life is essentially the unfolding of this "first intuition of the world". His moving evocation of his childhood is not justified through being a piece of fine writing; it is the embodiment of his spirit. Poets are not unique in being capable of delicate and imaginative experience of this type—if they were, their autobiographies would be interesting only as exotic specimens. But they are the people whose work and life centre in and evolve out of this type of attentiveness, they are pledged to it.

I have indicated in Chapter 3 the historic importance of the autobiographies of Wordsworth and Goethe, as the first to probe into the specific nature of their poetic activity and its peculiar function in their lives. They establish a pattern that has maintained itself since. Yet these writers had a larger intention than the delineation of a gift. Even with Wordsworth's narrower scope, his purpose is the evolution and self-recognition of a soul in its self-identification with mankind and the universe; in this his poetic gift is embraced and from it his poetry gains its substance and justification. Goethe's purpose is all embracing; he tells of his imagination and feeling, of how and why experiences turned into poetry, but also gives a history of his times, a history of literature and thought, the development of his own life and thought, and is ultimately concerned with a general problem arising from his total experience, the relation between freedom and necessity, between the infinitude of what is given him and the particularity of what he makes of it, between conscious intention and the "daemon" within him. In both men, the response to life is a total one, and the poetic activity is seen as a peculiar response within this larger one.

A considerable number of later autobiographies are similar in general intention, for instance Chateaubriand's, Gorki's, or Sean O'Casey's. These were men intimately concerned with social and political life, and they do not view their lives, as poets, as essentially different in character from those of their fellows; rather, they feel that they experience what other people go through, but more intensely, more profoundly, with less prejudice and inhibition. But, in this century, in many autobiographies of imaginative writers the focus has altered. They have tended to centre their attention more on what is distinctive about them as poets, not on what they have in common with others. They may live in the thick of events, yet like Stephen Spender be in the end primarily concerned with the problem of how being a writer affected their specific attitude and behaviour. Their chief pre-occupation is their peculiar mode of experience, of response to the world, as poets.

So there has arisen the autobiography of the poet as a man engaged in a special way with the world. I do not say, as a man with a special profession, for poetry is never a profession like others, however well a man may do by it. Trollope wrote (after an excellent account of his childhood) the story of himself as a professional writer, a "literary man", with the ups and downs of his career, his business accounts, and advice to aspirants. It is interesting enough, but one is uncomfortably aware that he is deliberately trying to bluff us, to hide his real secrets from us. Kipling failed in a still more difficult task, for his real distinction, outside his more fanciful work, lay in his vivid portrayal of men sustained in work by moral obligation. But he makes his autobiography largely the story of his career and opinions, and it is often downright and obstreperously obtuse. What we most dearly want to know about is not the writer's success, not even the inside story of his writings, but the evolution of his mode of vision in terms of his successive engagement with the world. It is no accident that autobiographies with this theme began to appear in numbers from the beginning of this century, for it was then that the "problematic" of the artist, defined in its most pointed form by Nietzsche, became a frequent matter of discussion and manifested itself in the most varied types of artistic expression.

One might imagine that visual artists and musicians might have made a particular contribution to this theme in their autobiographies; they often represent "the artist" in imaginative literature. In fact, their autobiographies are singularly unenlightening. Many are interesting as reminiscence, as a record of artistic circles, though they are often more engaging anecdotally than in any other way. Epstein's, less anecdotal and more seriously

K

autobiographical than most (for instance, than Augustus John's), is however baffling in respect to his peculiar gift. It seems that artists working in these symbolic media cannot find the words for experiences transmuted into these media; or perhaps the experience is not reducible to words. Epstein modestly attributes his failure to "lack of habit in explaining":

> I lack the habit of giving verbal expression to my efforts or aims in sculpture. There is a language of form which is sufficient to itself as there is a language of music, and any inarticulateness is not due to any vagueness in my own mind, but only to lack of experience in explaining, and as an outgrowth of that, my tendency of mind not to care to explain what I find so clearly expressed in the work itself.

Epstein on occasion does trace, as far as he can, the genesis of particular works, but it is noticeable that the account itself is given in symbolical terms. For instance, the impulse to his sculpture Consummatum Est comes from the alabaster block itself and the Crucifixus section of Bach's B Minor Mass. It is difficult to see how such experiences could be rendered verbally; and if the difficulty is so great with the origin of particular works of art, it must be still greater with the artist's whole manner of apprehension of the world. In both respects the imaginative writer has an easier task, since he works in the medium of words. The autobiographies of Yeats and Henry James are brilliant in their perception of their task and its execution.

In Yeats's autobiographical writings, particularly *Reveries over Childhood and Youth* (1915) and *The Trembling of the Veil* (1922), there are the materials of the conventional autobiography. His childhood in Sligo and his upbringing in artistic circles foster his natural imaginative tendencies. He recalls persons and incidents, evokes scenes. His imaginative, mystical bent leads him towards religious occultism on the one hand, on the other to symbolism in art. His discovery of Ireland gives his poetry a needed content, just as it gave him a purpose as a man. Political, imaginative, and personal purposes are fused in his creation of an image of Ireland, that is to be, he believes, a means for the recreation of an Irish culture and nation; at the same time it creates that personal unity of Being that he thought must be found "emotionally, instinctively" within the framework of a "unity of culture". His consciousness of the contradiction between his aims and actual reality leads him to his general theory of the Mask, which sustained his poetry as well as his life. We can follow Yeats through the turmoil of Irish literary and political life to the point where he is assailed by doubts about the value of his cultural and political work, this "heterogeneous labour", and where he comforts himself with the reluctant assertion that a man cannot be a mere poet—"there must be a man behind the lines written". In this respect the autobiography is a sincere and moving document, which must retain historical and biographical value. Yet there is something else here that particularly engages our attention.

It is indicated in the final sentences of the *Reveries*:

> For some months now I have lived with my own youth and childhood, not always writing indeed but thinking of it almost every day, and I am sorrowful and disturbed. It is not that I have accomplished very few of my plans, for I am not ambitious; but when I think of all the books I have read, and of the wise words I have heard spoken, and of the anxiety I have given to parents and grandparents, and of the hopes that I have had, all life weighed in the scales of my own life seems to me a preparation for something that never happens.

The statement is not easy to understand. Yeats does not say that what he has done is not adequate to all the hopes and effort put into it, but that the result "never happens". Now, much did happen, and he was fully aware of its value—his poetry, his work for the Irish National Theatre, the consolidation of an Irish national consciousness. What he must mean is that the efforts and the results are not commensurate, what happened cannot be measured against what was prepared and intended. We should understand him rightly, I think, if we generalise and conclude that the poet, different from other types of men, does not find his fulfilment in leading a movement, discovering a truth, founding a National Theatre and so forth, but in an incommensurate activity, in recording his imaginative experience, in his poetic work.

We can compare another statement. Yeats recalls a painting of his brother's:

> When I look at my brother's picture, *Memory Harbour*, . . . I recognise in the blue-coated man with the mass of white shirt the pilot I went fishing with, and I am full of disquiet and of excitement, and I am melancholy because I have not made more and better verses.

Here Yeats explicitly asserts a relationship between two quite disparate things. There is no logical or moral obligation involved; it is an obligation to reality which arises simply and solely from his poetic calling. If in this case Yeats says he is "melancholy" because he has not written better verses, we can be sure that it was not the quality of the verse that caused him disquiet. Rather, it was that intangible, disturbing relationship between poetry and life, whose results he summed up later as "something that never happens".

Yeats tells us that he was often haunted by a memory of childhood and could not rest till he could speak of it, and it was this feeling of oppression that brought him to write his autobiography. It has to be sharply distinguished from the burden of guilt that impelled Rousseau to confess, and arises from a much more obscure and complex feeling of indebtedness to the past, an indebtedness of the imagination above all. Franklin tells of his ancestry, for instance, just to give the facts; Gibbon in order to give himself prestige; Darwin to acknowledge a moral influence; Galton to discover his genetical inheritance. But none of these motives has any particular significance with Yeats. He recalls older members of his family because of the images he made out of them, because of their permanence in him as images. He writes typically of his grandfather, William Pollexfen:

> Even today when I read *King Lear* his image is always before me, and I often wonder if the delight in passionate men in my plays and in my poetry is more than his memory.

Yeats's account of his childhood and youth is disconnected not simply because all early memories are spasmodic. It is so because he was not primarily concerned to trace a consistent personal development, but because his early years lived on in him as a set of bright images. He occasionally gives outstanding examples of the working of his imagination. When the boy read in the newspaper of an athlete who was called "the bright particular star of American athletics", he tells us that the phrase "threw enchantment over him, and that he followed with fascination the subsequent career of the athlete: "I was nursing my own dream". His story is that of his dream, so strangely related to the reality of experience.

So in Yeats's autobiography these two elements are curiously combined and curiously dissociated. It has a dream-like flow, yet is concrete and precise; it combines delicate suggestion with a robust wholesomeness; the young man is "engaged" and yet elusive, attached yet impersonal. One can understand why Spender should speak of Yeats's "detachment",[1] but the detachment does not mean personal isolation, not dislocation (Yeats calls himself "a most gregarious" man), for it goes along with passionate attention to the outside world, a devotion that seeks objectivisation in a series of forms until it fills itself with the ideal image of Ireland and seeks to unite image and reality in cultural and political co-operation. It is detachment in the sense that the relationship between outer activity and experience and his essential being as a creator of images is indefinable; they are linked opposites.

With Yeats there is relatively little direct statement of the poetic mode of experience; its peculiarity appears above all in the manner of the writing. With Henry James, a novelist, we have a full and explicit elaboration of the imaginative mode of being.

The tone of Henry James's autobiographical volumes tempts one to think that the exceptionally favoured circumstances in which he grew up secured a tranquil progress towards the realisation of his literary tastes. His parents were well off and most generous to the children, his father a philosopher who venerated the human spirit, his brother William a most affectionate as well as brilliant and inspiring companion. They had a large circle of attractive relatives and friends. The boy Henry was encouraged to follow his own gifts and interests, never pressed for time or money or "results". In fact, there were stresses enough, tension with the father whom he learnt to appreciate only late in life, with America and its philistinism, and above all the suffering of an essential loneliness, the consciousness of being strangely detached from others and their business, of dwelling in his imagination.

These sufferings scarcely appear on the surface of the autobiography, and they are usually mentioned only when James wishes to assert the positive gain they brought. So he describes the "bewildered anxiety" of his early school-years:

[1] Stephen Spender, *The Creative Element*, 1953, 120.

139

What happened all the while, I conceive, was that I imagined things—and as if quite on system—wholly other than as they were, and so carried on in the midst of the actual ones an existence that somehow floated and saved me even while cutting me off from any degree of direct performance, in fact from any degree of direct participation, at all.

Here, clearly, the "saving" is a retrospective judgement; the "cutting off" must have been the boy's main feeling, a feeling of estrangement that one can divine throughout, once one has comprehended James's standpoint as an autobiographer. Now, an old man, he is free of resentment against the suffering itself. So he writes only of the "felicity", the "amenity" of his life, in the sense that all becomes for him, in retrospect, "consecrated", as the destiny to which he was born, as the stuff of his consciousness and the grounds of his achievement. Absurd therefore to criticise, to resent—

> The beauty of the main truth as to any remembered matter looked at in due detachment, or in other words through the haze of time, is that comprehension has become one with criticism, compassion, as it may really be called, one with musing vision, and the whole company of the anciently restless, with their elations and mistakes, their sincerities and vanities and triumphs, embalmed for us in the mild essence of their collective submission to fate.

James began his book as a memorial to his brother William, as a family book. As reminiscence it is extraordinarily rich, and indeed whole sections are devoted to his father, his brother, his cousin Mary Temple. But he found it rapidly and unavoidably turned into the story of his own consciousness, written through memories that continually "swarm" and "multiply", and it is remarkable how tightly bound this wealth of memories is. He once speaks of a "moral affiliation" that forces him to record his memories, a feeling of indebtedness that recalls Yeats's feeling of obligation towards the pilot in his brother's picture. It is not moral in any normal sense, but a sense of grateful indebtedness to life. Some of the people he describes had already been used as material for his novels, and in speaking of them he expresses this "moral affiliation"—"I scarce know whether most to admire, for support of one's beautiful business of the picture of life, the relation of 'people' to art or the relation of art to people."

So James rapidly perceived that reminiscence had to be enlisted in another task, which as he set about it seemed to him "difficult and unprecedented and perilous".[1] He formulated it as "the personal history of an imagination", a story of inconceivable complexity and indirectness:

> I lose myself in wonder at the loose ways, the strange process of waste, through which nature and fortune may deal on occasion with those whose faculty for application is all and only in their imagination and sensibility.

It is not an analysis of the imagination or the feelings, but the story of the swarming world that filled this imagination. His mode of apprehension is revealed more through the musing involutions of his style than through any direct statement.

It might be suggested that James's purpose took shape in some degree in relation to the *Education* of his friend Henry Adams, the story of the acquisition of an outlook. The nemesis of Adams's conception of his life's purpose was, that it might be proved untrue by events, and in fact, by the time James was writing his autobiography, Adams was already despondently aware that this might be the case. When James sent Adams a copy of *Notes of a Son and Brother* in 1914, Adams wrote to him about the futility of old age; but James, who had never shared Adams's optimism, refused to agree: "I still find my consciousness interesting . . . Being mine yields an interest I don't know I can tell you."[2] The expression is modest, but the challenge is absolute. For Adams much of his past was useless waste; perhaps, if his present political philosophy was proved to be wrong, all was waste. For James, all the past was significant, not because of a definable result, certainly not because his literary work had profited by it, but in itself. The same contrast appears when he describes how his brother William thought their early visits to London, Paris, and Geneva, were idle and useless, while he himself found that he was "much to profit" from this "wondering and dawdling and gaping". It seems a direct challenge to Adams when he asserts that they were "an education like another"—

---

[1] *Letters*, ed. Lubbock, 1920, ii. 213.

[2] *Letters*, ii. 373–4, and F. O. Matthiessen, *The James Family*, 1948, 669. *The Education of Henry Adams* had been privately printed in 1907.

No education avails for the intelligence that doesn't stir in it some subjective passions, and on the other hand almost anything that does so act is largely educative.

James's "subjective passion" is the focus of his narrative. It is not a record of reminiscences but "a tale of assimilations small and fine; out of which refuse, directly interesting to the subject-victim only, the most branching vegetation may be conceived as having sprung".

One can detect three interwoven strands in James's autobiographical method.

First, there is the feeling of "affiliation" to the past, to the persons that populated his world—"the blest group of us [he is speaking of late boyhood], such a company of characters and such a picture of differences, and withal so fused and united and interlocked, that each of us, to that fond fancy, pleads for preservation". Pleads, that is, not on the grounds of achievement, but simply by virtue of their being—like his cousin Mary Temple, who emerges in the book as a figure of almost legendary naturalness and grace. This delight in being, being for its own sake, is reiterated at the beginning of *The Middle Years*, when James hears something warning him not to try to record the multifarious experiences that befell him on his first adult visit to England:

I stop my ears . . . however, under the pleading reminder that just those days began a business for me that was to go on ever so much further than I then dreamed . . . I foresee moreover how little I shall be able to resist, throughout these Notes, the force of persuasion expressed in the individual *vivid* image of the past wherever encountered, these images having always such terms of their own, such subtle secrets and insidious arts for keeping us in relation with them, for bribing us by the beauty, the authority, the wonder of their saved intensity. They have saved it, they seem to say to us, from such a welter of death and darkness and ruin that this alone makes a value and a light and a dignity for them, something indeed of an argument that our story, since we attempt to tell one, has lapses and gaps without them. Not to be denied also, over and above this, is the downright pleasure of the illusion yet again created, the *apparent* transfer from the past to the present of the particular combination of things that did at its hour ever so directly operate and that isn't after all then drained of virtue, wholly wasted and lost, for sensation, for participation in the act of life, in the attesting sights, sounds, smells, the illusion, as I say, of the recording senses.

This means reminiscence, like the witty story of his visit to Tennyson, when the Bard read to him *Locksley Hall*, "taking even more out of his verse than he had put in". But it is not anecdotal reminiscence, for the memories stock his mind with their "saved intensity", have as living vivid images "value and light and dignity". The liveliness of James's memory and descriptions is in itself a convincing testimony to his imaginative nature.

The second strand is already implied in the manner of his remembering: the meaning these memories have for him. These encounters are recorded not simply because they occurred, but because they "signified". This cherished term of James has an almost unlimited range of meaning, and perhaps the most important thing about it is that it is unlimited. It means an accretion of knowledge, of insight, but is not limited to knowledge of a particular type, education for instance in Henry Adams's sense. Only occasionally can the actual accretion be formulated. The meetings with Tennyson, for instance, were "revelational" because Tennyson was "utterly un-Tennysonian", "neither knowing nor communicating knowledge", because he revealed to James "what a Bard might and mightn't be"—"he thereby changed one's own state too, one's beguiled, one's aesthetic".

But when James speaks of his imagination as something "to which literally everything obligingly signified", he does not essentially mean intellectual understanding. He means, that everything became a revelation of existence, and in this sense became symbolic. This is why he recalls with such love and precision his early life, his homes, his schools, the theatre in New York, the events of the Civil War; out of it all emerges a picture of American life as he experienced it, and the multiplicity of persons and relationships is its essence. His longing for Europe, his sickness as he calls it, grips him precisely because of the richer complexity of its reality as contrasted with the raw, modern world of America. In the Liverpool waiter, the London landlord, the German pension, the French servants, whole worlds of human relationships and possibilities thrust themselves on his understanding. Typical is his description of the glimpse he has as a boy, lying ill in a provincial inn in France, of a peasant-woman

working in the fields beneath a castle: "supremely, in that ec-
static vision, was 'Europe'". It is a vision quite different from
Wordsworth's of the woman on the fell (see above p. 44); there
is no mystical illumination with James. It is for him an illumination through a symbol, in "the bright unity of an experience", of
a complex range of human realisations and relationships, ec-
static because it means so vast an accession of imaginative understanding.

And the third strand is James's identification of his own character as an artist, one of "those whose faculty for application is all
and only in their imagination and sensibility". This is always
evident in the negative form of detachment; the intensity of his
attentiveness seems necessarily to posit a lack of involvement. In
contrast with his father's restless enthusiasms and moral passion,
and his brother William's purposeful and intelligent energy,
James's quality is always that of the onlooker. Accidents con-
spired to make him so, and it seems symbolical that a mysterious,
undiagnosed illness prevented him from participating like so
many of his companions in the Civil War. Feeling in him never
appears as more than affection; and his devoted observation of
human relationships almost precludes social and moral criticism.
It would be absurd to think James morally easy-going, and once
or twice he does allow us to glimpse his shrewd judgement, for
instance the distaste with which he discerned in London the
"obsequiousness" of the common people and the arrogance of
the privileged. But the purpose of his autobiography is rather to
under-emphasise all emotive and moral involvement in order to
stress his detachment, and thereby to bring out most sharply
the correlative, the intensity of his observation, his joy in ob-
serving, the supreme quality that distinguished him, the artist.

This positive aspect of detachment, its possibility as one sort
of human attitude, is first realised by him, he relates, at a play,
a crude dramatisation of *Uncle Tom's Cabin* in New York. He
describes affectionately the "rude art" of the sensational acting
and effects, but the main point is his discovery of the quality of
his family's enjoyment:

> However, the point exactly was that we attended this spectacle just
> in order *not* to be beguiled, just in order to enjoy with ironic detach-
> ment and, at the very most, to be amused ourselves at our sensibility

should it prove to have been trapped and caught. To have become thus aware of our collective attitude constituted for one small spectator at least a great initiation; he got his first glimpse of that possibility of a 'free play of the mind' . . . So he is himself at least interested in seeing the matter—as a progress in which the first step was taken, before that crude scenic appeal, by his wondering, among his companions, where the absurd, the absurd for *them*, ended and the fun, the real fun, which was the gravity, the tragedy, the drollery, the beauty, the thing itself, briefly, might be legitimately and tastefully held to begin. Uncanny though the remark perhaps, I am not sure I wasn't thus more interested in the pulse of our party, under my tiny recording thumb, than in the beat of the drama.

This capacity for "the free play of the mind" was awakened first in an aesthetic experience, and it becomes the ground of his own artistic work, his stories. His artistic character is made up of absorption and withdrawal, and his work involves, as he says, an "interpenetration" of reality and mind, "the constant quick flit of association . . . between the two chambers . . . of direct and indirect experience". In his withdrawal he becomes capable of all that others experience, learning to know "the fun of living by my imagination and thereby finding that company of friends, in countless forms, could only swarm about me. Seeing further into the figurable world *made* company of persons and places, objects and subjects alike: it gave them all without exception chances to be somehow or other interesting."

James's volumes do not form a typical autobiography of an artist any more than he himself was a typical artist. He was a novelist of a particular time, and his autobiography is his own. Even in this century, when many imaginative writers have made the theme of their autobiographies the peculiarity of the artist's relation with the world, their story has been markedly different from James's, and in particular they themselves have been often much more wholly engaged, emotively, morally, socially. Gide writes primarily of his emotive, moral, and intellectual development, and the climax to which *Si le grain ne meurt* leads us, with the grief and liberation that the death of his mother meant to him, is the discovery and assertion of himself as a moral personality, the discovery of "the tables of my new law". Edwin Muir's search is more like Wordsworth's than James's, the search

for the soul and the images it projects round itself. Stephen
Spender is preoccupied by the problem of reconciling social and
moral responsibilities with his need to remain intact. William
Plomer seems to find himself in a circle of artist-friends of integrity. For all these writers, their poetic gift is embraced in a
deeper purpose. With James, the artistic gift is primary, and other
personal or moral commitments are considered only in so far as
they contribute to it.

It would not be hard to see James's autobiography in fact as
dominated by a certain conception of the artist that was widely
held at the turn of the century, not so different from that in Joyce's
fragment *Stephen Hero* and its refinement, *A Portrait of the Artist*.
But it is more than a social document. What makes it important
in the context of autobiography is that the one specific artistic
activity, the "free play of mind" that transmutes reality into
image, is here the sole theme. The character of the experiences on
which such activity feeds varies greatly, and often includes
much that James's character excluded; but the activity itself is a
condition of the artist's being. James's life itself, his curious dis-
position, his self-willed exile, helped to make this theme pre-
dominate, but even more the view he took of his life in his old
age, his determination to see himself thus in his autobiography,
because he saw his imaginative work as the positive gain, the
distillation of so much distress. The outcome of his continuing
encounter with life was in fact his literary work, an imaginative
projection by which he could, as he said with a surprising echo
of Goethe, so different a man, "lay the ghost" of reality.

James's autobiography is significant in that it offers the fine
essence of the artist's operation on reality, and of the operation
of reality on the artist. That is, it tells us in elaborate detail
how reality, and what reality, becomes significant for the artist.
Other sorts of men can record reminiscences of the countless
impressions the world makes on them. But for James this wealth
is a capital, not a mere hoard; it is the substance of his public as
well as his private life. Everything "signifies". As his mind fills
with this experience, something happens to him himself. There
grows the realisation of the value of being as being, the tender
solicitude for human reality. There is no further purpose than, in
piety, though clear-sightedly and without illusions, to celebrate

existence as such, personality in its variety and self-achievement, and from this attachment to derive an "immortal comfort". He puts this theme explicitly in a passage concerning a visit to George Eliot:

> I find it idle even to wonder what 'place' the author of *Silas Marner* and *Middlemarch* may be conceived to have in the pride of our literature—so settled and consecrated in the individual range of view is many such a case free at last to find itself, free after ups and downs, after fluctuations of fame or whatever, which have divested judgment of any relevance that isn't most of all the relevance of a living and recorded *relation*. It has ceased then to know itself in any degree as an estimate, has shaken off the anxieties of circumspection and comparison, and just grown happy to act as an attachment pure and simple, an effect of life's own logic, but in the ashes of which the wonted fires of youth need but to be blown upon for betrayal of a glow. Reflective appreciation may have originally been concerned, whether at its most or at its least, but it is well over, to our infinite relief—yes, to our immortal comfort, I think; the interval back cannot again be bridged. We simply sit with our enjoyed gain, our residual rounded possession in our lap; a safe old treasure, which has ceased to shrink, if indeed also perhaps greatly to swell, and all that further touches it is the fine vibration set up if the name we know it all by is called into question—perhaps however little.

Other types of autobiography are bound by the logic of an intellectual, moral or practical purpose; the artist's autobiography, whatever its range, has to follow this "logic of life". The significant aspects are so complex and of such multiple radiation that imaginative writers often despair of recounting them—just as in their lives, like Goethe or Yeats, they feel the danger of succumbing under their weight. There is a good deal of truth in T. S. Eliot's statement that "the progress of an artist is a continual extinction of personality". But the artist's autobiography becomes possible and distinctive when, as with James's, the personality is marked not so much by its private adventures as its peculiar eager response to the impacts of experience, when at all moments we see the *how* as much as the *what* of this response.

X

"Man in all the truth of Nature"

IT may seem strange that only at this point do I attempt to write about autobiographies of the whole man, the proper theme of autobiography; and I must admit that I did not wish or expect to arrange my chapters thus. But my reluctant conclusion is that, in face of the great richness of modern autobiography in so far as it tells of the development of a specific gift and task, its success in representing the whole man is relatively meagre. I do not think this is due to the technical difficulty of combining many threads in a story; it arises above all from a certain falling short in respect of the whole personality. With the greatest number of autobiographies, this is simply an inadequacy in the persons writing, a lack of moral responsibility towards their task, a lack of awareness and insight. But many of the most scrupulous autobiographies also betray an uncertainty or hesitancy in respect to themselves. It is with relief, we feel, that they can write about their achievement, their gift, their attitude, solid, comforting realities as compared with themselves.

This in no way implies that modern life is short of personalities; they are as variegated and marked as ever they were. And I do not think it is due solely to the growing division of labour, to social and psychological specialisation. Perhaps what is most striking and decisive about the great autobiographies of this type, those of Rousseau, Wordsworth, and Goethe, is the attitude the man has to himself, a trust in himself, whether it is unthinkingly naïve (as in Cellini) or philosophically grounded. They believe that thus they had to be, thus they were appointed to become, thus nature had shaped and pre-destined them, thus they fulfil the law of their being. They know when, as Rousseau puts it, they "cease to be themselves". They are conscious too that they are working to a larger design, often expressed in metaphysical terms, as when Rousseau imagines himself standing proudly before the throne of God, or when Wordsworth and Goethe express their trust in an embracing cosmic purpose, which sustains them even if, as in the case of Goethe, it is recognised to be a postulate. A statement of Goethe's in his essay on Winckelmann sums up the basic belief (the meaning is complicated by the fact that the German "wenn" can mean either "if" or "when", so that a telling ambiguity belongs to the opening phrases):[1]

> If (When) the healthy nature of man works as a whole, if (when) he feels himself in the world as in a great, lovely, noble and worthy whole, if (when) a feeling of harmonious ease grants him a pure and free delight, then the universe, were it capable of conscious feeling, would rejoice to have reached its goal and admire the peak of its own growth and being. For what is the purpose of all the outlay of suns and planets and moons, of stars and Milky Ways, of comets and nebulae, of worlds created and to be created, if at the end a happy man is not unreflectingly to rejoice in being alive?

It will be noticed that the confidence of the assertion is qualified by being framed as a question as well as by the "if" or "when" of the opening.

Within this confidence, however qualified, the great autobiographies of the classical age unfold; they are attached both to the earth and the stars. It is difficult to say how far the assurance of a teleological purpose determines the confidence in the identity of the self, and how far it is the latter that produces the former. But certainly they are intimately linked, and in later autobiography both decline together. In Stendhal we already see both the uncertainty of the self—"What am I?" instead of "What I am"— and the utter absence of any metaphysical certainty and feeling of destiny. One might say that in this sphere too Darwin replaces Newton or Leibniz or Spinoza, and while one can trace a man's historical evolution, its objective reaches out into the uncertain— in the individual case, as in the general, man is "the undefined animal", as Nietzsche put it.

[1] Goethe, *Winckelmann und sein Jahrhundert* 1805.

The majority of outstanding modern autobiographies therefore conceive of self-fulfilment as the fulfilment of a task or group of tasks, a calling or profession. Or some theme is established which imposes an objective. In many this theme is their representativeness; they feel their experiences and development to be typical of their age, their nation, their class. Wells, for instance, blurs the specific and mercurial quality of his personality in order to etch his life more sharply as an epitome of his times; this it is that in his eyes gives point to his life. Koestler concentrates attention on his political beliefs and activities. If the writer simply tries to establish himself as a "personality", his work tends to be vain, crude, or philistine, redeemed only by the interest of his reminiscences or by the significance of some particular achievement. Denton Welch's account of himself painfully lost in an unrelated world is highly specific and an extreme case, yet it represents a fundamental situation of a loss of shape and meaning, both in the individual and in the surrounding world.

Clearly few people are content to admit so bleak a conclusion as Welch's. Yet they face great difficulties if they wish to sum up their lives and yet avoid an unreflecting empiricism or the refuge of reducing themselves to the accomplishment of a task. They can write sincere and in part illuminating accounts, yet the whole tends to lack both fullness and definition. One of the most sincere autobiographies of this type is that of the German writer, Hans Carossa, which continues over several volumes and is in fact his chief literary work. In this too it betrays a general situation; the autobiography is not a companion to the life's work, but is this itself, a continuous search to find the self and the meaning of the life. Carossa was a doctor and a poet, but his autobiography is not essentially the story of how he became either. It is the story of how he learnt to acquire a moral being, for instance how as a child he was painfully cured of his belief in magic, or how he was "healed" after being relegated from school on a false charge of homosexual relations. But Carossa's theme of the growth of insight, which is at the same time a process of healing from error, while it can sustain the account of his childhood, begins to show itself unsatisfactory as the boy grows. The problem of personality is reduced too much to a question of balance and humaneness, the person loses in concreteness, and so too do the circumstances through which he passes. Maturity brings a certain enfeeblement, a certain obliteration of the personality, that goes well with his profession as a doctor but indicates renunciation in respect to the totality of himself as of society. It is significant that Carossa's personality and his world appear much more vividly in the books outside the autobiographical sequence proper, in which he describes his experiences in the First World War (a diary worked over) and his fortunes and misfortunes in Hitler's Germany.[1]

It is easier for those writers in whose lives the pressure of outward circumstance is so heavy that it concentrates their energy and shapes their direction. The six volumes of Sean O'Casey's autobiography are an outstanding example. O'Casey became a distinguished playwright, a professional writer. Yet, differently from James and Yeats, and from Joyce and D. H. Lawrence in their autobiographical novels, he does not see his autobiographical purpose as the story of the emergence of a writer. This of course is necessarily included, yet the theme hardly appears before the fourth volume, *Innishfallen Fare Thee Well*; and even then his dramatic work is not seen as the fulfilment of his destiny, but as one element of his experience and activity. In fact, as he becomes a writer, the character of the autobiography involuntarily begins to change, the story loses in concrete substantiality; convictions which had the massiveness of experience now thin out into opinions and opinionativeness; and when O'Casey leaves Dublin, inconsequent reminiscences, tender or hilarious, take the place of autobiography. The four earlier books are not reminiscence, but life regained, relived passionately with all the intensity of a man still fiercely engaged.

O'Casey takes great liberties with the autobiographical form. Simply that he writes about himself in the third person allows him to slip repeatedly beyond what the child could have known about himself or others, beyond what was available to later enquiry too. He tells us what was going on in other people's minds, for instance the "inner monologue" of his sister Ella on her wedding day. We are often aware of a novelistic or dramatic technique in the imaginative reconstruction of dialogue and the composition of "scenes". There is little retrospective reconciliation with figures of the past, for O'Casey is fighting over again,

[1] *Rumänisches Tagebuch*, 1924, and *Ungleiche Welten*, 1951.

L.

from a point of vantage, the battles of his past. Yet it would be as pedantic to judge the autobiography on grounds of formal propriety as it would be wrong to resent its polemical spirit. If these are faults, they belong to O'Casey himself.

The autobiography is the story of Ireland from the early 1880s in so far as this boy lives it. Growing up in calamitous poverty, physically and mentally crippled by illness, he suffers the impact of society in its most cruel violence, and his life is therefore very much the story of his circumstances. Round him his brothers and sister succumb, painfully, and in the wider circle of the neighbours there is the same poverty, fecklessness, spasmodic revolt, and degradation. The odd recollections of the child, the dissociated incidents of early boyhood, guided and composed by the man's insight, build up into a picture of Ireland altogether—poverty and wealth, deprivation and culture, Irish nationalism and English imperialism, catholicism and protestantism, the Green and the Orange. In bitter struggle, often suffering from the ferocious or maladroit interventions of the rich and the poor, the privileged and the outcasts, the boy makes his way towards an understanding that is expressed rather in passionate belief and activity than in idea, through confusions of allegiance to devoted participation in the Workers' Union and the Citizen Army. As his radical Left Wing views begin to isolate him politically, so he turns to imaginative work, to his plays; and through them he becomes still more sharply separated from all parties and coteries until he feels he must leave Ireland.

Few autobiographies can tell of a harder and more desperate childhood and youth, yet one can think of few that are less depressing. What is characteristic is at all times the fierce energy of O'Casey's response and the exhilaration of fight. This spiritual energy is the very element of the books, and far more fundamental than any particular social doctrine, and it makes the work far more than a social document. It is expressed in numerous ways. It is there in O'Casey's dreamy questionings as a lad, his liking for games, his love of adventure stories, as it is in his later love of books; it is ever-present in his alert attentiveness to the outer world. It makes him at one time a sturdy protestant, later a piper and teacher of Gaelic in the Gaelic League, a patriot, a rebel, a socialist. It appears too in the people around him, in its political forms, the emotional upsurge of rioting mobs, in fanaticism and idealism, in the toughness of the Hurley players, in innumerable variations from his tram-conductor friend to Connolly and Jim Larkin. But it appears too in less obvious forms, in the extravagance of fantasy with which the simplest of people react against the weight of poverty and humiliation, in the pretty dresses of the girls, even in drinking and virtuoso Irish swearing.

There is a scene in *Pictures in the Hallway* where O'Casey describes how scavengers come to clear the household middens, carrying their foul loads through the living rooms, depositing the contents of the baskets in the street, and leaving behind them filth and a hideous stench. The women do what they can, saving the old oil-cloth on the floors, washing and scrubbing afterwards. But O'Casey manages to make the occurrence exhilarating rather than repulsive and depressing. His mother and a neighbour complain, but the vigorous inconsequent embroidery of their imagination is their way of overcoming, and the "dung-dodgers" themselves pause in their work to chat about the performances at a music-hall. This is not comic relief, but the spontaneous protest of these living people against a hostile reality.

The style expresses this same living and vigorous spirit. There is little factual objectivity, always the imagination is in play. O'Casey wishes to give us the quality of the boy's experience, through the medium of his thoughts, feelings, and imagination, and helps out only occasionally with a historical explanation. The language is as complex as the mind of the boy—it is shot through with the Biblical phraseology of his protestant upbringing, garbled Latin scraps from his catholic surroundings, the popular songs of the music-hall and the Irish movement, scraps from poets, from Yeats, Keats, Shakespeare and so on. Often O'Casey falls into Irish brogue, or into Joycean punning of an extravagant exuberance. Irish legends and Biblical stories are repeated in a language part sublime and part slang, at the same time far in the poetic distance and crudely down to earth. So that the language reflects much more than the boy could have been aware of, for it puts his consciousness into the context of his whole world as O'Casey now recollects and understands it. The language itself thus reveals the direct operation of the mature man, placing the past into the perspective of his understanding and judgement. Few writers have been able so candidly and yet so subtly to fuse in their autobiographies the past and present consciousness of the writer.

It is this mode of narration, this style, that tells us it is the autobiography of an imaginative writer, rather than anything explicit about literary ambitions and gifts. There is here none of the dedication to art that is the basic principle of the accounts of James, Yeats, or Joyce. O'Casey heard of the Abbey Theatre for the first time, he tells us, when the riot occurred over the production of Synge's *Playboy of the Western World*, and it was many years still before he was to begin writing plays. A navvy, a proletarian, he felt out of place in literary and artistic circles. He became an imaginative writer only when he became stranded among the Irish patriotic movements, unconcerned about the differences between Free Staters and Republicans, hating the senseless violence, so engaged with the sufferings of the people that he repudiated the actual parties and became an isolated and odd communist, "a voluntary and settled exile from every creed, from every party, and from every literary clique". Through his writing alone he felt he could "get a word in edgeways". And this isolation had another effect. For the first time he now had time for himself, and could find a purpose in himself—a purpose not antagonistic to the social purpose which had hitherto filled his life, but not identical with it: "He had shifted away from the active Ireland, and was growing contentedly active in himself. Instead of trying to form Ireland's life, he would shape his own. He would splash his thoughts over what he had seen and heard; keep eyes and ears open to see and hear what life did, what life had to say, and how life said it . . ." (*Innishfallen*, p. 118).

There is in the volumes hardly any explicit preparation for this discovery of his vocation. Only once, so far as I can see, in *Drums under the Windows* (p. 262), is there any earlier reference to a feeling of dedication, which he adduces on this occasion to justify his fear of taking part in violent political demonstrations—"for he wanted to live, feeling an urge of some hidden thing in him waiting its chance for an epiphany of creation" (the Joycean term is telling). It is the manner of his writing, the form in which his life is presented, that makes this development seem natural. Even in what might be called the lack of discipline of the narrative there is a rapturous exhilaration of spirit that outdoes the crushing weight of circumstances, and one feels that in this uncontrived, passionate, imaginative revolt lies the secret of the boy's ability not only to survive the physical pressure of poverty and squalor, but also to emerge from conventional and organised forms of self-defence. His departure from his people and his old life seems as integral and inevitable as Joyce made Stephen Daedalus's appear in *A Portrait of the Artist*.

But the last two volumes of O'Casey's autobiography, in which he tells of his fortunes as a writer and his private life and opinions in England, are a sad disappointment. His arguments with critics and producers, his continued feud with the catholic hierarchy, his ideas, lack direction, and have none of the compulsive reality of the childhood and earlier life. In this his work betrays the real problem of modern autobiography. He tells of "the struggle of a soul", as Powys called it. But the ground of this struggle was Ireland, was in the circumstances of his life. They pressed on him, distorted him, shaped him, intensified his powers, gave him his purpose. He recognised this, and told his story as the story of the whole society. But once he was removed from these compulsions and they lived on in him only as ideas, his autobiography loses its unity and drive. We do not feel that he found himself in the end, that he discovered and came to terms with some inner meaning which might have shown itself in a harmonious feeling of fulfilment. Removed from oppressive but sustaining circumstances, the self becomes haphazard, inwardly uncertain.

This uncertainty is not a question of social attitude. When he wrote his autobiography O'Casey was confident that society was moving purposefully and meaningfully towards a goal, a socialist commonwealth, and that his own work had meaning in this wider pattern. What is lacking is a rootedness of the individual life of a different sort, a sense of fulfilment of a personal destiny. We see the same lack in Sir Osbert Sitwell's five volumes, though here it is accentuated by other factors. For Sitwell our modern epoch is in every respect "cruel and senseless", and he frequently inveighs, like a crusty Tory, against modern democracy which is destroying in his view all he most clings to. He therefore deliberately evokes a more gracious and exhilarating past, charming settings, notable and eccentric personalities. His books have the advantage of a life spent in distinguished circumstances—though he is too sincere, and was always too much of a rebel, to idealise and embellish. But about himself he is reticent, almost savagely stand-offish. One must respect his avowed intention of not allowing us to share his sufferings as a child, and one could condone his reticence if such private feelings were irrelevant to the course of his life. But in fact his life therefore becomes obscure and incalculable. If he gained attractive material from being born into the upper class, he lost greatly in that there was no unambiguous pressure on him. Pressures there were—from his family, especially his father, from convention—but they were highly personal, whimsical, perhaps absurd, and they did not force him in any particular direction except that of ostentatious revolt. As a result, his life-line seems arbitrary, difficult to understand, the outcome of many impulses that did not grow into one major impulse. The dominant seems to have been his love and belief in art, yet even this expressed itself rather in an inconsequent revolt of avant-gardism than in any substantial achievement. With all his gifts and self-confidence, he seems to swerve continually away from himself, and in the end to devote himself with relief to reminiscence. And one might say that what fascinated him in his eccentric father, and led him to write a portrait of him that is far more brilliant than his self-portrait, was precisely the fact that his father was so inwardly secure, in his craziest schemes and opinions so confident of meaning.

There are many autobiographers who have felt the need of a personal fulfilment beyond the personal task or the social purpose. J. C. Powys, most endangered by its absence, and most keenly aware of its need, illustrates the acuteness of the problem. When he sees the task of autobiography as the story of "the struggle of a soul", and condemns the general run of autobiographies as "tedious", he is repudiating the normal purpose of showing how a man finds his social place and personal gift. When he says that "the only interest of events . . . is a symbolic one", he is insisting that all events worth recording must be related to this struggle of a soul. At the end of his autobiography he can justifiably assert that his life has a social content and meaning—the book is "the history of the 'de-classing' of a bourgeois-born personality and its fluctuating and wavering approach to the Communistic system of social justice". But its real centre lies elsewhere: "I feel that the deepest thing in life is the soul's individual struggle to reach an exultant peace in relation to more cosmic forces than any social system, just or unjust, can cope with or compass".

Powys's social revolt is therefore only a part of his general revolt against superficial beliefs and values. He accentuates the odd, neurotic, vicious elements in his character—indeed he admits that "I have made myself out at once more of a sinner and more of a fool than I really am"—in order to get to the absolute reality of himself. He does not hesitate to speak of his "manias", to call himself a "madman". In this "madness" lie both his specific self and his link with "cosmic forces", for, the Nietzschean writes, "a person's life-illusion ought to be as sacred as his skin". So he seeks, in defiance of propriety and sane realism to discover that metaphysical ground in which his personality is anchored. But, however much one may sympathise with his revolt and his truthfulness, the result is not what he aimed at. We see the desire to believe, not the belief, we see the passionate urge to round off his personality, but not the "exultant peace" that would have marked his success. The degree of neurosis involved, the eccentricity of his mystical experiences, so utterly remote from the calm confidence of a Wordsworth, indicate how difficult in modern times it is to achieve his purpose and to find meaning in personal fulfilment.

The central problem of Edwin Muir's autobiography lies in the conviction that his life, even his personality, are a "deviation" from his true self. He is aware of a hiatus between the real man and the outer shape of his life. What is distinctive and peculiar about each one of us is what he calls our myth or fable, but he despairs both of living it and of writing it: "I should like to write that fable, but I cannot even live it; and all I could do if I related the outward course of my life would be to show how I deviated from it". It is true that his story is for the reader something of a "dry legend", the meaning of which lies elsewhere, outside the book, in what is missing. The face he paints is, as he says, "plausible", yet that of a stranger to himself. His remarks on personality indicate a radical scepticism with regard to autobiography itself.

He says of a friend:

> If he had lived, he might have become a personality, for he had a trace of vanity in him, and perhaps every one who deliberately shapes himself into a personality has somewhere a deep frustration and a saving vanity. For this reason we end by making allowances for the man of personality, circumspectly coasting round him, forgiving him many things which we should not forgive a genuine human being, even acquiring a sort of appreciation of his quality as a thing *made*, his own creation . . . Our real task is not to cultivate but to get rid of personality.

I do not think that Muir was thinking here of the vulgar notion of personality, the sort of thing we mean when we speak of "television personalities", even though he speaks of persons who "deliberately" shape themselves into personalities. I take the statement in its widest meaning, indicated in the final sentence, as an expression of Muir's awareness of a lack of consonance between the outer life and achievements of a man and inner meaning. It is in this respect a statement that challenges the possibility of autobiography in its deepest sense, and certainly is very relevant to the general character of modern autobiography.

It may be thought that I am biassed in singling out auto-biographies with a mystical bent. But their mysticism, which I do not share, springs from a need and awareness that is commonly felt, though rarely with such acuteness as by them. That is, an awareness of essential distinctiveness and a need to see one's life as the fulfilment of this distinctiveness; at the same time a need to feel that such fulfilment is a meaningful process in itself. Innumerable modern autobiographies show this process of becoming, but the imperative "become that thou art" is given sense from outside, in such forms as, fulfil a religious or moral or social duty, find a shape for your gift. I do not want to appear ungrateful for them, or unappreciative, and it is only with reluctance that I observe that the self-fulfilment they record, the special and distinctive achievement that as it were gives such lives their justification, asserts itself as a substitute for a general inward imperative and an immanent self-evident meaningfulness.

This basic spiritual uncertainty is expressed in these auto-biographies by an uncertainty of pattern. As long as the writer remains in the sphere of childhood, we can observe a pattern of self-discovery, largely because he must rely on fairly meagre memories, and memory itself performs automatically a sifting process, recalling moments of significance in the general spiritual growth of the child. But for later life, when memories begin to throng and evidence to accumulate, a severe process of selection has to be made. If the principle of selection is a particular achievement, the memories can be accordingly chosen and organised, as one sees with Freud, James, or Wells, for instance. But if the writer has a more general objective, his personality as a whole, the choice is infinitely more difficult, more elusive. It is greatly helped as long as outside pressures continue strong and unambiguous, as with O'Casey; but once they relax, the pattern tends to disintegrate. What I have called the relapse into reminiscence occurs, as with David Garnett, and these reminiscences may seem fortuitous and insignificant in respect to the writer, and to be justified essentially in respect to some other person, like Osbert Sitwell's father. O'Casey's account of a visit to Cambridge in wartime is uproariously funny, but meaningless as autobiography; Muir's account of his life in post-war Prague is irrelevant.

In a sparkling essay, V. S. Pritchett has noted this lack in modern autobiography:[1]

> If we look at modern autobiographies of all sorts, we see that they are best when they are fragmentary: unabashed introspections like Mr. Cyril Connolly's account of Eton, or sweeping statements like George Orwell's. Or, when they reject ordinary chronology and are autobiographies ruled by a subject: T. E. Lawrence's *Seven Pillars*. Modern autobiography fails when it has no attitude, when it has no special subject which rescues the self from the cliché of having lived. There is no credit in living; the credit is in being able to specify experience.

Pritchett's explanation is in the main a psychological one: we are bewildered by excessive awareness and by the multiplicity of the selves within us, "we have worn out the first person singular in watching other people", "we find no ground under our feet when we start to write"; and so "we produce the normal autobiography: the life, the busy record of family, friends, career and events, without a self to support its tacit self-importance".

[1] "All about Ourselves", *The New Statesman*, May 26, 1956.

It is this conviction that urged André Gorz to his pitiless self-examination in *Le Traitre*. Austrian-born, half-Jewish, forced as a boy to flee from Hitler, Gorz pursues two strands of determination in his character, the psychological and the sociological; he can understand himself by Freud or by Marx. But in either case he himself is nothing, merely a victim of conditions. Where is his real self, his free humanity? Everything he has done and thought, even the philosophical investigation he has spent ten years on, can be seen as a mechanical product. Like most people, as Sartre writes in his introduction to the book, he becomes the prisoner of himself, and every act fortifies the bars. And consequently, Gorz's account of his earlier life (his autobiography was written when he was thirty-three) is not the means for discovering himself in the life he lived, but a means, he hopes, through understanding the past, to free himself from the chain of cause and effect, to "grasp reality", and to change into a real self. Here that "normal autobiography" of which Pritchett speaks is not the end, but of use only if it is a means of overcoming and transcending the personality involved. But with such a conception, the frontiers of autobiography are reached. The true self is no longer embodied in the life, and it is characteristic that Gorz speaks of himself as an object, in the third person, almost disdainfully, except in his philosophical reflexions at the beginning and end of his book.

I do not think one can evade the conclusion that the supreme task of autobiography is not fulfilled in modern autobiography. It has of course rarely been fulfilled, and it is hazardous to postulate a cause or causes when a single exception may utterly disprove a rule. I have already suggested that the lack of great autobiography in certain earlier periods may be ascribed to the fact that certain social periods are unpropitious to autobiography, in particular those in which social life is so violent and unpredictable that personal life itself is subject to the violent caprice of external events. This is true to some extent today, particularly in the autobiographies of men and women tossed about by fearful events. But what more profoundly affects modern autobiography is a general lack of relationship between personal and social being. Perhaps it is this that is meant by Yeats's remark, that "all life weighed in the scales of my own life seems to me a preparation for something that never happens". Special achievements do happen of course, but what is felt is that the whole being is not fulfilled, that there is renunciation, which to the keenest consciousness and conscience may even appear to be a betrayal of self.

It is not only the uncovering of psychological and sociological determinants by Freud and Marx that makes the individual unsure of himself—Rousseau and Goethe, after all, knew of such determinants. The self-distrust that is so marked in many modern autobiographies, and that leads in some cases, despite absolute confidence in the worth of some particular achievement, to an almost cynical estimation of the core of the self, suggests a malaise that is due to the nature of modern living altogether.

XI

The Autobiographical Novel

THE autobiography offers an almost unlimited opportunity for the exploration of personality—not solely of the author's, but also of the people with whom he is intimately involved. It can be shapely, with its outstanding "symbolic" incidents, its organic sections (the chapters), and a conclusion which may be that of fulfilled age or a situation at which the established personality stands collected and poised. With all this, it is free of the conventional exigences of "literature", it needs no plot, no spurious liveliness, and can devote itself truthfully to its theme, the slow assimilation of experience and emergence of a character. Even if the autobiographer makes demonstrable errors in respect to himself and others, these still are true evidence of himself, and truer to human nature than the absolute knowledge that the novelist often pretends to. Autobiographers accept certain limitations that are imposed by tact or by the laws of libel, but making allowance for these, it might seem that autobiography offers a better instrument for inquiry into the truth of personality and personal relations than does imaginative literature, in particular the novel. Certainly the range of experience described in autobiographies is astonishing, and sometimes too strange for fiction.

H. G. Wells indeed found work on his *Experiment in Autobiography* so "real and satisfying" that it gave him a distaste for novel-writing. He was fully aware of the pitfalls besetting the autobiographer. He recognised that memory is faulty, and that it inevitably charges past experiences with a meaning they acquire only in retrospect, and he several times discusses the danger of deluding oneself about oneself, and of substituting an ideal self for the real. He knew too that much has to be obscured in the interest of living persons. Yet, in spite of his success in using autobiographical material in his novels, he came to the conclusion (vol. ii, 502) that as mankind "matures", as it becomes more possible to be frank in the scrutiny of the self and others and in the publication of one's findings, biography and autobiography will take the place of fiction for the investigation and discussion of character.

Wells's opinion was based on a simple conception of the novel as a means to investigate personal relations. It is reinforced by the more complex considerations of Stephen Spender. He tells us, in *World within World,* that he thought of putting his experiences into the form of a novel, but decided on autobiography because it would mean a more honest relationship between him and his work, and between the reader and the author. The autobiography would not allow him to escape from the harsh reality of himself, and would not invite the reader to forget his real existence:

> The writer of fictitious autobiography offers the truth about himself within the decent and conspiratorial convention of contemporary fiction, which invites the reader to identify himself with the writer-hero. Reader-writer walk together in a real-seeming dream alliance leading into gardens inhabited by Stephen Daedalus and Marcel.

Spender is aware that autobiographers, simply by admitting us to their intimacy, do win our sympathy, even if they do not go further and make outright appeals to us to take their side. He himself deliberately fends against this by the severity of his own comments on his behaviour. But here he is referring to something more profound than this overt sympathy. In an imaginative work, a novel, we readers involuntarily identify ourselves with the hero and suspend judgement. We do not take him as we would any contemporary, and in particular do not feel under the necessity of making moral judgements on his actions. The novel-hero is removed from the actual world, and we do not conceive of him as existing outside the pages of the novel. What happens in the novel should be self-sufficient and completed, while the autobiographer must refer us continually outwards and onwards, to the author himself and to the outcome of all these experiences.

These contentions of Wells and Spender have to postulate the possibility of candour. It is true that modern autobiography has considerable freedom to expose the reality of our thoughts and behaviour, in particular sexual relations, with a frankness formerly and usually evaded. One should not forget that in this respect all modern writing owes a particular debt to earlier autobiography, to Cardano and Rousseau for instance. Yet the worth of autobiographies is not measured by the amount of candour with which all aspects of life are revealed. Wells and Spender are reticent in some respects, and one is even grateful to them for this. But, overlooking this problem, and assuming that absolute candour is possible, and accepting the thesis that the purpose of the novel is the investigation of character, can it be maintained that the autobiography offers such scope that it can replace the imaginative form?

The novel has apparent advantages that can be summed up as technical and may rapidly be enumerated. In the novel, events occurring outside the range of the author-hero may be evoked and imaginatively re-lived, not merely adduced, postulated, or explained. The thoughts and hidden motivations of other people may be exposed. How presumptuous and absurd it is, by contrast, when Havelock Ellis writes in his autobiography that he knew his wife perfectly and that she kept nothing from him! To this sort of knowledge only the creator of imaginary characters can lay claim. Scenes and conversations may be constructed as a vivid actuality, not as something thinned out and coloured by memory. The hero may be described from outside, or through the refractions of other persons, and thus become rounder and more clear-cut, while there is always a core of darkness in the hero of the autobiography.

There is a difference that cuts deeper, in that the novel is complete in itself while the autobiography always reaches forward to the man writing. The experiences described by the autobiographer both belong to a precise past and refer forwards, are selected and given a peculiar slant because of this ultimate purpose, so that many autobiographers have been puzzled by the problem of how to reconcile the immediacy and indeterminacy of an actual past experience with the need to detach from it just what in it is the seed of the future man. We find indeed novelistic techniques being used by autobiographers in order to try to escape from this dilemma. George Moore confuses his time-scheme and creates isolated scenes in order to reproduce situations in their indeterminate freshness. Richard Church begins *Over the Hill* with such a scene (echoed at the beginning of the second volume), as if he wished to capture the multiple radiation of a moment and escape from the teleology of the autobiography. The method cannot be kept up, however, and both writers have to return to an earlier period and underpin the isolated scene—Moore, more wayward, found he had to fill his third volume with rather indiscriminate supplementary material about his early life.

Of course, the fact that many novels are told in the first person indicates that there are also advantages in telling a story through the eyes of a participant. It is an ancient literary device, used in the *Odyssey* and the early Greek novel, as by Defoe, and abundantly employed in the modern novel. No method can convey the peculiar quality of life as the individual lives it so convincingly as the story seen through his eyes. This is how we all know the world, since one's relationship to oneself is unique and utterly different from one's relationship to any other person. The novel has a wider scope than the autobiography, for it can adopt this method as well as others. When on the other hand autobiographies are written in the third person, like those of K. P. Moritz or Sean O'Casey, the result is at times disturbing, for the author, positing an objective relationship to himself, misrepresents the true character of life as seen from inside. There is contradiction between form and view-point. There is contradiction of an allied kind when Denton Welch, though he writes in the first person, eliminates himself as a reflecting consciousness in order to reproduce the shock of experience as barely and directly as possible.

In the character of the form itself, then, there are certain limitations inherent in autobiography that mean it can never supplant the novel as a means for the investigation of character. But questions of artistic form always imply some deeper problem and purpose. There are innumerable novels which build on a particular personal experience of the author, and one might examine why it is that authors feel impelled to transfer it to fictional characters in an invented situation and impose on it a fictional outcome.

It is more pertinent and economical to restrict an examination to a few autobiographical novels which are in content and scope close to autobiography proper.

KELLER'S *Green Heinrich* (1879–80)

The great autobiographical novel of the Swiss author, Gottfried Keller, tells in the first person the story of a boy whose ambition to become an artist is the expression of his incapacity to come to terms with reality, and who in the end abjures art and devotes himself to the welfare of the community.[1] To some extent it resumes the actual career of Keller, who after a long period of artistic effort became secretary to the Cantonal administration in Zürich—though Keller himself continued to write and after fourteen years resigned his public office in order to devote himself to his literary work. But Keller's intention was not autobiographical; he used the material of his life, he said, "not because it is mine, but in spite of the fact that it is mine". It is not primarily a novel about an artist, for Keller stated that he was concerned with "the human behaviour, the moral fate" of his hero. That Green Heinrich is an artist is simply a fact, which meant consequently that Keller had to discuss his moral dilemma in terms of his artistic efforts and ideas; but he said that what he hoped to do was to show "the general relevance in these apparently remote and professional matters". Thus he felt at liberty to use the material of his own life very freely. But the moral theme of his book did grow out of his own experience, was a fundamental result of this experience, however much his own life varied from that in the book and even, one might say, failed to realise the potentialities of itself. So if he uses his life freely, he does not do so arbitrarily. In an autobiographical essay he writes that in the novel he had let "the meagre seeds grow fully", and that the later parts, which diverge further from his actual life than the childhood, "supplement" or "complete" reality. That is, the additions, alterations, inventions are logically bound to his character. I will take one example to show his method and its purpose.

In his late teens, the hero has a curious double love-affair, with

[1] I have discussed this book, regrettably little known in England, in my *The German Novel*, Manchester Univ. Press, 1956.

a delicate, rather ethereal girl, Anna, who dies of consumption after a protracted illness, and a robust young widow, Judith. Both relationships are boyish and romantic, but distinct in character, and their contemporaneity demonstrates most strikingly his dilemma between the attractions of the ideal and natural. We can discover in Keller's life the originals. Anna seems to be a projection of a cousin who died early, and Judith an amalgam of one or two maturer women he later loved. But Keller himself never found any response to his love. He was a very small man with a huge head, and acutely conscious of his physical oddity, and perhaps because of this was shy, bristly, and clumsy in his relations with women. Now novels often can provide a cheap compensation for Keller's sort of unhappiness, and the love between Heinrich and Anna and Judith might have been just wish-fulfilment. It is in fact something very different. It tells us of the real resources of feeling in the boy, which in life were frustrated by the accident of his appearance and manners. A true autobiographical account would have told us about the frustrations, and one might have guessed at the capacities that were choked. The love that in the novel is released takes us into the heart of his character, illuminates it, and is in a sense truer than life.

A comparable example is the love of Lucy Snowe for M. Paul in *Villette*. Charlotte Brontë herself perhaps became conscious of her love for M. Heger only after leaving Brussels, and could express it only indirectly in her letters. But, in order to show her whole range and spiritual resources, she needed to postulate for the novel an expressed and answered love. Without this brief happiness we could scarcely have imagined what potentialities there were in this repressed and controlled English teacher.

Both books exemplify the artistic process that Henry James discusses in some of the prefaces to his novels, particularly in that to *The Spoils of Poynton*. His imagination was repeatedly fired, he tells us, by some anecdote from real life—or rather, by the situation that lay at the root of the anecdote. But he rejects the anecdote itself, the actual story and dénouement, and imposes on the situation invented characters and an invented outcome, guided by what he calls "the sense of life" or the search for "the secret of life". For actual life, with its "classic ineptitude", is "all inclusion and confusion", it "persistently blunders and deviates"; while art draws "the right truth out of the so easy muddle of wrong truth". This conflict of truths is never more clearly in evidence than in the autobiographical novel.

The actuality of their lives would have been, for Keller and Charlotte Brontë, a "wrong truth". They know themselves to be other than they were in actuality, and obey the "sense of life" instead of the historical facts. In so doing, they do something more. Overcoming what in their characters and circumstances they felt to be fortuitous, they also make their heroes and their novels more generally true, more illuminating about personality in general, more relevant to everyone. And in this process a curious transformation occurs that distinguishes art. Our relationship to the heroes becomes something different from that to the subject of an autobiography, or to any real person. We walk with the hero in a "dream-alliance", we imaginatively participate in his actions, thoughts, and feelings, we do not stand outside, considering whether he was sensible, good, deluded and so on. Above all, our moral relationship to the hero is different. Not that the moral sense is in abeyance. Keller in particular criticises outright the moral behaviour of his Green Heinrich, and invites us to participate in this criticism. But we see his life as something that had to be thus and could not have been otherwise. We refer his errors, when they occur, back to ourselves, not to him, and think of him as living for us, not for himself. If all art is, as Thomas Mann said, "criticism of life", it is criticism through a widening of consciousness, of the moral sensibility, of this kind. The serenest, most theodicy-like autobiography cannot dare to raise the author-hero into a realm of being so removed from practical moral judgements. The artistic imagination sees the individual *sub specie humanitatis*.

Sons and Lovers

Like many autobiographies, D. H. Lawrence's *Sons and Lovers* arose out of his need to make his reckoning with his past life— Middleton Murry called it "a heroic effort to liberate himself from the matrix of the past". It is constructed out of the stuff of his life, and Lawrence was deeply concerned with its veracity. He submitted parts of it to Jessie Chambers (the Miriam of the novel) and adopted many of her additions and corrections, and the truth of much of the novel has been checked by the evidence of other living participants. That Lawrence continued to be concerned with it as a true historical account is evident from his statement, made later in life, that he would have liked to re-write it "in fairness to his father", whom he had learnt to understand better.

It is not autobiography however, neither in technique nor in content. Careful as Lawrence was to try to reproduce past events, even conversations, as they actually were, he represents them not retrospectively, but as actually taking place. He invents situations, and adds data which could never actually have been available to him, such as, for instance, the thoughts of his mother as Paul Morel lies in his cradle. He writes about himself in the third person. He simplifies the family, omitting his eldest brother and younger sister, adding a younger brother. Paul remains at one job throughout, whereas Lawrence remained at the surgical goods' manufacturer's for a few months only, and then, after illness, began to train for a teacher. He gives us little or no indication of his lively intellectual interests in this period, and makes the hero's painting much more original than his own was at that time (he was then, in the main, only copying reproductions).

Some of these alterations are readily understandable. Lawrence wanted to give the story a direct impact as living experience, not as spent experience. He simplified in order to single out the most significant events. He wrote in the third person because he felt the imperative need to view himself from outside. This is the sort of objectivisation and simplification we find in Benjamin Constant's *Adolphe,* where the author reduces himself to his capacity to love, and his beloved to a mere "function of the hero", as a recent editor, J. Mistler, puts it. But some changes in *Sons and Lovers* indicate a wider variation from an autobiographical purpose. If Lawrence had been concerned, like the autobiographer, to tell us how he became the man he is, he would have been obliged to tell of his intellectual development, and to have mentioned, at least, the influence of Schopenhauer, Huxley, and Nietzsche. In fact, the novel does not lead in this direction at all. It was not written to tell us about a certain author, Lawrence—he was young and practically unknown at the time; had it been, it would have betrayed the sort of vanity Lawrence never suffered from. It is one of his earliest novels, and necessarily had to stand by itself.

One can recognise two linked purposes that inspired the alterations he made in the structure of his life. He was seeking to show the emergence of his personality from the entanglements of his love for his mother and Miriam, and was therefore primarily concerned with this "soul-making", to use Keats's phrase, not so much with intellectual development. At the same time he was concerned, perhaps at first unconsciously, with the representativeness of his life; its significance grew for him as he recognised in it the story of the youth of his time—"It's the tragedy of thousands of young men in England", he wrote to Edward Garnett. The closer he got to the heart of his emotional entanglement, to his essential problem, the more representative he felt he became.

In the book, Paul's love for Miriam culminates in physical union. But it entirely accords with what we know of Lawrence that Lawrence's love for Jessie Chambers remained "pure", as the latter later insisted, and largely because of Lawrence's fanatical devotion to the idea of "purity". Why did he make this change? I would suggest that it was because he did not want to ascribe the failure of their relationship to particular, rather juvenile ideas, but sought to trace it back to a more fundamental cause, to a complexity and frustration of being. In the same way, the suppression of the intellectual interests of the young people must be ascribed to a desire to concentrate on basic emotive relationships not on ideas that were necessarily less substantial and less representative.

Certain stylistic features betray the same intention. We remember Miriam in a series of attitudes—her fear of the swing, her suffocating love for her little brother, her caressing of flowers. None of these is likely to be historically untrue. But because they are singled out and put into relief, they sharply delineate that aspect of her character that is decisive within the framework of Lawrence's theme. They become symbolic to a degree that autobiography, in which incidents also acquire a symbolic character, can rarely allow itself. This search for symbols which condense a whole group of relationships becomes conscious with Lawrence, and leads to outright invention. When the mother lies dying, Paul puts her and the family out of the misery of her protracted suffering by giving her an over-dose of morphia. It is an action typically untrue of life, yet typical of the novel, for in it is symbolised that meeting-point of love and hate for the mother, that victory over her and affirmation of his own life, that is the substance of the book. It gives a dramatic climax, uncharacteristic of actual life, which sums up the book as it rounds it off. Very typically, we forget as we read to ask ourselves whether Paul's action is morally justifiable.

Many modern autobiographers become pre-occupied with their lives as representative of their generation, as I have pointed out above (pages 57–8); Wells represents his life, for instance, as a "sample" in its social setting and its ideological effort. Lawrence's use of the novel form cannot therefore be ascribed simply to this intention. Partly his choice is due to his conviction that its fundamental characteristic lies not just in a social or ideological situation, but essentially in an emotive nexus, which had to be delineated more sharply than the actual real events allowed for in themselves, and therefore required artistic re-arrangement and invention. Partly it is due to his youth at the time of writing. In Wells's case, as in that of most autobiographers, life itself had effected this discriminating and arranging process, since he could see the line of his life leading to what he had become much later. Lawrence, still faced with uncertainty as to what he was and would become, had to rely for self-knowledge on an intuitive apprehension of his unrealised potentialities. He gave his story an auto-biographical form because he felt his individuality to be unique and specific; but he had to go beyond the actuality also, in order to uncover what was only potential.

A Portrait of the Artist as a Young Man

As with *Sons and Lovers,* independent testimony has established that Joyce's *A Portrait of the Artist as a Young Man* is substantially true to historical fact. For some part of the novel we have in addition the check of Joyce's autobiographical fragment, *Stephen Hero,* and it is enlightening to compare the two records.

Stephen Hero covers Joyce's university life. It is far fuller than the account in *A Portrait.* Friends and family are described in greater detail, Stephen himself has more pre-occupations, and his development is far less sure and direct than in the novel. In the latter, the conception of Stephen as a budding artist is established very early, and as this central quality is singled out, so other characteristics and relationships are reduced and moulded so that the world in which he lives is presented as nothing but the stimulus and foil to the working out of his artistic destiny. Thus the squalor and poverty of his circumstances never appear simply, in their oppressive impact, but are always balanced by the linked antithesis of his poetic response—just as the delicate beauty of the Elizabethan lyrics that he loves and imitates is linked in his mind with the squalor of Elizabethan times. In *Stephen Hero* we are aware of the almost stifling atmosphere in the Daedalus home; in the novel, its sordidness is described only at a moment when it is functionally necessary, when it appears as the counterpart to Stephen's dream of beauty. Stephen's ties with his mother are not shown as a long and complex struggle between affection and inner calling, for they are not much more than indicated in the course of a long conversation with his friend Cranley, where Stephen relates his artistic gift to his lack of feeling, his failure to know "what the heart is and what it feels". Emma Clery, in *Stephen Hero* a very real girl, loses all substantiality in *A Portrait,* and properly takes her place in a symbolic series of woman-figures some of whom exist only in the mind of Stephen Daedalus.

Thus *A Portrait* condenses the actual Joyce to a central and basic characteristic, the artist, and reduces the world round him to functional expressions of his inward drive. The composition of the novel is similarly determined. It is no doubt a simplification to divide an autobiography up into chapters, but Joyce goes even further in *A Portrait.* We are presented with a series of sequences, in each of which the experiences involved (some told in the form of reminiscence) are bound tightly together and illuminate one another. Between the sequences too there are subtle connexions, not so much historical and psychological as symbolical, in particular the series of women-images, hardly real in themselves, that denote his creative search for beauty. Thus too, the significant high points are visions of beauty, the flight of birds, the poem he creates.

The novel is indeed a "portrait", that is, an artistic vision of himself, subtly composed and mysteriously illuminated like a Rembrandt. Joyce is only concerned with himself as an artist, as a man dedicated to art, capable of nothing significant except the creation of beauty. There is no need to say that this was fundamentally true, this was his essence; but in representing it he has distilled his actual existence, his ties with the world, its impact on him, down to its finest substance. *A Portrait* is not a search for an actual Joyce and an actual Dublin; both are now only a medium for the emergence of an artistic gift. We have seen in other autobiographical novels the uncovering in imagined situations of what in life remained hidden or frustrated, and with that a move away from the particular to the representative. With Joyce the process is taken still further, in that the individual is taken as the artist in himself and his life is understood as an "epiphany" of this particular type of man. It remains particular, vivid, individual, but nothing is haphazard or indifferent, nothing is described simply because it happened. Only that part of real experience can claim to be included that illuminates the theme.

*   *   *   *   *

It seems superfluous to remark that autobiographical novels should properly be compared only with the autobiographies of poets or artists, since authors of novels belong to this category. This does not mean that the "heroes" of such autobiographical novels have to be artists or would-be artists, for the author may not be concerned with what is specific to him as an artist, but with something more generally shared. But it does mean that he is concerned with inward problems and struggles, with emotive experiences, moral values, an imaginative ideal. He differs from many autobiographers in that he singles out a central issue in his character as his distinctive feature, but not from all, for so do Gibbon, Freud, and Croce, among many others. What is different is that the narrative centres on a spiritual problem, and that the resolution of this problem is a decisive act which establishes the character finally. Unlike Freud, Croce, or Wells, who follow up the development of an intellectual task, and ignore whatever does not fit in, the novelist clings to experience and portrays spiritual growth, even if the latter defies intellectual measurement. This is another way of saying that, while the autobiography leads to something known, the author's present position, the novel is its own goal and is complete in itself as a rounded experience. The novel, like all art, in this respect represents an ideal, for while every-one has such experiences, they are in life not only confused by a thousand discrepancies, but are embedded in a process of growing that, of its nature, forbids us at any moment to recognise a state of completion and fulfilment. That autobiographers are in general reserved about such inward experiences is due, I believe, not to tact or shyness, but to the consciousness that the feeling of fulfilment that may accompany such experiences is negated by the character of life as process.

It was with the consciousness that the important thing in his life was a subterranean spiritual unity, often unrelated to his actual activities, that Edwin Muir wistfully speaks of what he could do if he were writing an autobiographical novel instead of an autobiography. He writes of the permanence of childhood images and their way of re-emerging throughout later life, of their "correspondences" which interpret his real identity, and continues:

> If I were writing an autobiographical novel I could bring out these correspondences freely and show how our first intuition of the world expands into vaster and vaster images, creating a myth which we act almost without knowing it, while our outward life goes on in its ordinary routine of eating, drinking, sleeping, working, and making money in order to beget sons and daughters who will do the same. I could follow these images freely if I were writing an autobiographical novel. As it is, I have to stick to the facts and try to fit them in where they fit in.

When Muir decries the idea of personality and of development in response to experience, he is likewise asserting that true growth is simply an unfolding and that the outer life is accidental, a "dry legend". The statements are extreme and indicate how it was that Muir found his true medium in poetry rather than the autobiographical novel. Joyce, with something of the same purpose as Muir proposes, was able to delineate his inward "myth" by re-casting imaginatively his outward circumstances. But Muir's remarks do point to a real distinction between autobiography and the autobiographical novel.

The distinction is alive in the very structure of the two types of writing. In the novel, everything is tightly bound, everything is closely related to the theme. Now this is true in part of the auto-biography. Henry James repeatedly speaks of everything in his life "signifying", bringing some accretion of understanding and insight, a continuous, almost imperceptible assimilation. But such assimilation takes a different form in the novel. It is there expressed not simply in understanding, but also in events that can rightly be called symbolical. The novel demands a narrative structure much more coherent and firm than the autobiography, a sequence of symbolical events, and a significant climax such as we have in *Sons and Lovers* and *A Portrait of the Artist*.

Life itself does not proffer many such symbolical events. They do occur, and are recorded in autobiographies. It is perhaps characteristic that they occur most clearly in autobiographies with a single spiritual theme, like Augustine's, where they are often turning points in the actual life of the man. But even in such autobiographies, they often remain detached from actual action. Newman, lying dangerously ill in Italy, found the idea of a Mission rising spontaneously in his mind—"I have a work to do in England"; but the meaning he gave these words in retrospect seems somewhat forced. A man's spirit may cry out for concrete expression, but the "epiphany" rarely takes shape, and his development will usually occur in an obscure, complex, almost intangible fashion. This was the cause of Gide's despairing exclamation, "the most important thing, being without contours, escapes capture". And when he tried to make up for the lack of significant incident by "fine" evocative writing, Valéry detected insincerity. It is significant incident, like Miriam's fear of the swing, related as it is to other similar incidents, that reveals a character and relationship in all its complexity, not just subtle analysis, evocative description, or ruminating reflexion. This the novelist can invent and heighten by his mode of composition.

I have suggested that by inventing situations the autobiographical novelist can reveal in a person what in life may be hidden and only latent. One must go further. Is it right to say Lucy Snowe's capacity to love was there, before it actually was in being? Is it not truer to say that only the invented circumstances of the novel could make us believe in its existence, and that without them it did not "exist" at all? Latency can only have a meaning in retrospect, after what was "latent" has become patent. If the right circumstances are not there, certain characteristics must remain for ever unknown, even unsuspected. The inventions of the autobiographical novelists indicate in fact a general principle of the novel. All are based on experience of life, of course, and many on particular and identifiable originals of character or incident. Commonly the characters are put into situations which can be called extreme, that is, situations in which the posited potentialities of the character have the utmost room to develop. They therefore become more intense, more active, better or worse than is the case in life. One thinks of Goethe's method in *Werther*, Proust's throughout his novel series, but also of novels remoter from autobiographical reference like *Madame Bovary* or *War and Peace*. These extreme situations, extreme pressures, have to be invented if human potentiality is to be plumbed, in the same way as the physical properties of a substance can only be discovered under extreme tests.

But this limitation of the autobiography cannot be ascribed solely to the lack of invented extreme situations, and it is necessary to reconsider what was said earlier in this chapter on the implications of the I-form. In the autobiography there is a lack of vivid impact in respect to the hero, not only to our view of him, but also in his own sight. Reviewing his life, writing in the first person, the author necessarily treats himself with a certain bias. I do not mean here a moral bias, that he must embellish his good qualities and excuse his bad, or *vice versa*, but that he must essentially be acquainted with intentions, motivations, the inside view, rather than with the actual product, the actual act as it strikes others. No-one is a hero to his valet—and, Hegel retorted, that is the fault of the valet; and to ourselves we are all valets in some degree. In the autobiography we can never reach the intensity and precision of view that is the prerogative of others. It is clear that this subjective view has a profound truth in it, and for this reason novelists have often adopted the first-person narrative. But it is only part of the truth. We also exist as objects for others, in our impact on them, and it is perhaps the great achievement of such a novel as *War and Peace* that here a multitude of people are seen both from inside and outside, and because of this acquire so intense and vivid a life. The autobiographer can neither get inside other people nor outside himself.

So it is that autobiography, a remarkable instrument for the investigation of the truth of a life, also imposes restrictions on this investigation. It cannot experiment, it cannot invent conditions in order to exploit all the possibilities of the subject, it cannot see the author's impact on others. It comes nearest to doing these things when the author himself has recklessly given himself up to his inward urge, like Augustine, Cellini, Teresa, Rousseau, but such dedication is rare, and even with them is not unconditional. In nearly all autobiographies we are aware through hints of stifled resources, particularly in the sections dealing with childhood, but these hints are not often realised in behaviour and activity, and sometimes as it were disqualified by them.

So Wells's claim for biography and autobiography must be rejected. There are limits to the "truth" of autobiography, if one thinks of truth not as the realised actuality of a life but as its whole potential range. Life must restrict in a thousand ways, and without the resources of invention, of art, we should remain ignorant of much that is decisive in man. If one remains true to the facts, too much eludes. Perhaps this was at the back of Proust's mind when he told Gide, "You can tell anything but on condition that you never say 'I' ". For in *A la Recherche du Temps Perdu* Proust transposes himself into a hundred people and situations. Gide levelled at him the traditional invective against the artist when he called him "that great master of dissimulation". He was right on the surface, for if one sees the novel as a confession or a source-book for Proust's own life, one falls into trap after trap. But he was wrong in the other sense, for it shows all that Proust was capable of, the multiple modifications possible to his being. Gide's autobiography is more honest, but infinitely less profound.

One must therefore disagree with Dilthey's statement, quoted approvingly by Misch,[1] that the autobiography is "the highest and

[1] W. Dilthey, *Gesam. Schriften*, vii, 199.

most instructive form in which the understanding of life is re-vealed to us". Unless Dilthey meant, not the understanding of life in its whole extent, but the understanding of how to live, how to manage. What it can do is to show how men, at grips with powerful forces within themselves and in their circumstances, can come to some sort of terms with them, can establish out of them all some sort of positive achievement. And while this means surrender to a dominant force within them, it means at the same time a compromise between other potentialities and the demands of life. This compromise is not a deliberate choice or decision, it is the actual result of their lives. Thus it is that significant autobiography is a product of maturity. A young man cannot shape his autobiography without imposing rather arbitrary limits on his conception of himself. For him the autobiographical novel is much more appropriate, where he both interprets himself and invents situations to reveal what he feels is his potential reality. On the other hand, for an old man to write an auto-biographical novel would smack of the sentimental. Not only would it indicate a futile revolt against himself, but it would miss the very point of autobiography, that it can tell us how one comes to terms with reality, how one has found the way to the realised self. It is through art that man discovers his infinite range. The objective of autobiography tends rather towards practical wisdom.

XII

The Structure of Truth in Autobiography

THROUGHOUT this study I have returned again and again to one central problem: what is the range of truth in autobiography, how is it organised to form a work we can read as literature, for itself, not merely as a supplement to something else? The particular content of an autobiography has been discussed in general only in so far as it bears on this problem.

Now I know that autobiographies are written and read for the sake of the information they provide, information about the author, about his times. Their interest is inexhaustible. One can take delight in the records of quite trivial people, not only because of what they tell us, but even because of themselves as human beings. One is perpetually astonished, delighted, perhaps horrified, in any case instructed by the variety of human existence, of personality and of circumstance. They are a valuable corrective to historiography, which cannot allow its attention to wander too far from what is common to a people and a period, from general determinants and a general outcome, and must ignore much of what is specific in the individual. I have no doubt done less than justice to this aspect of autobiography and to many autobiographies that I have read with appreciation of their content and respect for the men whose lives are described in them.

I cannot believe, however, that information of this type, psychological or historical, suffices to create autobiographical stature. Certainly it is impossible to review autobiographies from this point of view. The mass of heterogeneous information they give defies estimation and summing up. As historical documents they have to be studied and checked with the most sceptical discrimination. Catherine Burr, in one of the earliest books on autobiography, tried to estimate what contribution they had made to our knowledge of human nature, but, quite apart from the fact that their most valuable contribution is often the involuntary self-revelation of the author, any such investigation results only in a heap of indiscriminate facts. Such a purpose leads, too, to faulty valuations, as when Mrs. Burr finds that Goethe's *Poetry and Truth* is "tedious", because it tells us little that is psychologically startling—thus ignoring the main concerns and interest of one of the greatest autobiographies. Such particular purposes lead naturally to a blurring of the distinction between autobiography and such related but distinct literary forms as memoirs, diaries, and letters.

More recent critics have felt the need to look for what is specific to autobiography. Some have tried to group them according to the attitude of the author, or his motivation in writing, for instance the desire to chronicle, to confess, or to expound. The method does not lead to any very firm conclusions, however, since motives are usually mixed; and in any case motivation does not seem to provide a clue to the differences we discover in the form of autobiographies. Latterly some, like Wayne Shumaker in his full study of English autobiography, and Gusdorf in his searching essay, have seen the problem as one of a particular literary form. This is how I have tried to see it. If however I posed the question as an aesthetic one, its implications go very far, for in the development and varieties of this form, even more than in the actual content of the works, we have significant evidence of the modulations of a civilisation. In fact, one might say that, of all literary forms, it is the one least affected by national characteristics and most indicative of a common European culture.

Autobiography is a distinctive product of Western, post-Roman civilisation, and only in modern times has it spread to other civilisations. It postulates a pre-occupation with the self that may, and often does, deteriorate into vanity, complacency, self-indulgence. But in its best examples, of which there are many, it holds the balance between the self and the world, the subjective and the objective. It is inspired by a reverence for the self, tender yet severe, that sees the self not as a property but a trust. It is not concerned just with the moral personality, like the Stoics, but with the self in its delicate uniqueness. Hence it seeks to trace its historical identity, in all its particularity. Informed with the consciousness that the self escapes definition— "individuum est ineffabile"—it reveals it not so much by contemplation and analysis as through its encounters with the world.

In all this it betrays a general situation in which the individual feels himself to be responsible for himself. It cannot be an accident that in its earlier manifestations it owed much to the Christian confessional, not simply as a relieving confession of sin, but as a means to reach an objective relationship to oneself. With Petrarch and the post-Renaissance world it delivers itself from the direct religious connexion, and becomes a rendering of accounts as such, a result of a need to establish "what manner of man I am". The search is a puzzling one, and its theme may become the Stendhalian "what am I?" rather than the more serene "what I am". It is often provoked by a recognition that other men want to know the answer, as with Augustine himself, with Petrarch, Gibbon, Freud, and so many, and the very act of publishing acknowledges this motive of satisfying a public demand. But it may be promoted primarily by a personal need, a personal need for confession or clarity, arising perhaps from that simplest yet most profound realisation of ageing, as when Cellini is "startled to realise that I really am fifty-eight years old", or that more obscure pressure that Yeats speaks about when he writes that he is haunted by the past till he can speak of it. In all cases it must involve a personal pressure, for good autobiography is always more than a mere exposition to the public of something already known to the author. It is for this reason that Arthur Koestler's two volumes leave us dissatisfied. They are packed full with lively experience, and tell of a development of general significance—the author's progress from pledged devotion to Communism to his spirited repudiation of it. Yet, shrewd as the author is, his book lacks the quality of great autobiography, largely because he is so certain and clear, at times cocksure, about his wisdom. He writes the book to inform and enlighten others, not at all for his own sake.

The purpose of true autobiography must be "Selbstbesinnung", a search for one's inner standing. It is an affair of conscience, and in its immediate source and purpose suggests something of a metaphysical urge, or at any rate something that cannot be reduced to a rational or social function. One may hold that conscience is a natural product of social living, the subjective form of an ethos without which no complex society can maintain itself. But in autobiography conscience has developed beyond the obligation towards a social, and one may add religious, set of values, and has become obligation to oneself, to one's own truth, and in this respect has become a principle that may be burdensome or hostile to the needs of social life.

Thus it makes a challenge: that the author is to be judged by his inner quality, his soul, if one may use the term in its widest meaning, the underlying source of his achievements. It is a most risky enterprise, as risky one might say as lyric poetry, and it reveals as inexorably as poetry the quality of the soul. Riskier perhaps than other forms of literature, where the work exists apart from the author; for here, as Montaigne says about his essays, criticism of the work is criticism of the author.[1] Hence too it is in fact not at all a suitable vehicle for the exposition of a doctrine, for by its very form we are led to appreciate the ideas and insights expounded in it (e.g. with Augustine, Wordsworth, Croce, Schweitzer) not in their objective truth but as true for this particular man, as true of him. If Darwin's or Freud's theories were proved to be false, it would not affect the quality of their autobiographies; or inversely, it is the quality of their spiritual personalities, as recorded in their autobiographies, that provides the sufficient guarantee of the truth of their doctrines.

The life is represented in autobiography not as something established but as a process; it is not simply the narrative of the voyage, but also the voyage itself. There must be in it a sense of discovery, and where this is wanting, and the autobiography appears as an exposition of something understood from the outset, we feel it is a failure, a partial failure at any rate. Remembering is itself a creative act, and the recording and ordering of memories even more so, but I mean here a discovery of a more fundamental sort. We expect something of the shock that Henry

[1] Montaigne, *Essais*, ed. Villey, Paris 1923, iii, 28.

James records when he writes in the middle of his autobiography that he discovers with surprise that he is engaged in writing "the personal history of an imagination". Without this sense of discovery, the very nature of living is distorted, for life is always an expedition, perhaps a groping, into the unknown. The act of writing it is a new act of the man, and like every significant new act it alters in some degree the shape of his life, it leaves the man different. Sartre, in his preface to Gorz's *Le Traître,* generalises from complacent autobiographies when he says that autobiography is "a style of death", that is, that it devitalises both the past and the present. On the contrary, good autobiography represents a new stage in self-knowledge and a new formulation of responsibility towards the self; it involves mental exploration and change of attitude.

Autobiography therefore has a function far beyond the pleasure of reminiscence or reflexion on an interesting set of experiences. For old men, in particular, it often acquires the meaning of a theodicy. In the religious autobiography this has the simple form of a conviction that the life accomplishes a divine plan as well as an inner calling, but there is often something of this conviction present even where there is no such explicit belief in divine direction. Goethe's could lead him, in the last Book, to reflections on the "daemonic" element within him that worked out its destiny without his control—"it was like chance, since it evinced no sequence of causality; it resembled Providence, for it hinted at coherence"; and in his profound poem on the mystery of personality, *Urworte.Orphisch,* it is not fortuitous that he uses an astrological metaphor:

Wie an dem Tag, der dich der Welt verliehen,
Die Sonne stand zum Grusse der Planeten,
Bist alsobald und fort und fort gediehen
Nach dem Gesetz, wonach du angetreten.[1]

If there is no such cosmic confidence, autobiography still seeks to reassure through establishing, not just the public significance of what has been achieved (if it is confined to this, it lacks a personal

---

[1] "As on the day that gave you to the world the sun stood greeting the planets, you straightway prospered, and on and on, according to the law that governed your arrival."

function, and must appear flat, uncreative), but the wholeness of personal identity. In an old man like Darwin, viewing his life "as if I were a dead man in another world", it rounds it off; in others, like Wells or Croce, it resumes its wholeness in order to prepare for future work, it reassures in order to add a heightened meaning and unity to the future.

Self-knowledge is then a primary motive of autobiography. But what sort of self-knowledge? Clearly all autobiographies tell us, consciously and unconsciously, of the curious ways of the heart and mind, of the double aspect of life as accident and providence, freedom and law. Yet do we judge them according to the amount of psychological insight they show? It is true that some enjoy great prestige because of their psychological insight. Augustine, Rousseau, Moritz and others noted down psychological processes up till then ignored, and their autobiographies are landmarks in the history of psychological understanding. I have already made the claim that it was the autobiographical form that made such discoveries possible and released psychological thinking from conventional categories. Yet many important autobiographies do not noticeably advance our knowledge of the workings of the heart and mind, and in many cases the authors are silent or blissfully ignorant concerning inward movements and responses that might have been readily understandable to their friends.

In all autobiographies there is a cone of darkness at the centre, even in those so outstanding as psychological documents. Can one say that Augustine discovered anything about the sources of a man's relations with his mother, his friends, his religion? No, though these relations are described with such delicacy and profundity. Rousseau, as Hume observed, for all his brilliant insight, was surely as naïve in regard to himself as a man could be. Goethe had such a distaste for the "pathological" that he seems to close up forbiddingly when he comes to the borders of such regions, and it was with difficulty that Freud could find an incident in Goethe's account that yielded some evidence of complex unconscious processes. Whence came Harriet Martineau's impulse to do good? Darwin's nervous illness leaves us so puzzled that it has provoked several attempts to diagnose it. Does Henry James disclose how it was that he had so curious an attachment for and detachment from social reality? What was the impulse of Wells's search for the key to the social process? Does Gide, analytical as he is, even try to find out why he is determined to find the tables of his new law? One might even say that the most analytical autobiographers, like Cardano or Stendhal (especially in the *Souvenirs d'Egotisme*), most elude our grasp. Gorz, who ruthlessly pursues his reactions with all the resources of Freud and Marx, discovers contrary and crossed motives, which themselves change in character and function as they assert themselves in his life: what begins as an inferiority complex becomes a means to recognise a general social situation. It seems to be required of the autobiographer that he should recognise that there is something unknowable in him, and we should agree with Augustine when he remarks: "Although no man knoweth the things of a man but the spirit of a man which is in him, yet there is something of man which neither the spirit of man that is within him knoweth". When we speak of self-knowledge through autobiography, we must mean some peculiar sort of knowledge.

The autobiography is a story, the story of a life in the world. The numberless impulses and responses of a person have to be reduced to a main strand, and only that which is effective, realised, can be considered worthy of being elaborated. The elaboration takes the form of the recording of experiences, events, actions, of thoughts and feelings that involve action and decision. What is important has to have a shape, an outward shape in the narrative, and this shape is the outcome of an interpenetration and collusion of inner and outer life, of the person and society. The shape interprets both. This is the decisive achievement of the art of autobiography: to give us events that are symbolic of the personality as an entity unfolding not solely according to its own laws, but also in response to the world it lives in. So that these events are symbolic of a whole group of things. Through them both the writers and readers know life. It is not necessarily or primarily an intellectual or scientific knowledge, but a knowing through the imagination, a sudden grasp of reality through reliving it in the imagination, an understanding of the feel of life, the feel of living. Barea puts it well in his Foreword to *The Track*:

N*

I wanted to discover how and why I became what I am, to understand the forces and emotions behind my present reactions. I tried
to find them, not through a psychological analysis, but by calling
up the images and sensations I had once seen and felt, and later on
absorbed and re-edited.

Autobiography provides us then with what Susanne Langer
defines as the achievement of art, "the intuitive knowledge of
some unique experience", which as such is representative of the
character of life altogether.[1] Its symbols are not invented by the
imagination, but chosen and arranged by the evaluating memory.
Muir and Spender both say it is impossible to know oneself.
What they mean is that one cannot come to a scientific or "discursive" knowledge of oneself and the meaning of one's life.
But their autobiographies do give a different sort of knowledge,
an intuitive knowledge that is quite as true as any other sort, and
as important as far as the job of living is concerned.

Autobiographies fail if the authors lack insight or seriousness,
wholeness, of character. But they frequently fail too because they
do not create that significant meeting-place between the individual
and the outer world, that illumines both. One asks, why is
Margery Kempe's autobiography inferior to Saint Teresa's,
and the answer is not just that Teresa understands herself better
than Margery, for there are unfathomable obscurities in Teresa.
Nor is the difference due solely to the devoted and stern
determination with which Teresa tested herself at all stages, the
deep seriousness of her character. It is also, and significantly,
due to the almost consistent fortuitousness of relationship, in
Margery's life, between her actions, the incidents of her outward
life, and her inward conviction and urge. The incidents of her
life's journey, with an occasional exception, are wayward and
trivial, and rarely rise to the level of symbolic event in which her
character and her world are suddenly embodied; while in Teresa's
Life almost every step has this symbolical relevance. In other
words, Teresa's personality seems to bind her outer experiences
and her inner world together; Margery's moves in a haphazard
world which itself then makes the personality seem haphazard and
wayward.

[1] Susanne K. Langer, *Feeling and Form*, 1953.

The purpose of autobiography is lost when the mass of reminiscence makes us lose trace of the distinctive personality of the author. Its peculiar sort of knowledge is also absent when the personality fails to find its correlative in the outer world, when in Gusdorf's phrase there is no "projection du domaine intérieur dans l'espace extérieur". This is the failing of Nietzsche's *Ecce Homo*, so rich in psychological and philosophical observation, but utterly unplastic, shimmering, bewildering; because of the utter lack of environment, of other people, there is no clear inward personality. Jouhandeau's *Essai sur moi-même* has the same sort of elusiveness. Perhaps it is not accidental that there is in this type of self-investigation at times a somewhat repellent complacency, due not to self-approval necessarily but to self-engrossment. The autobiographical method proper seems to be more objective as well as more true, in that it can give its due importance to the outer world. Thus it is misleading to talk of the "self-love" of autobiographers (Pritchett); most of us love ourselves too dearly to be autobiographers.

So infinite is the response of a man in any given situation, so interwoven past and present, that it might be considered that the truth of a personality at a given moment could be given only by the most detailed and in reality never-ending uncovering of all its fibres—a refined, almost static analysis of a type that Virginia Woolf attempted in the novel. If this were so, autobiography would be condemned as a most clumsy instrument, if not as an outright misrepresentation of life. At best, the complexity of such moments of experience is suggested in certain autobiographies—particularly those of imaginative writers—by the evocation of a situation. But even here, the author does not linger to dissect, but hurries on with his story, even if like Yeats he is not concerned to give many of the connecting links between one situation and another. All autobiographies must, like novels, have a story-structure. But it would be wrong to suppose that this imposes a regrettable limitation on their truthfulness, on their range of truthfulness. It is their mode of presenting truth. They are, like novels, cumulative structures, and we experience them as wholes, so that at any moment the earlier parts, the earlier experiences, are present in the reader's mind. The reverberations from past experiences do not need to be explicitly recalled afresh at every moment, nor does each new situation need endless dissection. In all new events the author's past experience is recalled objectively in the shape of formed behaviour, feeling, thought. Thus events build on events to construct the achieved personality.

What is decisive for the art of autobiography is the relationship of the parts, the mutual reflection of all elements in their evolution, the intimate and dynamic identity of experiences and events with the writer, with the writer as the object of the book and as author. One should speak of autobiography in terms of a type of "Gestalt" theory. Its truth lies in the building up of a personality through the images it makes of itself, that embody its mode of absorbing and reacting to the outer world, and that are profoundly related to one another at each moment and in the succession from past to present. The value and truth of autobiography—and its value is always linked with its truth—are not dependent on the degree of conscious psychological penetration, on separate flashes of insight; they arise out of the monolithic impact of a personality that out of its own and the world's infinitude forms round itself, through composition and style, a homogeneous entity, both in the sense that it operates consistently on the world and in the sense that it creates a consistent series of mental images out of its encounters with the world.

What is troubling about this way of looking at autobiography is that it may seem to bring it too close to imaginative art and obscure the fact that it tells of events whose truth may be tested from other sources. Historians have necessarily to check and often to correct autobiographical statements, and autobiographers are deeply concerned to correct current and anticipated misapprehensions. Matters of detail do not trouble us much, where the autobiographer has erred through forgetfulness, ignorance, even prejudice or polemical intention. Nor does it matter that the biographer may have to amplify or explain. Ernest Jones's large biography of Freud in no way disqualifies Freud's autobiography, though it adds much to our knowledge of Freud. The really troubling question affects the central theme of autobiography. We like to ask, does the author's representation of himself as a personality correspond to what we can get to know of him through other evidence? It is a question that can never be asked regarding a work of art. We do ask it of autobiography, and we are comforted to hear, if we cannot carry out investigations ourselves, that for instance George Sand's *Histoire de ma vie*, or Joyce's *Stephen Hero*, is substantially true, that is, true as a portrayal of the intimate self and of the decisive relations with others.

It is a most complex question, for we do not wait for confirmatory evidence before deciding on the worth of an autobiography. The great autobiographies are works that stand by themselves, and are appreciated without reference to the actual lives and works of the authors. It would seem that this quality of truth must emerge from the text itself. I have already suggested, in Chapter 5, that there are occasions when a fault can be detected. Vanity and triviality show themselves immediately, and style in general is the most revealing element in any autobiography. Often authors tell us unmistakably that they are going to be reticent, and deliberately put limits to their confiding communication, as with Trollope or Osbert Sitwell. The problem becomes difficult when the author has the candid intention of telling all the essential truth. Sometimes we are helped to detect an omission. Harriet Martineau drops a significant hint about the difficulties of the brother–sister relation, and this enables us perhaps to supplement her story with a missing factor, her love for her brother James. I have suggested that this omission is a fault, but there are occasions when such omissions may be justified. That Henry James only allows us once to glimpse his unhappiness as a young man is not misleading, since he is concerned not with his life and personality as a whole, but with "the personal history of an imagination".

But there are autobiographies in which the author seems to be candidly giving us himself, dropping no clues as to reticence or bias, and bringing his life and actions into a consistent harmony with his personality; and yet external evidence may show him to be deeply mistaken about himself, or skilfully scheming to deceive us. Is it possible that we can fall into such a trap, and succumb to his conscious or unconscious wiles? Consistent misrepresentation of oneself is not easy. The outward course of a life corresponds most subtly to the character, and if crying dissonances are to be avoided in the distorted narrative, the only way to achieve one's aim is to make the self opaque, to erase;

gaps and obscurity reveal the false intention, perhaps accompanied by other stylistic evidences of something wrong, bluster, rhetoric, flatness, digressions, and so forth. But while one can on occasions measure the truth of a story in this rather concrete way, and can say the internal evidence shows that such and such an autobiography is not truthful, one comes up here against a more general problem, which can best be elucidated by examples.

A little time after the publication of G. G. Coulton's *Fourscore Years*, his daughter Sarah Campion published her *Father*. It is the book of an affectionate woman who found that Coulton's account was, in important features, not true of the father she knew. She fills in the domestic pictures of an eccentric, obstinate, and tyrannical husband and father, and those who knew Coulton will recognise the faithfulness of her picture. It is more important that she shows that the rather reasonable controversialist that appears in Coulton's *Fourscore Years* was in fact a man repeatedly obsessed by certain issues, and that when engaged in controversy "he was a dear man who had temporarily lost his reason and become something quite fiendish in consequence". Again we should incline to admit that the daughter is right. There is no doubt that Coulton, whose most endearing quality was his transparent, almost childlike honesty, never had the least intention of touching up his picture; all that one can say is that, when writing his story, he was utterly unaware of certain sides of his nature and behaviour. And this ingenuousness is a serious drawback in an autobiography in which the author says that life is above all "a test of character", and that his chief interest in reading other autobiographies is "the attempt to disentangle what a man was from what he would have liked to be and what he shows to the world". While his book is delightful and fascinating as a book of reminiscences, remembered with amazing sharpness, as an autobiography it is not true to himself.

If we had not known Coulton, and if his historical writings and pamphlets, and the book of his daughter, had all vanished, should we accept his autobiographical portrait without reserve? There are some indications of his eccentric and fierce temperament in it, but I think we should have overlooked them, and have thought of him as he would have us do. But we should never consider this work to be a great autobiography. It lacks intensity; the mildness of his mood of reminiscence affects also his account of his religious and moral difficulties and his interests. In softening himself he reduces the quality of the whole book; the self is not a problem and a search. This is the fate of the great mass of estimable autobiographies. Their untruth is evident not in particulars but in their lack of probing, in their relaxed mood.

And still, one has to be dissatisfied with such a conclusion. The evidence of Coulton's controversies and pamphlets is valid, as is that of his daughter. But also his own evidence. Sarah Campion did not wish to say, her father's picture must be supplanted by hers, but, the one must be supplemented by the other. The curious meals he used to cook himself in his College rooms seem comic and odd to the others; to himself they were sensible and rationally planned. Is the inside view wrong because it conflicts with the outside? Was it fanaticism and obsession that pursued him in his campaign for conscription and his polemic against Roman Catholic historiography, or was it commonsense and a determined love of truth? It is not easy to answer. But what is certain is, that the inside case has as full a right to be presented as the outside, and there is no tribunal that can establish which was right and which was wrong. This is the fundamental problem, and it is explicitly discussed in H. G. Wells's *Experiment in Autobiography*.

Wells was continually dogged, as he wrote his autobiography, by the unquiet feeling that he might be imagining himself to be quite other than he actually was. His idea of himself, he says, as "a pre-occupied mind devoted to an exalted and spacious task", seeking detachment and "a dignified peace of mind", is not what he is but "what I most like to think I am". He warns the reader not to accept at its face value this conception of himself, this "mask", this *persona*, as he calls it. He is much else, and much that is contradictory. But the *persona* is not untrue either: "it is the plan to which I work". And it may be that the mask may become the true face. The question to be decided by the *Autobiography* is, is this *persona* "sufficiently consistent and developed to be the ruling theme of the story"? Wells believes he can answer, yes.

Wells tells his story as that of "a worker concentrated on the perfection and completion of a work", and this work is "a drive to make a practically applicable science out of history and sociology". Few autobiographies so brilliantly fuse a general theme with the actual particular experiences undergone, the "history of my sort and my time" with the personal story. But his very consistence makes his dilemma more acute. I will take one example. At the beginning of the second volume Wells describes his divorce and re-marriage in terms of his general intellectual development from small, narrow-scope living to "a longer reach of motive", from a family purpose to that of a citizen of the world. His divorce is neatly "explained" in these terms, and the two women involved symbolise the two worlds. But he brings himself up with a jolt. There are other motivations here, he recognises, as for instance the search for a more satisfactory sexual life, and he discusses the group of novels he wrote at this time on the theme of the personal adjustment of man and woman. Yet he clings to his main theme, and we note that his account is determined by this interpretation. He tells us hardly anything of later sexual relationships, and I do not think this is due to consideration for persons or the law. For, while he mentions, it is true, certain attitudes like his militant patriotism during the First World War, and his temporary religious faith, he treats them outright as aberrations and lapses. He admits that "the consistency of my present *persona* has been achieved only after a long struggle between distinct strands of motivation", but he never leaves us in doubt about what he considers the main strand. In fact, the whole of his life is told as the story of his *persona*, and he was so conscious that he had neglected or subordinated other facets of his being that he belatedly confesses his fault in the Envoy: "I have not done any sort of justice to the keen interest of countless subsidiary happenings, to the fun of life . . . I may have failed to convey my thankfulness to existence".

Even without such a lead, acquaintances of Wells would have been aware that the Wells of *Experiment in Autobiography* was not exactly or fully the man they knew. Frank Swinnerton, a longstanding friend, describes in his own *Autobiography* a Wells who is in many respects a supplement to that other, and comments on the difference. His conclusion is that Wells was "much more agreeable, impulsive, inventive, and irritable than that other man . . . Readers of Mr. Wells's *Experiment in Autobiography* would gain from that book no impression of the author as he is seen by his friends." One need not add how differently he would be seen by his enemies! But, while Swinnerton adds to and corrects the picture Wells gives of himself, he also makes the acute comment: "Autobiographers, in pursuing the truth, fail to catch the likeness". That is, he recognises here that the public view, the likeness, is not the whole truth, and not necessarily truer than the inside view; and that the autobiographer must have some other object than the presentation of himself as he may appear to others.

We must add a further consideration. The autobiography is not simply a statement of what a man was and is. Like others, Wells's is in some sort a polemical statement, another contribution to his life's work, not a résumé of it. It is an active contribution, not a closing of accounts. Its object is wisdom, not just self-knowledge or self-exposition; the latter is a means to the former. He concludes it with words that indicate the psychological function of autobiography in general:

> I began this autobiography primarily to reassure myself during a phase of fatigue, restlessness and vexation, and it has achieved its purpose of reassurance. . . . My ruffled *persona* has been restored and the statement of the idea of the modern world-state [the ultimate goal of his work] has reduced my personal and past irritations and distractions to their proper insignificance.

So it is that the autobiography is not a portrait, and its motivation is quite other than that of the biography. The autobiographer is not simply uncovering facts and relationships that an outsider must necessarily be unacquainted with, but presenting an order of values that is his own. He must necessarily establish a sort of ideal image of himself, and arrange things according to his blue-print, as Wells calls it. Not that he idealises himself, sees himself better than he might appear to others; but that he establishes an over-riding purpose, which he finds, perhaps to his surprise, has become expressed and grasped in the shape of his life. He presents an inner core, a self beneath the personality that appears to the world, that is his most precious reality since it gives meaning to his life. Others are content with his outer personality and its meaning for them, its social meaning; and sometimes they resent this other self and suspect its genuineness.

Does the autobiographer thus delude himself? Our judgement on whether he is right is guided by evidence, by the record of his doings, their consistency, the manner in which they are told. This is what I have called the "Gestalt" theory of the autobiography. But all scientific terms are misleading, or run the danger of being misleading, when applied to our relationship to human beings. We do not judge an autobiography solely upon the evidence of the facts but also upon our intuitive knowledge of the distinctive character of life as experienced by ourselves individually. Everyone else appears distinct, shaped, ascertainable, and their actions conform to a forseeable plan; we ourselves retain as an essential part of ourselves something undefined and undetermined, and seem to ourselves to be always capable of the unexpected and unforeseeable. Even if in retrospect we can see our character as genetically and socially determined, in the present we are always aware of the power of choice and decision, and we can see a truth in a young man like Gorz's tormented longing, despite the consciousness of determination, for a "free human act". It is the problem at the bottom of Sartre's existentialism: the repudiation of the view of man as an object, a thing, since the property of man is precisely that he can surpass himself and assert his freedom; and Sartre might have applied to the great auto-biographers the phrase from *L'être et le néant*, "man constitutes himself as what he is in order not to be it". Autobiographers however are nearer to the truth of experience than Sartre in that they establish this power of man not as an abstract and discontinuous freedom, but as a realisation of an inner self that is as much compulsion as it is freedom. It is not at all arbitrary, but presents itself to reflexion as a "daemon" or "persona" or "life-illusion". In every case, this dynamic creative element is as true as anything else about us, though it may be invisible to others, and is the driving force of a life as seen from inside by the man living it.

Not all autobiographies postulate this inner personality, though I believe all good autobiographies demonstrate it. Perhaps one can say that it is the will to find expression for it, and to justify the life in relation to it, that determines the worth of an autobiography. For it is this that gives depth and weight to the assessment of a life, a feeling of responsibility to the inner creative power. However this power is interpreted by the author, as immediately experienced in the consciousness his feeling of being pledged to something within has a metaphysical character. And here too one comes up against the contrast between autobiography and art. For the lack of this feeling is not of course simply a fault in the writer's conception of his literary task. It must first have established itself in his life; and most lives are too fragmentary, too much of a compromise, to claim this. Gertrude Stein puts a common enough point of view when she writes (in *Everybody's Autobiography*): "Anyway autobiography is easy like it or not autobiography is easy for any one . . ." But she is wrong like it or not—though everybody might be able to write memoirs. True autobiography can be written only by men and women pledged to their innermost selves.

There is no final and complete truth about a man. We all know how different a familiar landscape or a person appear to us after we have seen them portrayed by a good artist. Picasso even said, when looking at his portrait of Gertrude Stein, that though she was not like it, she would become so. So also the man changes as he writes his autobiography, and must share in some degree Montaigne's conviction, "I have not made my book more than my book has made me". The biography, in being more objective, that is, in seeing the person concerned as an object, misses the specific dynamic truth of the autobiography; and we know too how, with the change of time, biographies have to be re-written. There is no tribunal which can deliver a final judgement. It may be a question of all against one; but what vote can decide that Rousseau is wrong and the rest right? Beyond factual truth, beyond the "likeness", the autobiography has to give that unique truth of life as it is seen from inside, and in this respect it has no substitute or rival.

Bibliography

AUTOBIOGRAPHIES

This list includes all autobiographies mentioned in the text, but not by any means all I have examined. For a more extensive bibliography, see the under-mentioned works of Misch, Shumaker, Beyer-Fröhlich, and others. Where possible I have listed English translations of foreign autobiographies. The place of publication, if not mentioned, is London.

ABELARD, *Historia Calamitatum. Oeuvres complètes,* ed. Gréard, Paris n.d.

ADAMS, H. *The Education of Henry Adams,* Boston and New York, 1918.

AKSAKOFF, S. *Years of Childhood,* trans. Duff, 1910 (World's Classics). *A Russian Schoolboy,* trans. Duff, 1917.

ALFIERI, V. *Memoirs* (trans.) 1810.

ATTLEE, C. *As it happened,* 1954.

AUGUSTINE, SAINT. *Confessions,* trans. Pusey, New York, 1952.

BABUR. *Memoirs,* trans. Beveridge, 2 vols. 1912–22.

BAREA, A. *The Forge,* 1941; *The Track,* 1943; *The Clash,* 1946.

BAXTER, R. *Life and Times,* ed. Calamy, 2 vols. 1713.

BEAUVOIR, S. DE. *Memoirs of a dutiful daughter,* trans. Kirkup, 1959.

BUBER-NEUMANN, M. *Von Potsdam nach Moskau,* Stuttgart, 1948; *Als Gefangene bei Stalin und Hitler,* Stuttgart, 1958.

BUCHAN, J. (Lord Tweedsmuir). *Memory Hold-the-Door,* 1940.

BUNYAN, J. *Grace Abounding to the Chief of Sinners,* ed. Venables and Peacock, Oxford, 1925.

CARDANO, G. *The Book of my Life,* trans. Stoner, 1931.

CARLYLE, T. *Reminiscences. Selected Works,* ed. Symons, 1955.

CAROSSA, H. *Eine Kindheit,* Leipzig, 1922; *Rumänisches Tagebuch,* 1924; *Verwandlungen einer Jugend,* 1928; *Führung und Geleit,* 1933; *Das Jahr der schönen Täuschungen,* 1941; *Der Tag des jungen Arztes,* 1955.

CASANOVA, J. *The Memoirs,* 2 vols. 1922 (Navarre Society).

CATHERINE THE GREAT, EMPRESS. *Memoirs,* trans. Budberg, 1955.

CELLINI, B. *The Autobiography,* trans. Bull, 1956 (Penguin Classics).

CHATEAUBRIAND, F. R. A. de *Mémoires d'Outre-Tombe,* ed. Lavaillant, 4 vols. Paris, 1947.

CHURCH, R. *Over the Bridge,* 1955; *The Golden Sovereign,* 1957.

CHURCHILL, W. S. *My early life,* 1930.

CIBBER, C. *An Apology for his Life,* 1740 (Everyman's Library).

COLETTE, S. G. *Mes Apprentissages,* Paris, 1936.

COLLINGWOOD, R. G. *An Autobiography,* 1939.

CONNOLLY, C. *Enemies of Promise,* 1938, revised 1949.

COULTON, G. G. *Fourscore Years,* 1943.

CRAIG, E. GORDON. *Index to the Story of my Days,* 1957.

CROCE, B. *An Autobiography,* trans. Collingwood, 1927.

DARWIN, C. *Autobiography,* ed. Barlow, 1958.

ELLIS, HAVELOCK. *My Life,* 1940.

EPSTEIN, J. *An Autobiography,* 1955.

FONTANE, T. *Meine Kinderjahre,* Berlin, 1894; *Von Zwanzig bis Dreissig,* Berlin, 1894.

FORD, F. MADOX. *Return to Yesterday,* 1931.

FRANKLIN, B. *Autobiography,* ed. Bigelow, 1872.

FREUD, S. *An Autobiographical Study,* trans. Strachey, 1935.

GALLACHER, W. *Revolt on the Clyde,* 1936.

GALTON, F. *Memories of my Life,* 1908.

GANDHI. *Mahatma Gandhi; His Own Story,* ed. Andrews, 1930.

GARNETT, D. *The Golden Echo,* 1953; *The Flowers of the Forest,* 1955.

GHIBERTI, L. *Comentarii. Leben und Meinungen des L.G.,* Basel, 1941.

GIBBON, E. *Memoirs,* ed. Lord Sheffield, 1827 (World's Classics).

GIDE, A. *Si le grain ne meurt,* Paris, 1928. (*If it die,* trans. Bussy, 1950).

GIRALDUS CAMBRENSIS. *Autobiography,* ed. and trans. Butler, 1937.

GOETHE, J. W. *Aus meinem Leben*: *Dichtung und Wahrheit,* 1812–31; *Die Italienische Reise,* 1786–8; *Campagne in Frankreich,* 1792; *Werke,* Gedenkausgabe, vols. 10, 11, 12, Zürich, 1948–50. (*Poetry and Truth; The Italian Journey; Campaign in France*).

GOLDONI, C. *Memoirs,* trans. Black, 2 vols. 1828.

GOLLANCZ, V. *My Dear Timothy,* 1952; *More for Timothy,* 1953.

GORELL, LORD. *One man—many parts,* 1956.

GORKI, M. *My Childhood,* trans. Foakes, n.d.

GORZ, A. *Le Traître,* Paris, 1958.

GOSSE, E. *Father and Son,* 1907.

GRAVES, R. *Goodbye to All That,* 1929; revised 1957.

GUBSKY, N. *Angry Dust,* 1937.

GUYON, MME DE LA MOTTE. *Autobiography,* trans. Allen, 2 vols. 1897.

HAMANN, J. G. *Gedanken über meinen Lebenslauf. Schriften,* Berlin 1821–43, vol. 1.

HAMNETT, N. *Laughing Torso,* 1932.

HARE, AUGUSTUS. *The Story of my Life,* 6 vols, 1896–1900.

HARRIS, W. *Life so far,* 1954.

HAYDON, B. *Autobiography,* 1853 (World's Classics).

HERBERT OF CHERBURY. *The Life,* ed. Dircks, 1888.

HOBBES, T. *Vita,* 1672.

HUDSON, W. H. *Far Away and Long Ago,* 1928.

HUME, D. *Life,* 1776 (in *Essays,* World's Classics).

JAMES, H. *Autobiography,* ed. Dupee, 1956 (*A Small Boy and Others,* 1913; *Notes of a Son and Brother,* 1914; *The Middle Years,* 1917).

JOUHANDEAU, M. *Essai sur Moi-même,* Paris, 1947.

JUNG, J. H. *Jung-Stillings Lebensgeschichte,* Berlin, 1777–1817 (Reclam).

KEITH, A. *An Autobiography,* 1950.

KEMPE. *The Book of Margery Kempe,* ed. Meech and Allen, Oxford, 1940.

KIPLING, R. *Something of Myself,* 1938.

KOESTLER, A. *Arrow in the Blue,* 1952; *The Invisible Writing,* 1954.

KÜGELGEN, W. *Jugenderinnerungen eines alten Mannes,* Berlin, 1870.

LEHMANN, J. *The Whispering Gallery,* 1955.

LEONHARD, W. *Child of the Revolution,* 1957.

LOW, D. *Low's Autobiography,* 1956.

McDOUGALL, W. *Autobiography* (in *A History of Psychology in Autobiography,* vol. 1, 1930).

MARTINEAU, H. *Autobiography,* 3 vols. 1877.

MAUGHAM, W. S. *Of Human Bondage,* 1915; *The Summing Up,* 1938.

MILL, J. S. *Autobiography,* 1873.

MOORE, G. *Hail and Farewell,* 3 vols. (*Ave,* 1911; *Salve,* 1912; *Vale,* 1914).

MORITZ, K. P. *Anton Reiser,* Berlin, 1785–90 (World's Classics).

MUIR, E. *An Autobiography,* 1954.

NEWMAN, J. H. *Apologia pro vita sua,* ed. Ward, Oxford, 1931.

NICHOLS, B. *Twenty-Five Years,* 1926.

O'CASEY, S. *I Knock at the Door,* 1939; *Pictures in the Hallway,* 1942; *Drums under the Windows,* 1946; *Innishfallen Fare Thee Well,* 1949; *Rose and Crown,* 1952; *Sunset and Evening Star,* 1954.

O'SULLIVAN, M. *Twenty Years A-Growing,* trans. Thomson, 1933 (World's Classics).

PETRARCH, F. *Letter to Posterity, The Secret,* trans. Tatham, *Works,* 2 vols. 1926.

PLOMER, W. *Double Lives,* 1943; *At Home,* 1958.

POLLITT, H. *Serving my Time,* 1940.

POWYS, J. C. *Autobiography,* 1934.

QUINCEY, T. DE. *Autobiography. Collected Writings,* ed. Masson, 1896, vols. 1 and 2.

READ, H. *Annals of Innocence and Experience,* 1940.

RENAN, E. *Souvenirs d'enfance et de jeunesse,* Paris, 1883 (Nelson).

Bibliography

RESTIF DE LA BRETONNE. *Monsieur Nicolas, Oeuvres,* vols. 7 and 8, Paris, 1932.

RETZ, CARDINAL DE. *Memoirs,* trans. 4 vols. 1774.

ROUSSEAU, J.-J. *The Confessions* (1782) trans. 1904. (Also Penguin Classics, trans. Cohen.)

RUSKIN, J. *Praeterita,* 3 vols. 1899.

SAINT-EXUPÉRY, A. DE. *Terre des Hommes,* Paris, 1939. *Pilote de Guerre,* Paris, 1942.

SAINT-SIMON, L. DE R. *Mémoires,* Paris, 1947 ff. (Pléiade).

SALIMBENE. *The Chronicle. From St. Francis to Dante,* trans. and ed. Coulton, 1906.

SCHWEITZER, A. *My Life and Thought,* trans. Campion, 1933.

SEUSE, H. (SUSO). *The Life of the Servant,* trans. Clark, 1950.

SITWELL, O. *Left Hand, Right Hand,* 1945; *The Scarlet Tree,* 1946; *Great Morning,* 1948; *Laughter in the Next Room,* 1949; *Noble Essences,* 1950.

SMITH, L. PEARSALL. *Unforgotten Years,* 1938.

SNOWDEN, P. *An Autobiography,* 1934.

SOREL, C. *Histoire comique de Francion,* 3 vols. ed. Roy, 1924.

SPENCER, H. *An Autobiography,* 2 vols. 1904.

SPENDER, S. *World within World,* 1951.

SSU-MA-CHI'EN (SE-MA TS'IEN). *Mémoires historiques,* ed. Chavannes, 5 vols, Paris, 1895–1905.

STANISLAVSKY, C. *My Life in Art,* trans, Robbins, Boston, 1927.

STEIN, G. *The Autobiography of Alice B. Toklas,* 1933; *Everybody's Autobiography,* 1938.

STENDHAL. *Souvenirs d'Egotisme,* ed. Stryienski, Paris, 1892; *The Life of Henry Brulard,* trans. Stewart and Knight, 1958.

STEPHEN, J. *The Memoirs,* ed. Bevington, 1954.

SWINNERTON, F. *An Autobiography,* New York, 1936.

TERESA, SAINT. *The Life,* trans. Cohen, 1957 (Penguin Classics).

THOMSON, J. J. *Recollections and Reflections,* 1936.

TISCHBEIN, W. *Aus meinem Leben,* ed. Brieger, Berlin, 1922.

TOLLER, E. *I was a German,* trans. Crankshaw, 1934.

TOLSTOY, L. *Childhood,* 1852; *Boyhood,* 1854; *Youth,* 1857; *A Confession,* 1882; *Recollections,* 1902, 1908; *Works,* Centenary Ed., trans. Maude, vols. 3, 11, 21.

TROLLOPE, A. *An Autobiography* (1883), Oxford, 1950.

TROTSKY. *My Life,* 1930.

WEBB, BEATRICE. *My Apprenticeship,* 1926.

WELCH, D. *Maiden Voyage,* 1943; *Brave and Cruel,* 1948; *The Voice through a Cloud,* 1948.

WELLS, H. G. *Experiment in Autobiography,* 2 vols, 1934.
WORDSWORTH, W. *The Prelude,* ed. de Selincourt, 1928.
YEATS, W. B. *Autobiographies,* 1955 (*Reveries over Childhood and Youth,* 1915; *The Trembling of the Veil,* 1922; *Dramatis Personae,* and other pieces).
ZWEIG, S. *The World of Yesterday,* 1943.

BOOKS AND ESSAYS ON AUTOBIOGRAPHY

BEYER-FRÖHLICH, M. *Die Entwicklung der deutschen Selbstzeugnisse,* Leipzig, 1930.
BURR, A. B. *The Autobiography,* 1909.
CLARK, A. M. *Autobiography,* Edinburgh, 1935.
DOBRÉE, B. *Some literary autobiographies of the present age, The Sewanee Review,* 1956, no. 4, vol. lxiv.
GARRATY, J. A. *The Nature of Biography,* 1958.
GOOCH, G. P. *Political Autobiography* (*Studies in Diplomacy and Statecraft,* 1942).
GUSDORF, G. *Conditions et limites de l'autobiographie* (*Formen der Selbstdarstellung,* ed. Reichenkron and Haase, Berlin, 1956).
KLAIBER, T. *Die deutsche Selbstbiographie,* Stuttgart, 1921.
MAHRHOLZ, W. *Deutsche Selbstbekenntnisse,* Berlin, 1919.
MAUROIS, A. *Aspects de la biographie,* Paris, 1928.
MISCH, G. *Geschichte der Autobiographie.* Vol. 1, *Das Altertum,* Leipzig and Berlin 1907; new enlarged edition 1949. Trans. as *History of Autobiography in Antiquity,* 2 vols., 1950.
Vol. 2, *Das Mittelalter,* 2 parts, Frankfurt, 1955.
PASCAL, R. *The Autobiographical Novel and the Autobiography, Essays in Criticism,* 1959, No. 2, vol. ix.
Autobiography as an Art Form (*Proceedings of the 1957 Conference of FLLM,* ed. Böckmann, 1959).
PRITCHETT, V. S. *All about Ourselves, The New Statesman,* May 26, 1956.
PRYCE-JONES, A. *The Personal Story* (*The Craft of Letters in England,* ed. Lehmann, 1955).
SHUMAKER, W. *English Autobiography,* University of California Press, 1954.
SPENDER, S. *Confessions and Autobiography* (*The Making of a Poem,* 1955).
STEPHEN, L. *Autobiography* (*Hours in a Library,* 1892, vol. 3).
WETHERED, H. N. *The curious art of Autobiography,* 1956.

Index

Index